The ABCs of Globalism

Globalism

A Vigilant Christian's Glossary

Bill,
may this work
be a blessing to
you.
In His service,

by

Debra Rae

"Debra Rae"

HUNTINGTON HOUSE PUBLISHERS

Printed in the United States of America.

Huntington House Publishers
P.O. Box 53788
Lafayette, Louisiana 70505
or visit our website at:
www.huntingtonhousebooks.com

Library of Congress Card Catalog Number 96-79608
ISBN 1-56384-140-1

Dedication

This effort is dedicated to my father who presently is experiencing in eternity what, through the years, I have passionately studied and prepared for, but have yet to know experientially. It is also dedicated to my mother, without whose encouragement this work might have languished.

Contents

B

C

D

I

J

K

L

M

N

O

P

R

S

T

U

V

W

Introduction
The Plan of God

A Christian's Life Journey

Most Christians have heard it said rightly that God has a plan for their lives, a marvelous one at that. Not surprisingly, our journey's itinerary is found in the first book and first chapter of the Bible (Gen. 1:26-27), and its glorious destination is spiritual maturity, wholeness, completion (Eph. 4:13). You see, Christ Himself is formed supernaturally within the yielded believer (Gal. 4:19).

The Lord has not left us bereft of a road map for this sometimes perilous journey. Indeed, He has given us His Spirit-breathed Holy Word, and He even provides the worthy vehicle of His Son, Jesus Christ, for are we not in Christ? Paul lets us know further that He is first among many who follow (Rom. 8:29) throughout this caravan of life. God's grace provides for rest stops and spiritual refueling in the Word, prayer, and fellowship; and He has thoughtfully supplied us with the safety belt of free will.

The compliant Christian's life journey results in total fulfillment of the Plan of God to be fabricated over time into the very likeness, or inner character, of God. Our model, of course, is Jesus Christ, first in position and first in time, according to Philippians 2:9-11 and Romans 8:29, respectively. "Many sons," ourselves included, follow the prototype, Jesus (Rom. 8:17, 29-30).

We are of good cheer and in perfect peace and confidence on this tribulation-ladened journey. Why? Because Jesus, having gone before, has deprived the world of its power to harm (*Amplified*, John 16:33).

The travel route for this journey of journeys is pictured, perhaps, in the Old Testament Tabernacle, portable sanctuary that served as a place of worship for Israelites from the time of wilderness wanderings to the building of Solomon's magnificent

Temple. This Tabernacle was divided clearly into sections. Sacrificial animals were slain in the Outer Court. Having washed at the laver, one entered the Holy Place with its altar of incense. The Most Holy Place, the *naos,* housed the Ark of the Covenant, God's throne in the midst of Israel. It was entered on the Day of At-one-ment once a year, and then by the High Priest alone.

As Christians on the Lord's life journey for us, we are blood-covered and cleansed in the Outer Court of sacrifice. The Lamb's sacrifice of shed crimson blood atoned flawlessly for our red-as-scarlet sins (Isa. 1:18). In accepting this truth, Christ becomes our personal Savior, and we, in turn, become His willing servants. We remain servants of this King of kings, but our journey to God-likeness does not end here. We move on into the commitment of friendship in the Holy Place as we learn of the Master's doings (John 15:15). We speak, as it were, face-to-face with Him at the altar of incense (Rom. 8:26), having been cleansed at the laver with washing of water by the Word (Eph. 5:26).

But the best is yet to come. Servants we are, and friends, too, but remember the rending of the Temple's veil (Matt. 27:51). Because of Jesus, we now have access to the very *naos,* the Holy of Holies. In fact, the Bible tells us our Spirit-filled bodies constitute the *naos* itself (1 Cor. 6:19). As God's throne was in the midst of Israel in the Ark of the Covenant, God resides in the ark of destined-to-be-glorified mankind (Rev. 21:2, 23). Such ones commune in the bridal chamber of the Most Holy Place of spiritual intimacy with *Yahweh-Ishi* (or "husband," Hosea 2:16-20).

In summary, the travel route on this divine life journey starts with blood-covering and cleansing in the Outer Court of servanthood, moves on to commitment in the Holy Place of friendship, and culminates in intimate communion of bridal chamber love in the Most Holy Place. Through this journey of maturation, over the course of a Christian's life, the "many sons" who follow Jesus Christ are made experientially perfect (that is, whole, mature, complete). Christ is formed within until, ultimately, the body is transfigured (1 Cor. 15:53), the soul redeemed, the spirit purified, and Christ's at-<u>one</u>-ment prayer of John 17 is gloriously and experientially answered in full.

Servanthood

Blessed we are indeed to be on the Christian's life journey toward spiritual completeness (Eph. 4:13), as anticipated in the first chapter of the first book in the Bible (Gen. 1:26-27). We enter this journey only through the blood-sprinkled way of the Outer Court of sacrifice, where Christ's crimson blood renders lily white our scarlet sins. Now, thus cleansed, we emerge as His servants, not because we are forced, or for compensation, but rather, as His voluntary love slave, or *doulos.*

Even as Philemon's slave, Onesimus, became a new creation in Christ and was honored subsequently as a beloved brother, partner, and co-heir with Paul in Christ (Philemon 16), we, too, are similarly honored. Onesimus means "profitable." Although we are unprofitable in ourselves (Luke 17:10), we indeed are profitable. Why? Because we walk in the footsteps of our Master, Who, for a season, emptied Himself and took on the *morphe,* or nature, of a slave (Phil. 2:7; John 13:16; 15:20).

The Old Testament pictures beautifully our new covenant position as Christ's love slave. For example, in the old covenant, the poor could be sold into slavery. In like manner, we who were poor in spirit were sold into the slavery of sin. The good news is that in the seventh year (seven being the number of spiritual perfection), slaves were set free. So it is with us. We who were distanced from the Kingdom and, therefore, without hope, are now made nigh to God by the Blood of Jesus Christ (Exod. 21:1-11; Lev. 25:39, 47; 2 Kings 4:1; Eph. 2:12-14). Unlike slaves in an oppressive world system, we who the Son sets free are truly free (John 8:36). In war, human booty was taken into slavery. At the end, Christ shall have put all enemies underfoot, and His Kingdom will be delivered up as willing war booty unto the Heavenly Father (Num. 31:25-47; 1 Cor. 15:24, 27).

King Jesus is always our supreme example (Isa. 42:1-4; Matt. 12:16-21; 23:11). Both He and the lesser king, David, picture servanthood (1 Sam. 16 to 1 Kings 2:11 and 1 Chron. 11-29). For example, David shared with Christ the posture of servanthood in his humble Bethlehem birth (1 Sam. 16:1; Matt. 2:1), as well as the label of servanthood—that is, beloved. Even as Christ was the "beloved son," David's name means "beloved" (1 Sam. 18:30; 2 Pet. 1:17). Both earmark servanthood with the laying down of self for the sheep (1 Sam. 17:34-36; John 10:14), and both paid the price of servanthood—suffering exile (1 Sam. 19:10; Matt. 2:14), persecution (Ps. 17:1; Isa. 50:6), and malcontents (1 Sam. 23:12; Isa. 50:6). As Christ's love slaves, walking in the footsteps of the Master, we are called, as was King David, to humility, death to self, and suffering. In turn, we are accepted among the beloved (Eph. 1:6) and made members in particular of His Body (1 Cor. 12:27).

In this picture of servanthood, both Greater and Lesser Davids were Divinely anointed (1 Sam. 16:13; Luke 4:18-19) to seek and save the lost (1 Sam. 17:45-51; Luke 19:10). We are joint (or equal) heirs of God the Father with Christ (Rom. 8:17); our mission, in turn, is to fish for men, bringing them into the Kingdom under God's mighty anointing (Acts 1:8). Having identified with Christ in being least of all (Luke 9:48), we do not remain as such, for our destiny is, eventually, to be exalted and glorified, as were the Greater and Lesser Davids of Scripture (2 Sam. 5:1-5; John 17:10).

Both David and Christ were "men after God's own heart" (1 Sam. 13:14); both kept their gaze heavenward. As Christ's love slaves, we are men and women after God's own heart. Our gaze is upward. As such, we are blessed to serve Him continually all the days of our lives; however, servanthood is not the end of the matter. The Lord does not want us to remain exclusively His slaves, for the servant does not know the intricate thoughts and deeds of his master. Jesus has called us friends because He communes with us on a deeper level than servanthood, telling us all things that He hears of the Father (John 15:15). Our Christian life journey does not remain in the Outer Court of servanthood. We move on in commitment to the Holy Place of friendship, where we speak face-to-face with Him at the altar of incense (Rom. 8:26), having been cleansed at the laver of the washing of the Word (Eph. 5:26).

Friendship

As early as the first book in the Bible, God lets His people know that He has a glorious plan for each one. The Hebrew text affirms God's plan to fabricate over time willing ones among humanity into the very likeness, or inner character, of God (Gen. 1:26-27). Believers in Christ are among the "many sons" who follow their altogether lovely prototype, Jesus (Rom. 8:17; 29-30).

Blood-covered and cleansed in the Outer Court of servanthood, Christian disciples walk in the footsteps of their worthy Master Whose *morphe,* or nature, was that of a servant (Phil. 2:7).

It is no surprise that many are content to remain servants for this One. But Jesus said, "No longer do I call you servants, for the servant knows not what his lord is doing. But you I have called friends, because all things which I heard from my Father made I known unto you." John 15:15 in no way undermines our calling as love slaves. It is, however, a significant road sign on the Christian's life journey, and it is pictured, in type, through the life of Saul's son, Jonathan.

Jonathan served David selflessly and self-sacrificially. Whatever David asked of him, Jonathan was willing to do (1 Sam. 20:4). As a good servant, he was with David when there was hardly a step between David and death (1 Sam. 20:3-4), and he pled David's case before the king himself (1 Sam. 19:1-7). As Jesus came not to be ministered unto, but to minister (Mark 10:45), Jonathan served David by warning him to hide from Saul (1 Sam. 19:2), by fighting David's enemy, the Philistines (1 Sam. 14:1), and by encouraging David in God at Horesh (1 Sam. 20:32-35). Christ serves us in all these ways and more. He is the Ever-present One (Matt. 28:20) Who responds to prayer (John 15:7). He pleads our case before the Father (Rom. 8:34), and He faithfully warns us (John 8:24), fights our spiritual battles (Luke 4:34), and encourages us (Heb. 4:15-16), as typified by Jonathan and David.

Jonathan's relationship with David transcended that of a servant and master. It is said that Jonathan's love for David passed the love of a woman (2 Sam. 1:26); their very souls were knit together (1 Sam. 18:1). This type of love is not unlike Christ's love for us. Christ prayed to be one with His friends even beyond the knitting together of souls (John 17:21-23). Keep in mind that in Christ there is neither male nor female (Gal. 3:28). This all-surpassing love, therefore, is of an infinitely higher order than *eros* and in no way suggests romantic or homosexual affection. Let us see it acted out.

For his beloved David, Jonathan willingly surrendered all rightful claims to his father's throne (1 Sam. 18:4). In like manner, Christ knew the Father has no fellowship with sin; nonetheless, He became sin (2 Cor. 5:21), thus yielding His rightful claim to the Father's throne. As Jonathan, many have courageously given their earthly lives for friends, even strangers, but only One has willingly volunteered to take another's deserved place in Hell (Eph. 4:9). Praise God, Christ's strong crying and tears were, in fact, heard (Luke 22:42). The penalty of eternal separation from the Father was gloriously removed from Him and, in turn, from us (Heb. 5:7).

As Jonathan made a steadfast covenant with David, our Greater Jonathan has promised not to fail us, or give us up, or leave us without support. The *Amplified* version of Hebrews 13:5 reads, "I will not, I will not, I will not in any degree leave you helpless, nor forsake, nor let you down [relaxing My hold on you]. Assuredly not." This truly is an exceeding great and precious promise (2 Pet. 1:4).

In deep gratitude we sing the beloved hymn, "What a Friend We Have in Jesus." But consider this: Could Jesus reciprocate? Could He sing in earnest, "What a friend I have in Debbie, . . . or in Wayne, . . . or in Sally?" Let each of us purpose to pass through the blood-sprinkled Outer Court of servanthood that we might commune, as a friend, with our beloved Jesus at the altar of incense, or prayer, in the Holy Place of spiritual friendship. Let us further act out our friendship as Jonathan to our Greater David.

Bridehood

The travel route for the Christian's life journey is pictured in the Old Testament Tabernacle, which was divided into three sections—Outer Court, Holy Place, and Most Holy Place. As Christians, our divine journey starts with blood-covering in the Outer Court of servanthood. It progresses to heart-compelled commitment in the Holy Place of friendship and, ultimately, to intimate communion with our Heavenly Bridegroom in the Most Holy Place, hitherto available to the high priest alone, and then only once a year.

Although we always serve, we are called beyond servitude to friendship with our beloved Jesus (John 15:15). How indescribable the honor of serving and even befriending the altogether lovely One. Content we are, and content we should be. But our journey is not yet complete. With the rending of the Temple's veil (Matt. 27:51), all believers now have bold access to the Most

Holy Place of God's boundless grace (Heb. 4:16). In fact, our Spirit-filled bodies have actually become the *naos*, or Most Holy Place (1 Cor. 6:19). As God was in the Ark of the Covenant, He now resides in the of ark of destined-to-be-glorified mankind (Rev. 21:2, 23). As such, we enjoy bride chamber intimacy with *Yahweh-Ishi*, our Husband.

Some find it more comfortable to assume the posture of servant, or even servant friend. They cannot possibly relate to bridehood. After all, they are undeniably unworthy. Others respond as did the Shulamite bride of Solomon's Song. With eyes fixed on their Heavenly Bridegroom, and not on self, they heed His call to "rise up and come away" (Song of Sol. 2:10). Love is stirred as He pleases (Song of Sol. 2:7), but they are open and unreservedly responsive (Song of Sol. 5:6).

Such ones understand that spiritual intimacy is not romantic. It is not sensual or "of the flesh," nor is it in any way deserved. To those who heed this remarkable call, it is enjoyed, in measure, on this earth; however, it is more fully enjoyed throughout eternity. Then the Plan of God (Gen. 1:26-27) will be fulfilled; and our bodies will be transfigured, our souls redeemed, and our spirits purified—all experientially. We will be perfect (whole, mature, complete) in Christ and one with Him in answer to Christ's prayer of John 17:21-26. Indeed, when He shall appear, we shall be His suited mate (1 John 3:2), without spot or blemish (Eph. 5:27) and glorious within (Ps. 45:13; Rev. 21:11), all because of Jesus.

As this set apart Bride of Christ, we go beyond the blind obedience of servanthood, beyond even the enlightened cooperation of friendship, to experiential oneness of purpose and mind. The Heavenly Bridegroom is set as a seal upon our hearts as a divine mark of authenticity and ownership (Song of Sol. 8:6), and a precious spiritual union transpires. In it, we actually partake of the divine nature (2 Pet. 1:4), something so heavenly it transcends the senses (1 Cor. 2:9).

Truly eye has not seen, nor ear heard, what God has prepared for His Bride (1 Cor. 2:9). The progression, however, is simple and pure. As Rebekah heeded the call of Eliazar, sent by Father Abraham, we heed the call of the Spirit to wed the Greater Isaac. With the commencement of her journey to a far land, Rebekah entered a sacred betrothal with one she had yet to see, and so it is with us. As Rebekah lifted up her eyes at the first sight of Isaac, she lighted off her camel, leaving behind the last vestiges of the world she had so far known (Gen. 24:64). In like fashion, the Church will one day lift up her head at the Lord's *parousia*, or presence (Luke 21:28); and she shall meet her Bridegroom in the air. Their spiritual union will be complete, and so shall she ever be with Him (1 Thess. 4:17).

"Whosoever will" may heed the call. Yes, let us will to serve Him, for He is worthy. Furthermore, let us will to be His friend, for His arms are open wide. Even more, let us will to love Him with bridelike passion, for He is the soon-coming Bridegroom. Even so, come, Lord Jesus (Rev. 22:20), that we might victoriously conclude this splendid life's journey.

Satan's Counterfeit Plan

We have seen that God has a glorious plan for each one. "Whosoever will" may come and be a part of it. Whenever God does or gives something good, however, Satan has an analogous counterfeit. For example, God has given His holy music (Ps. 95:1); Satan, his unholy counterfeit of acid rock. God has His holy dance (Exod. 15:20; 2 Sam. 6:14; 1 Chron. 15:29; Ps. 30:11; 149:3; 150:4; Song of Sol. 16: 13; Eccles. 3:4; Jer. 31:4, 13; Luke 6:23; 15:25; Acts 3:8) and Satan, his unholy counterfeit.

Whereas God moves His people from glory to glory (2 Cor. 3:18), Satan moves his from degradation to degradation (Prov. 4:19). Christ is the Lamb (John 1:29, 36); Satan's emissaries are lambs in wolves' clothing (Matt. 7:15). Jesus Christ is the Prince of Peace (Isa. 9:6), but when worldly men cry, "peace," apart from Him, sudden destruction comes (1 Thess. 5:3).

According to Scripture, the Christian is destined to spiritual maturity, wholeness, and completion (Eph. 4:13), Christ Himself being formed supernaturally within the yielded believer (Gal. 4:19) until—in a very real sense—it is no longer the Christian who lives, but Christ within (Gal. 2:20). Yet, His awe-inspiring Deity and my frail humanity remain indisputably separate. In effect, He lives His life through the yielded believer to the extent that a believer, by decision of will, allows self to decrease that Jesus might increase (John 3:30) and that the Father might be given free reign through that one to complete Christ's work on earth. The Millennial rule of Christ with His Bride will usher in God's intended New International World Order. Then the earth will be full of the knowledge of the Lord as the waters cover the sea (Isa. 11:9); and Satan, at long last, will be bound.

Until then, the Devil is hard at work. His counterfeit scheme destines man to what the New Age occultists call "christhood," a position attained, not through the shed Blood of Christ, but rather through self-worth. Some believe that this clearly anti-scriptural concept is achieved through the ladder of reincarnation. Humans, they believe, are gods-in-the-making, moving toward "Christ consciousness." This Cosmic Gospel is unadulterated pantheism, which is the belief that god is the sum total of all that exists. There is no personal God, only a god- or life-force which flows through all living things. Therefore, mankind, plants and animals are all part of God, destined by a series of reincarnations, to become one with God and with the universe. A planetary quantum leap will signal man's evolution to full potential. Then will come the anticipated golden era of pseudo-peace and brotherhood in what is known as the Age of Aquarius. Misplaced belief in evolution, reincarnation, astrology, and Eastern forms of meditation will join arms with secular schemes to usher in Lucifer's New International World Order with its one-world political, economic, and religious components for this up-and-coming New Age.

God's Plan and Satan's Contrasted

God's work in our days will cause scoffers to marvel (Acts 13:41). In the spiritual realm, this work transforms the believer by renewing the mind (Rom. 12:2). In the natural realm, it magnifies the city of Jerusalem, which has been trampled underfoot until times of the Gentiles be fulfilled. Biblical prophecies affirm Israel will be led back to live again on her own soil, having been dispersed by Assyrians in the eighth Century B.C. (Jer. 23:7-8). It is no wonder that the enemy is manifestly anti-Semitic, identifying Jews (and Christians) as Forces of Darkness or Evil and, therefore, worthy to be destroyed as hindrances to the New International World Order for a coming New Age.

Whenever national Israel is addressed in Scripture, there is parallel application to spiritual Israel as well. For example, Jerusalem which is above is free. She is mother of us all (Gal. 4:26). This free Jerusalem represents the New Covenant. Its participants are brethren in a spiritual sense and the children of promise (Gal. 4:24, 28). The culmination of this spiritual picture is the presentation of the Bride of Christ, pictured as a holy city, the New Jerusalem. John sees her as one prepared and adorned for her heavenly husband while coming down from God out of heaven (Rev. 21:2).

God's plan for His own embraces both national and spiritual Israel. Satan's strategy pinpoints possibilities for deceiving, if possible, the very elect of God (Matt. 24:24). To do so, he engages hordes of demons and their dupes to undermine the good work of God. God's work in the Church moves her from glory to glory (2 Cor. 3:18). It will not be prevented, for the gates of hell shall not prevail against her (Matt. 16:18).

Satan's opposing work is by God's permission, allowing evil men and seducers to wax worse and worse—deceiving and being deceived—until their time is up (2 Thess. 2:11-12; 2 Tim. 3:13). Then shall that wickedness be revealed and subsequently consumed. Antichrist and his subversive schemes will be paralyzed with the brightness of Christ's coming (2 Thess. 2:8).

To accomplish His plan, God's intervention spans the gamut of fields. Not surprisingly, Satan comes alongside with his lying deceptions. The widely funded New Age Movement is an united worldwide coalition with an ungodly global platform. Advocates refer to the movement as "The Plan." As is the case with secret societies and Wicca (modern witchcraft), seven branches of its "Great Work" address these major fields: political/ environmental/ geographic; religious/ moral; educational; scientific/ medical; military/ technological; cultural/ social/ philosophical; and economic.

Politically

A Christian's fitting citizenship is in Heaven (Heb. 11:16), for (s)he is in the world, but not of it (John 17:16). The believer's heart, then, is not tied to this world or its established system. With Christ Jesus, believers are joint ("equal") heirs of God Himself (Rom. 8:17). Their position is as royalty under King Jesus, the One to Whom all loyalty is due (Phil. 2:9-11). All other allegiances dim in comparison.

Recognizing that righteousness exalts a nation (Prov. 14:34), the Christian purposes to be a good citizen, shunning imitation of ungodly ways (Matt. 23:23). While using the world and its system without unduly abusing it (1 Cor. 7:31), the believer submits wholeheartedly to those appointed by God to rule on earth (Heb. 13:7, 17) when they do not oppose the highest authority, God Himself.

The world's hope, by contrast, is a destined-to-fail, but nonetheless, swiftly emerging New World Order, which will be celebrated for its one-world system of government, religion, and economics under one called Antichrist and his False Prophet (Dan. 2:19; 31). Big Government will likely be controlled by world financiers, who, as veritable "kings without kingdoms," will rule with Antichrist for "an hour"—that is to say, a predetermined and bounded time span (Rev. 17:12-13).

In preparation for a swiftly coming New Age, the politically astute seek to establish a presumed collective security with multilateral peace-keeping efforts (1 Thess. 5:3). Multinational planning commissions will eventually give way to world government by establishing economic interdependence among superpowers.

International power elites purpose to regionalize first Europe, then the world, while paving the way for world peace. Concepts of national sovereignty will be effectively dissolved, and these regions will be linked to a bio-regionally defined representative federal government.

Precursor coalitions include, but are not limited to, Old Rome revived through the new European Community (Dan. 9), the Islamic World Order in alliance with Russia (Gen. 16:12; Ezek. 38:1-8), and Asian alliances (See Armageddon: "Kings of the East.").

Environmental issues will likely provide the chief argument in favor of a world government.

Environmentally

Scripture promises a coming Day of the Lord (2 Pet. 3:10-12), which shall burn as an oven (Mal. 4:1), and thus end the time of the world's history (Isa. 2:10-11). In that day, God will accomplish His divine purpose of vindicating and delivering His people. It will be a day of both wrath (Isa. 13:6, 9; Jer. 46:10) and restoration (Isa. 14:1; Joel 2:28-32).

In accordance with Biblical prophecy, the earth will experience unprecedented shakings with the approaching of Christ's *parousia*, or presence, at the Rapture. Changes include varied global weather patterns, due in part to increased volcanic action (Matt. 24:7-8), and supernatural signs, shakings, and earthquakes (Luke 21:11).

Satan's plan for a New World Order will capitalize on guilt and fear surrounding environmental crises. According to some authorities, even the earth's atmosphere will become increasingly polluted (Luke 21:11; 25-26). Some claim that deforestation will deplete the air supply, and soil erosion will disrupt the earth's food supply, resulting in famines and water shortages (Matt. 24:7); others claim that manipulated, unwarranted fear of such occurrences will hasten Big Brother intervention.

Unbeknownst to radical environmentalists, however, woe is proclaimed upon the earth's inhabitants, not because of technology, industry, or an out-of-balance ecosystem, but rather because of the Devil himself (Rev. 12:12) and his flood of deception, lies, and persecution (verse 15).

Geographically

The true Church looks to a very special time on earth throughout Christ's Millennial Kingdom, a thousand-year universal reign of righteousness (2 Pet. 3:13). Then, "the earth shall be filled with knowledge of the glory of the Lord, as the waters cover the sea" (Hab. 2:14); and the whole creation will be delivered from the "bondage of corruption" (Rom. 8:21-22). This new dispensation of glorious liberty will be marked by restoration of "all things" previously taken by the devourer, Satan himself (Joel 2:25).

The world's agenda in contrast calls for dissolution of national sovereignty toward regional groupings with redistribution of the world's wealth. Eventually, this New World Order's companion one world religious system will require all who dwell upon the earth to worship Antichrist (Rev. 13:8).

Religiously/Morally

According to the Bible, the true Church—spiritual Israel—is destined to experience a great outpouring of God's Spirit (Joel 2:28). With spiritual gifts operating freely in what Joel identifies as a future time, she will experience a deluge of former (teaching) and latter (soul-ingathering) rains of revelatory insight (Dan. 12:4). This "latter rain" was birthed previously at Pentecost (Acts 2:16-18), but continues to heighten as the Rapture draws nearer (James 5:7-8). Worldwide preaching of the Gospel will accompany these phenomena (Matt. 24:14; Rev. 3:7).

No doubt God's people will deliver Holy Ghost anointed testimony in the face of escalating persecution. The time will come that whoever kills a consecrated Christian will believe (s)he has served God well in doing so (Mark 13:9; John 16:2). Despite elevated "Christophobia," the ever-increasing Body of Christ will be immersed, perhaps as never before, in a baptism of love (Eph. 4:16). So distinctive is this love that the Bible labels it "exotic" (foreign to the human heart)—(*Wuest*, 1 John 3:1).

Apparently the Church will receive some recognition and homage for Christ's love bestowed upon her (Rev. 3:9). For many believers, however, materialism will set in (Rev. 3:17ff). Despite these "lukewarm" within the true Church, there are always believers who escape pitfalls of religious conglomerates, syncretism, and social gospel (2 Tim. 3:5). They are the faithful who continue to ready themselves for the presence of their soon-coming heavenly Bridegroom (Matt. 24: 44; Luke 21:28). In anticipation, they comfort one another daily with hope of the Rapture (1 Thess. 4:18).

As they mature in unity of spirit and faith (Eph. 4:3, 13, 16), believers prepare to be raised up as a Warrior Bride (Eph. 4:12-13; Ezek. 37:10; Isa. 66:7-8; Rev. 19: 14). Before the flood of Great Apostasy released against them (1 Tim. 4:1), they stand firmly against their formidable foe. This vigilant Church body discerns rightly between the true and false Universal Messiahism rampant at the twilight of history as we know it (Dan. 9:27; Matt. 24:24).

Satan's Counterfeit:
The False Church (Cults), Matt. 24:11

Some bodies of believers demonstrate cult tendencies, but these churches may not necessarily be "cults." Certainly no church has full truth. By definition, a cult is a recently founded system of religious teaching, claiming to be "Christian," but erroneously requiring compulsive, unreasonable preoccupation with its human leadership. Moreover, a cult denies or alters essential Biblical doctrines.

Whereas "children of the Wicked One" (father of cults) are as tares, true believers are as wheat. Cults are sanctioned to grow side by side with the true Church, often undifferentiated, lest in gathering the tares of cults, wheat is accidentally rooted up (Matt. 13:24-30; 37-40).

When disagreements arise on finer points of doctrine, many in their zeal make a point of labeling brethren "cult members." It is the Lord's work to protect His true wheat, even if mistaken for tares; it is the Devil's work to "divide and conquer." This he does by seducing wheat to accuse and attack wheat—if not falsely, certainly presumptuously. As a result, confusion reigns; instead of applying spiritual dynamism to combat the real enemy, well-meaning but misguided Christians fight one another.

Brethren are forbidden to *anakrino*, or cross-examine as a prosecuting attorney, fellow brethren—themselves included (1 Cor. 4:3). Nonetheless, as "[wo]men of the spirit" (Rotherham), believers are to "try the spirits," investigating and making inquiry into "all things" that pertain to their faith (*Amplified*, 1 Cor. 2:15). Those engaged in this type of pursuit find that false churches have visibly proliferated especially since the mid-1800s. Strongholds are readily apparent in such gatherings as the apostate Jesus Seminar (2 Tim. 3:7) and the Freedom from Religion Foundation (1 Tim. 6:20-21).

Satan's Counterfeit: The "Godly" Unregenerate ("Fields White unto Harvest," John 4:35)

Men and women of faith may choose to use the description "pre-Christian" in reference to their yet-unregenerate friends, neighbors, and relatives. Religious pre-Christians, being conditioned by prayers of loved ones, may include groups linked to Zionism (Jer. 23:7,8), Islam (Gen. 17:20), or nominal Christianity (Rev. 3:15-16). The Lord's work on their behalf is clear: It is to bring them to a saving knowledge of Jesus Christ.

Satan's plan, however, is to thwart this endeavor. Descriptive of Satan, a Greek word for "evil" suggests active evil. So wicked are Satan and his emissaries that they are not content to suffer an eternity alone in hell. Rather, they would drag down with them all possible candidates. To this vile end, they double their efforts in fearful anticipation of their certain downfall at the brightness of Jesus' presence.

Satan's Counterfeits: The Occultists (1 Tim. 4:1) in Secret Societies, Wicca, and Luciferic/ New Age Movements (Rom. 1:25)

Even as born-again Christians know, love, and serve their precious Savior, practicing occultists know and serve the antagonist, Satan himself. Willing participants comprise an age-old occult coalition with an ambitious political platform to regionalize and then unify the world.

Ancient mystery religions—from the bowels of Babylon—birth these demonically inspired global goals. Marching in step with its occult alliances is the evolutionary holistic New Age Movement, which along with other groups, is fixed upon "balancing forces in the universe." This Babylonian concept is inspired by pantheism with its "all is energy" premise.

The Bible declares that a season will come when all nations drink of the wine of the wrath of Babylon's fornication (Rev. 14:8). It is for this reason that the Church must remain decidedly separate, touching not "the unclean thing" (2 Cor. 6:17). Her call is to fulfill God's plan to be presented a "chaste virgin," free from spiritual syncretism, unto Jesus Christ, her Lord and heavenly Bridegroom (2 Cor. 11:2).

Remaining separate, the true Church, Christ's spotless Bride, is spared union with a coming one world false religious system, depicted in Scriptures as a whore sitting upon waters representing "peoples, nations, multitudes, and tongues" (Rev. 17:1, 15). Allied with Antichrist, and demanding his worship (Rev. 17:12), this harlot is at the root of an imminent Great Apostasy (1 Tim. 4:1; 2 Thess. 2:3). Furthermore, this false worship earmarks "the lie" of 2 Thessalonians 2:11.

Morally

Christ's true Church is predestined to assume the "measure of the stature of the fullness of Christ" unto a "perfect [mature] man" (Eph. 4:13). Toward this glorious end, God is all the while effectually at work in the Church both to will and to do His good pleasure (Phil. 2:13). Though not without human frailty, followers of good eschew evil (1 Pet. 3:11-13; 3 John 11). They prove (or "put to the test") all things, holding fast to that which is good (1 Thess. 5:21).

In contrast, the Devil's plan for the world is moral relativism (Judges 17) leading to ungodliness, demonstrated as follows (2 Tim. 3:1-5):

1. Misplaced love of self, money, pleasures—unloving and lacking natural affection.
2. Misplaced self-image—being irreconcilable, boastful, arrogant, conceited, lacking in gratitude.
3. Misplaced loyalties—being disobedient to parents, treacherous, malicious in gossip, and apt to revile.
4. Misplaced godliness—having a form of godliness, but denying its power, and lacking self-control.

Educationally

The true Church anticipates "knowing, even as she is known" (1 Cor. 13:12); for earthly knowledge is destined to vanish (verse 8). The world, in contrast, rejects the knowledge of God for its own brand of politically correct dogma and moves toward establishing a New World Order (interdependent globalism), a new

race (one world; one species—genetically engineered and atti-
tude/ behavior modified), a new world religion celebrating what
the "heathen have to offer," and a new economic system (global
economics). The Rockefeller created Department of Health,
Education, and Welfare—along with other influential groups,
such as the Aspen Institute—bias education toward these goals.

The Outcome-Based Education (Goals 2000) Movement,
funded by New American Schools Development Corporation, is
creating an easily managed and controlled global work force of
automans, deliberately "dumbed down." Its emphasis is affective
development of emotions, attitudes, opinions—politically correct
ones, of course—toward collectivism and ultimately "oneness with
the universe." The esoteric philosophy in the New American
School strategy belies its sound link with New Age occultism.

Scientifically

Medical Science

Through the work of Christ at Calvary, the true Church
possesses "the children's bread" of wholeness (Matt. 15:30, 31).
God's peremptory plan for humankind is wellness.

However, through the entrance of sin, and as a part of its
curse, pestilence (Rev. 6:8) and plagues are increasingly manifest
in various places (Luke 21:11; Rev. 16:8-9). As recompense for
error of ungodly lifestyles (Rom. 1: 25-26), new and increasingly
deadly strains of disease associated with sexual sin will continue
to ravage the world's populace.

Medical and legal avenues make possible what pro-life advocates see as the murder of unborn infants (2 Tim. 3:2-3; Rev.
22:15). Parents "without natural affection" (Rom. 1:31) become,
as it were, "foes of their own households" (Matt. 10:36) when
they terminate life of their offspring for no more compelling
reason than convenience.

Drug abuse associated with religion (Greek *pharmakeia,* sorcery, or enchantment by drugs or magic) characterizes the false
religious system of John's Revelation on the Isle of Patmos.
According to the Word, all nations will one day be deceived with
sorceries (Rev. 18:23-24).

Among those to suffer the second death of Revelation 21:7-
8 are fortune-tellers (diviners), soothsayers (observers of times),

magicians (enchanters), sorcerers (witches), hypnotists (charmers), media possessed with spirit guides (consulters with spirits), clairvoyants or psychics (wizards), and media who contact the dead (necromancers) (Deut. 18:9-12). In seeking such familiar spirits, New Agers share their impending fate (Isa. 8:19-20).

Military Science (Matt. 24:6)

The true Church is depicted in Scriptures as a fighting army outfitted with the whole armor of God (Eph. 6:13-17) and engaged in the good fight of faith (2 Tim. 4:7). She prevails against rulers of the darkness of this world and spiritual wickedness (Eph. 6:12).

The world's warfare is of an entirely different sort. Its nuclear weaponry and chemical/biological warheads now make possible man's obliteration of the earth by fire (Isa. 24:1, 6). Armageddon is entirely possible and, from a natural standpoint, more probable than ever.

Technological Science

Knowledge of the things of God will increase dramatically as the Holy Spirit actively prepares the true Church for her glorious future (Dan. 12:4). Already the Church surpasses all knowledge known to man with the love of Christ (Eph. 3: 19).

The world's knowledge is diametrically opposed to God's. The Enemy will use modern technology to establish a worldwide super computer network (2 Tim. 3:7)—used by God's people for His glory, but correspondingly by globalists toward establishing a New World Order, destined to suffer forthcoming thermonuclear holocaust (Joel 2:30-31; Isa. 1:7-9).

Culturally/Socially/Philosophically/Psychologically

Culturally

In Christ, there is neither Jew nor Greek, bond nor free, male nor female. All who have put on Christ, having been baptized into Him, are uniquely one (Gal. 3:27-28). Their citizenship, training, concepts, manners, and tastes are heavenly (Heb. 11:16). God's plan is for unity and oneness within His true Church, for she is one body of believers with one selfsame Spirit; furthermore, her hope is categorically one (Eph. 4:4).

Satan's plan is to counterfeit this brilliant oneness. He works on unregenerate man to cause a sense of pseudo-oneness with his fellow man—even with the universe at large.

A popular advertising campaign uses the line, "This is my planet." Thus given a keen sense of belonging and ownership, the "natural man" of 1 Corinthians 2:14 is primed to assume "one mind" with the nations, eventually forfeiting power and strength to Antichrist. Gender, color, race, or creed matter not (Rev. 17:13, 15); Bible-believing, consecrated Christians alone fail to qualify as being among the world's celebrated diversity.

Socially

Scriptures picture the true Church as a many-membered body, each part precision tuned to function alone, but always in unity with its whole. Every joint supplies what is needed (Eph. 4:16) in perfect submission to its head, Jesus Christ (1 Cor. 12:12ff). It stands to reason that the basic unit of godly society is the traditional nuclear family, as defined in the Bible, for it mirrors God's relationship with His Church, the universal family of God destined to share eternity at their loving Father's side.

It is no wonder that the prince of this world hates traditional families. In Satan's scheme, responsibility and accountability take a back seat to pleasure while demonically-dulled natural affection gives rise to the cunning convenience of legal abortion on demand (2 Tim. 3:3-4). This enemy's tireless efforts result in godless children bent on disobeying parents (2 Tim. 3:2). Family members, who should love and support one another, become bitter foes (Matt. 10:34-35). God's gift of sexual union, reserved exclusively for a man and his lawful wife (Heb. 13:4), is exchanged for perversion and promiscuity, both subject to due recompense (Rom. 1:27; Luke 21:11). All contribute to the breakdown of the family, hence society at large.

Philosophically/Psychologically

The term "political correctness" is an umbrella under which a number of other "isms" huddle. Causes thus united include civil/gender/sexual orientation rights and radical environmentalism. The movement's program is to deconstruct Western civilization, specifically European/American culture. Anything "traditional" is the target—namely, traditional values, family, work ethic, the Constitution of the United States, and Judeo-Christian faith.

The antilogic of today's politically correct crowd is not new. Fifth century B.C. Greek philosophers called Sophists first developed it. They were atheists and early humanists known, perhaps not surprisingly, for attacking traditional religious beliefs. Protagorus was the leading Sophist who taught that "man is the measure of all things," which is the maxim underlying contemporary secular humanism. To move toward New Age globalism, national sovereignty must be abolished, cultures merged, and Judeo-Christian traditions undermined. Insiders to so-called politically correct Sophist antilogic are as those professing to be wise, while in fact they are foolish (Rom. 1:22). They are astute in evildoing, but of doing good in the sight of God they have no knowledge (Jer. 4:22). In the second epistle Paul addressed to Timothy, he aptly describes them in terms of prevalent last day attributes; men will be proud, trucebreakers, traitors, false accusers, and despisers of those that are good. Ever-learning, they never come to the knowledge of truth (2 Tim. 3:1-7).

Solipsism is a philosophical view that maintains that the self is the only thing that can be known to exist. The solipsist sees himself as the only individual in existence, assuming other people to be a reflection of his own consciousness. Solipsism embraces the notion that one must, therefore, feel good about oneself. It is part of the modern movement "inward" (to the New Age occultist, seeking one's "higher self").

In the last days, says Paul, "men shall be lovers of their own selves" (2 Tim. 3:1-2). Self-love and self-deification play important roles in preparing the world for Luciferic Initiation. The religion of Antichrist exalts self as "God" (1 Cor. 3:16; 6:19 with 2 Thess. 2:4).

Economically

The true Church is forever "profitable," though not necessarily financially affluent (1 Tim. 4:8). Wealthy or not, she is subject to temptation by increased goods (Rev. 3:17).

The world's planned economies smack of socialism and are destined to result in an ultimate dictatorship (Rev. 13:7) with world economic controls and redistribution of wealth. An imminent cashless society is paving the way for the Mark of the Beast, without which none can transact business (Rev. 13:16-17; 14:9, 11; 16:2; 20:4).

Summary

Despite scoffers and unbelievers, God is accomplishing a momentous work in our days. This work centers on Jerusalem—re-establishment of her people on their own soil, subsequent economic prosperity, and the rebuilding of the Temple. He is also at work in spiritual Jerusalem toward her restoration and maturation as the perfected Bride of Christ.

Enemies will be brought against both national and the spiritual Jerusalem; and, indeed, the last war of the world will start over her. Parallel works of God in the Church and of the Enemy span all fields. As God's Church prepares for Christ's presence at the Rapture, the world prepares for Antichrist and his False Prophet. The good news is this: The Bride will be snatched away to the side of her heavenly Bridegroom before full bloom of the New World Order, the destiny of which is sudden destruction (1 Thess. 5:3).

God's Plan (Gen. 1:26-27)	Satan's Counterfeit (2 Thess. 2:9ff)
Theocratic Kingdom (Rev. 12:10)	New World Order (Dan. 2:19; 31-45)
King Jesus (Rev. 15:3)	World Dictator (Antichrist) (2 Thess. 2:4)
Prince of Peace (Isa. 9:6)	Pseudo-peace Maker (1 Thess. 5:3)
Unity of faith (Eph. 4:13)	Unity in diversity (Rev. 17:13,15)
Unity of Christ's Body (Eph. 4:4)	Mystical, universal oneness (2 Cor. 6:17)
Man, partaker of Divine nature (2 Pet. 1:4)	Man, divine (Prov. 11:2)
Experiential peace (Gal. 5:22)	Proclaimed peace (1 Thess. 5:3)
Jesus, only way (John 14:6)	Many ways (Matt. 7:13)

All for glory of God (Rom. 12:1-2)	All for me and mine (2 Tim. 3:15)
Creation (Gen. 1:1)	Evolution (Rom. 1:25)
Glory to glory (2 Cor. 3:18)	Degradation to degradation (Prov. 4:19)
Creator all in all (Rom. 1:25)	Creation all in all (Rom. 1:25)
Man, Crown of Creation (Heb. 2:6-8)	Equality of life forms (1 Cor. 15:39)
Preeminence of Jesus (Phil. 2:9)	Preeminence of universal good (2 Tim. 3:5)
Holiness enjoined (Eph. 5:27)	Holiness disdained/ mocked (Acts 13:41)
Do His thing (1 John 2:17)	Do my own thing (Rom. 8:13)
Loving/hating as God does (Ps. 97:10)	Loving/hating as the world does (1 John 4:5)
Sexual purity (Col. 3:5)	Sexual permissiveness (Eph. 4:19)
Traditional Family (Prov. 8:22; 1 Tim. 5:14; 2 Cor. 12:14)	Alternative Lifestyle (Rom. 1:26)
Christ in believers (Col. 1:27)	God-force in all (2 Thess. 2:11-12)
Word, plumb line (Amos 7:8)	Man, measure of all things (1 John 2:16)
Woman, weaker vessel (1 Pet. 3:7)	Woman Power [Feminism] (Prov. 19:13)
Woman honored (Prov. 31:30)	Woman demeaned (Prov. 14:1)
Child humility/submission (Col. 3:20)	Child rights (Job 30:12)

Childlike childhood (1 Cor. 13:11)	Childless childhood (Gal. 4:1-2)
Absolute values (John 14:6)	Moral relativism (Judges 17)
Inordinate love of money, evil (1 Tim. 6:10)	Money, major life goal (Eccles. 10:19)
Love passing knowledge (Eph. 3:19)	Knowledge supreme (Dan. 12:4)
Humility enjoined (1 Pet. 5:5)	Pride applauded (2 Tim. 3:2)
Death to self (1 Cor. 15:31)	Ascent to Higher Self (Rom. 7:24)
All unrighteousness is sin (1 John 5:17)	Situation ethics (Judges 17)
Man accountable to God (Rom. 14:12)	Man accountable to self (Prov. 12:15)
Believers forgiven (1 John 1:9)	Believers suspected/accused (John 15:19)
[National, Spiritual] Jerusalem restored (Ezek. 37:19-22; Rev. 21:4)	[National, Spiritual] Jerusalem compromised (Matt. 24:15; 24)

A

Vigilant Christian's

Glossary

A

Abortion

Abortion is termination of a pregnancy before the fetus is grown sufficiently to survive outside the mother's womb. It may be involuntary (as in miscarriage) or deliberate, the latter being the issue in question. *Fortune* magazine estimates that the abortion industry grosses half-a-billion dollars annually. Methods include suction curette, prostaglandin pessary to induce labor, and the antiprogesterone pill (RU486). Ovrette is a chemical abortifacient. Mifepristone allows a woman to abort in a doctor's office instead of having a surgical abortion at a clinic.

Pro-choice advocates point to the large numbers of deaths and mutilations from back-street abortions which are certain to ensue, they claim, without unlimited legal abortions. In contrast, pro-life advocates believe that "My body—my right to choose" stops at an infant's right to life itself. Every person is endowed by the Creator with certain inalienable rights, the first of which is life. The latter belief affirms the Hippocratic Oath.

Perhaps no political issue exceeds in controversy that of abortion. Nonetheless, with the possible exception of Red China, the U.S. has the most liberal abortion laws in the world. Abortion-on-demand was legalized by the Supreme Court in 1973 (*Roe v. Wade*). Now a Christian, Jane Roe (pseudonym) today supports the pro-life agenda. Another U.S. Supreme Court decision (1989) gave state legislatures the right to introduce some restrictions. Today, anti-abortion activists concentrate their attentions on outlawing the late term procedure of partial birth abortion, deemed medically unnecessary by the American Medical Association.

Although federal health officials report the lowest number of legal abortions in about two decades, the Center for Disease Control has made no effort to determine how many illegal abortions were completed during the same time period. The Center admits that abortions are "selectively underreported." Yearly, there are 50 million abortions globally ("Facts in Brief: Induced Abortion," The Alan Guttmacher Institute, January 1997).

At the forefront of global efforts, the World Constitution and Parliament Association plans to funnel funds of the new global banking system to countries with zero or less population growth. Population control nestles under the banner of the United Nation's concept of "sustainable development," which marries philosophies of Thomas Malthus and Alfred Kinsey. The former purports that too many people on earth will outstrip its resources; the latter embraces need for, and the right to, nonproductive sexual gratification at any age (See Safe Sex). Contemporary champion of Malthusianism, Paul Ehrlich of Stanford University has provided the model, the Global Biodiversity Assessment, to implement policy of a treaty originated at the 1992 Earth Summit (See Radical Environmentalism).

Internationally active Planned Parenthood is the largest provider of abortion services in the nation. The U.S. government gives tens of millions of our tax dollars to Planned Parenthood and similar organizations. The fact that ninety percent of those who gather, write, and report our news support abortion may account for its seemingly ubiquitous approval (See Mainstream Media).

Biblical Perspective

Politically correct feminists have been led to believe that legal abortion serves as "a great equalizer," ushering women into a new age of enlightenment and freedom (See Genderism/Radical Feminism). It feeds instead into today's death culture. Whereas Satan is dubbed "a murderer" (John 8:44; See Lucifer), Jesus Christ is "the life" (John 14:6). Simply put, the Lord hates "hands that shed innocent blood" (Prov. 6:16a-19).

To further New Age globalism, the Judeo-Christian ethic with its celebration of life must be effectively undermined. No doubt *Roe v. Wade* has dramatically altered the moral fabric of American society, and that of the world at large. This comes at a price (See Values [Affective] Education). Whenever, contrary to the Plan of God, human life is perceived as expendable, the Enemy is released to carry out his counterfeit plan which circumvents the "abundant life" Jesus promised (John 10:10).

ACLU

Established in 1920 by Communist Jane Addams, Roger Baldwin, Norman Thomas, and others, the American Civil Liberties Union (ACLU) is allegedly a nonpartisan organization devoted to protecting basic rights set forth in the U.S. Constitution. Over a quarter-million dues paying members support affiliates in every state.

"Mainstream" Claim; Radical Agenda

(Dr. D. James Kennedy. *What Does the ACLU Really Believe?* [Ft. Lauderdale: Coral Ridge Ministries, 1995].) While reckoning itself "mainstream," the ACLU opposes laws banning polygamy; moreover, a California affiliate recently claimed that to teach, as a traditional American value, monogamous, heterosexual relations within legal matrimony actually violates the First Amendment.

The ACLU supports unconditional protection for flag-burners and voting rights for illegal aliens. It opposes secret CIA operations to rescue hostages (or to resist terrorist activities).

While fighting for legalized drug use, the ACLU sued to stop drug searches in Chicago's crime-infested public housing projects. Furthermore, the Union opposes searches of student lockers for drugs or guns, not to mention sobriety checkpoints.

"The American Sex Liberties Union"

(Dr. Beverly LaHaye. Newsletter. [Washington, DC: Concerned Women for America, 1997], 1-4). The ACLU goes beyond litigation to operate an aggressive public education program with mandatory sex education for all grades when, in fact, thirteen years are not necessary unless "how-to's" are introduced. Furthermore, the union opposes parental consent laws and rating movies to alert parents about sexual or violent content.

The ACLU supports abortion on demand, legalization of prostitution and child pornography, and gay rights to marry, adopt children, serve as foster parents, and participate in the Boy Scouts. (Jeffrey M. Peyton, Publishing Director. *Religious Rights Watch* [Chesapeake: Christian Coalition, 1998]. vol. 9, no. 4; vol. 9, no. 3.) It objects to medical safety regulation and reporting of

AIDS cases. While disallowing pro-life demonstrations, the ACLU has helped to restore Medicaid coverage of abortion for women in federal prisons.

"The Criminals' Lobby"

(Dr. D. James Kennedy, *Let's Tell the ACLU* [Ft. Lauderdale: Coral Ridge Ministries, 1995].) With the exception of the government itself, the ACLU has done more than any other entity to reshape public policy through court precedents. The union frequently takes an anti-police position—for example, in the Rodney King case. For all crimes except murder and treason, the ACLU opposes prison terms (Policy 242), preferring fines instead, even for rapists and child abusers.

Since its founding, the ACLU has defended almost every primary U.S. civil liberties court case. ACLU lobbyists in Washington are known for intensive, high-pressure scare tactics toward insuring "freedom of expression," "personal equality before the law," and "due process." Believing that people commit crimes because of poverty, the ACLU proudly represents prostitutes, drug abusers, and pornographers. Many agree with Former President George Bush that the work of the ACLU is to expand the rights of criminals. Bush labeled it "The Criminals' Lobby." Although the ACLU has eight policies on prisoners' rights, it has no policy to support rights of crime victims. (Dr. James Kennedy, Ph.D. Newsletter [Ft. Lauderdale: Coral Ridge Ministries, 3 July 1995]. 1-4).

"Anti-Christian Liberals' Union"

(Benjamin Hart, President. Newsletter. [Alexandria: Christian Defense Fund, 1997]. 1-4). While pushing for taxation of churches, ministries, and other charities, the ACLU promotes tax exemptions for Satanists (See Ancient Mystery Religions). Rightly dubbed the "Anti-Christian Liberals' Union," it opposes voluntary prayer and Bible reading in schools, sports arenas, and legislative assemblies. (Virginia Schnabel, Sr., Editor. *Blackmail in Washington Schools* [Olympia: Christian Coalition of Washington, 1995]. 1). The Union works to eliminate nativity scenes and other Christian symbols on public property. In 1995 the ACLU filed suit against the Honorable Roy Moore, a Baptist judge who posts the Ten Commandments and opens court with prayer led by a clergyman. More recently, it has filed a federal lawsuit to prevent Ohio's state motto, "With God, all things are possible," from being set into pavement on a Capitol grounds plaza. (Jeffrey M. Peyton, Publishing director. *Religious Rights Watch* [Chesapeake: Christian Coalition, 1997]. vol. 8, no. 10).

Fighting for the rights of proclaimed atheists, the ACLU opposes imprinting "In God We Trust" on our coins and use of the phrase "under God" in the Pledge of Allegiance. The Union objects to accreditation for science departments at Bible-believing Christian universities, homeschooling, and access for Christian school children to any publicly funded services.

Biblical Perspective

Scriptures prophesy that in perilous last days (2 Tim. 3:1), "evil men and seducers shall wax worse and worse, deceiving and being deceived" (verse 13). In harmony with Isaiah 5:20, true spiritual light (good) will be exchanged for darkness (evil). Those "wise in their own eyes, and prudent in their own sight," will "justify the wicked for reward" and effectively take away righteousness (verses 21, 23). By "the sleight of men and cunning craftiness," these lie in wait to "lead to a false path" (Eph. 4:14). Their so-called "mystery of iniquity" is already at work (2 Thess. 2:7) to topple the Judeo-Christian ethic for a more suitable counterpart for a coming New Age. In time, global allies at war with Christ and His disciples will be of "one mind" under submission to Antichrist (Rev. 17:13-14), whose mission will be to oppose godliness and support instead "self-god" (2 Thess. 2:4; See Pantheism), with man at the center of all things (See Humanism).

Adept/Initiated Adept

To the New Age occultist, the master is considered to be enlightened, or "to have fire in the eyes" (throwback to sun-worship). The term, "master," is synonymous with ascended master, adept/initiated adept, spirit guide/guide, the Hierarchy of Initiates/ Spiritual Hierarchy of the Earth/Planetary Hierarchy/the Hierarchy, and *Uburmenschen* (German).

Once embryo-gods, adepts have repeatedly undergone the process of reincarnation. Having achieved Luciferic Initiation, they claim to be highly evolved humans (See Evolution) who have mastered the so-called "science" of Esoteric Philosophy. Having triumphed over matter by supposedly mastering self, the adept's consciousness has shifted from self to group. One with God and the universe (See Pantheism), adepts are Custodians of the Plan and, therefore, equipped to watch over and guide humanity's spiritual progress.

To some mystics, adepts are spirit beings (actually demons) with whom they interact once having entered an altered state of consciousness. Spirit guides (adepts) are sometimes referred to as "guardian angels" (actually fallen angels, or demons) by self-proclaimed "Christians," such as Madeline L'Engle, a New Age author in residence at Upper Manhattan's Cathedral of St. John, the Divine. Known as the "Green Cathedral," "Big John" houses the Gaia Institute (See Radical Environmentalism).

Toward establishing the Anti-Christ New World Order, adepts work hard to extinguish Forces of Darkness/Evil (actually Jews and Christians) so that the old "Piscean Age" with its obsolete religion will give way to the Age of Aquarius, marked by a pseudo-golden era of peace and brotherhood, given the flowering of human potential apart from the one true God (See Humanism).

Biblical Perspective

Paul was an apostle not from or through men (i.e., via spirit guide), but by Jesus Christ and the Father (Gal. 1:1). He admonished the Thessalonians to "stand fast," being fixed firmly in every good word and work (2 Thess. 2:15,17) lest they believe the lie of self-god (verse 11), and thus buy into Antichrist's agenda for one world subjugation (Rev. 17:13-14). In the context of the latter-day "mystery of iniquity," Paul refers to the "strong delusion" of those who forsake salvation in wrongful pursuit of esoteric enlightenment (2 Thess. 2:10-11; See Antichrist and False Prophet). In contrast, the "perfect" (mature) man of Ephesians 4:13 attains "the measure of the stature that belongs to the fullness of Christ" (See Manchild Ministry). This is achieved, not by Luciferic Initiation, but by Jesus, Author and Finisher of one's faith (Heb. 12:2). Speaking truth in love, the mature believer grows up into Christ (Eph. 4:15); (s)he does not evolve into esoteric christhood, as New Agers purport.

Afrocentrism

The term political correctness is an umbrella under which a number of other "isms" huddle, Afrocentrism included. Simply put, the movement's program is to deconstruct Western civilization, specifically European/American culture. Afrocentrism's central theme is that whatever happens in the West is bad, but everything out of Africa is good (*Newsweek,* 23 Sept. 1991, page 46).

Afrocentrists believe that Abraham, Isaac, Jacob, Jesus, Joseph, Mary, Beethoven, Robert Browning, William Faulkner, Eli Whitney, and Huck Finn were all black. While at the same time claiming credit for achievements of Western culture, Afrocentrists condemn European/American culture. Even black scholar Frank Snoden of Harvard University admonishes Afrocentrists to cease mythologizing and falsifying the past (*Measure,* Jan. 1992, No. 102, page 10).

Those who challenge the movement are tagged racists and charged with seeking to preserve white, heterosexual male supremacy. Director of Harvard's African-American studies program Professor Henry Louis Gates, Jr. is arguably the most distinguished black scholar in the world; and he opposes this type of Afrocentric scapegoating.

No doubt Afrocentrism has much in common with activism of the sixties, but color lines are being drawn all the more today, this time by some blacks. While white institutions are quickly becoming integrated, traditionally black ones are being preserved. In fact, new black institutions (e.g., the Black Miss America Pageant) are even encouraged.

Anyone who questions the flawed logic of Afrocentrism is labeled "racist." According to politically correct antilogic, blacks themselves cannot be racist because they have "no power." Claims to Afrocentric ascendancy by the likes of Malcolm X and Black Panthers effectively topple this faulty reasoning.

Afrocentrists also protest as racist the National College Athletic Association's attempt to impose minimum academic standards through its Proposition 48. In so doing, Afrocentrists actually rob blacks of the sound education many of them want and deserve. Furthermore, Afrocentrists call SAT and ACT tests racist for failing to measure "Black potential" when achievement, not potential, is the point. Given that many first-generation Asian-

American immigrants perform best on these tests, the accusation that they are "culturally biased" does not ring true.

In tenor with Afrocentric goals, the school board of Oakland, California, has elevated Ebonics (Black English) to the status of an official language, considered to be part of the district's bilingual education program. Many blacks join whites in disputing this controversial policy.

Biblical Perspective

For the New World Order to take form, national sovereignty must be abolished, cultures merged, and Judeo-Christian traditions sabotaged. Such is the case with Afrocentrism, a component of today's Political Correctness Movement, whose agenda seeks to deconstruct Western civilization.

In His Eschatological Discourse (Matt. 24), Jesus clearly states that in the last days, *ethnos* (race) will rise up against *ethnos* (verse 7). Although racial wars define these godless latter days, God remains "no respecter of persons" (Acts 10:34). In Christ, there is neither male nor female, Jew nor Greek, bond nor free— black nor white (Gal. 3:28). Because it is not right to do evil that somehow good may come, reverse discrimination cannot possibly be a godly solution for the offense of bigotry (Ps. 34:14; Acts 10:28).

Afrocentrists nonetheless claim that Christianity plays a key part in keeping African-American minds in bondage. Not so. The "more sure word" admonishes diverse believers to "stand fast therefore in the liberty wherewith Christ hath made us free, and be not entangled again with the yoke of bondage" (Gal. 5:1). It is the flesh nature, not its color, that yields bondage (Gal. 5:19-21); true Christianity in action produces liberty, which the Bible aptly describes as glorious (Rom. 8:21).

Age of Aquarius

New Age theology teaches that every 2,160 years of cyclic time, a new age emerges with some new revelation. To the mystic, humankind represent "planetary light bearers" presently moving out of the Age of Pieces (Age of the Individual) into the Age of Aquarius (Age of Group Consciousness). This soon-coming age will be distinguished by group interplay and idealism.

According to esoteric philosophy, the old age with its anti-quated form of Judeo-Christian religion is even now giving way to a new, enlightened age, which promises unprecedented opportunity, peace, and worldwide collaboration. It will usher in unlimited well-being and universal brotherhood in a golden era of harmony with the universe (See Pantheism), paired supposedly with the full flowering of human potential (See Humanism).

Every New Age has a new Savior (Maitreya) to lead the world into discovery of the "higher self," or more accurately, "self-god." A Masonic work entitled *Freemasonry and the Ancient Gods* (1921) calls Aquarius "the sign of the perfected man." Antichrist typifies this enlightened, "perfected man" who, through Luciferic Initiation, discovers his own godhood.

Biblical Perspective

Promise of a coming Age of Aquarius counterfeits progressive ages outlined in the Apocalypse (Chapters 2-3) toward realizing God's Plan for maturity in Christ (Col. 2:10). The number "seven" symbolizes spiritual completion. While in the spirit on the Isle of Patmos, looking back in time to what yet is to come, John the Revelator addresses seven churches (Rev. 1:1, 3, 10, 11), which represent the entire body of believers.

For believers throughout history, and for individual Christians, the glorious Plan of God takes time to realize. Many authorities believe that each church of John's revelation represents a broader church age typified by a unique spiritual condition, a lesson to be learned, and a reward. For each, Jesus Christ is revealed in a extraordinary way. For example, the latter-day church of Philadelphia, or "brotherly love," points to today's church age of worldwide evangelism. Jesus is revealed as "One Who holds the world in His hands." "For having kept the word of His patience" (Rev. 3:10), and by means of the Rapture, Philadelphia saints will be "kept out of" (*ek,* in the Greek) the forthcoming global trial (Great Tribulation, instead of an anticipated New World Order of pseudo-peace).

Be sure that the Bible promises no counterfeit new age apart from absolute rule of the Lord, Jesus Christ (1 Tim. 6:14-16). Overcomers in Christ will obtain a more "exceeding great and precious promise," which is to partake of the Divine nature, having escaped corruption and vanity in this sin-bent world (2 Pet. 1:4).

AIDS/HIV

AIDS is an acronym for "Acquired Immuno-Deficiency Syndrome," which is among the most recent, and is certainly gravest, of sexually transmitted diseases. In the past fifteen years, the AIDS epidemic has killed over three hundred thousand in the U.S. alone. Even the conservative International AIDS Center at Harvard predicts that, by the turn of the century, as many as 110 million worldwide will have contracted HIV. No less than half, and more likely 100 percent, of those infected can expect to develop AIDS within ten years. (For sources, see Select Bibliography—Medical.)

Reliable sources say AIDS got its start in Haiti and Western Africa, both popular vacation spots for gays in the 1970s and 1980s. AIDS was first introduced to the United States in 1981, presumably through New York's male homosexual population (See Gay Rights).

AIDS is caused by an organism which in 1986 was universally renamed the HIV virus. HIV stands for human immunodeficiency virus, which is now known to be a retrovirus. That is, it progresses backward in the genetic code and is capable of changing its structure after taking over the lymphocyte released to fight it. Once a person has had the virus, he or she is infected, whether or not AIDS develops. Recent evidence suggests the presence of other diseases, particularly syphilis, is linked to full-blown manifestation of AIDS (Dr. John Cionci. *AIDS* [W. Columbia: Midnight Call, December 1997]. 20).

ARC (AIDS-related Complex) may often be considered pre-AIDS complex. The AIDS virus attacks the body's immune system, damaging its ability to fight other diseases. Hence, the patient becomes vulnerable to bacteria, protozoa, fungi, and the like. This can cause life-threatening illness that would not otherwise gain a foothold. Researchers from Rochester's Mayo Clinic showed that people who are HIV-positive have a higher risk of skin cancer, with increased risk of dying from it, than those not infected (Dr. John Cionci. *AIDS* [W. Columbia: Midnight Call, December 1996]. 15).

Medical journals are discussing outbursts of deadly mutant strains. The AIDS epidemic is at least partially to blame for a new strain of tuberculosis radically resistant to antibiotics.

The AIDS virus can be found in fluids and tissues of the brain and spinal cord. HIV is transmitted through body fluids, mainly blood and sexual secretions, but also through saliva, feces, and urine. Traces of the AIDS virus have been present in mother's milk. Because its life outside the body is short, the virus is not spread by casual contact.

Anal sex is often responsible for transmitting the virus, but HIV is not selective. Transmission threatens both men and women, boys and girls, especially high-risk groups (homo- and bi-sexual men, prostitutes, intravenous drug-users sharing needles, hemophiliacs and surgical patients treated with contaminated blood products).

The number one killer of people between the ages of twenty-five and forty-four, AIDS has no known cure. About a dozen medications are used today in the treatment of HIV. The drug, AZT, or Azidothymidine (with the trade name Retrovir), supposedly delays the onset of AIDS and diminishes its effects until the point at which the drug itself becomes toxic. Study of the therapeutic vaccine called "GP160" showed it to be ineffective.

Dr. Paul Cameron is the scientist who first proved second-hand tobacco smoke to be dangerous. In *Exposing the AIDS Scandal,* he contends that the mainstream media is withholding vital facts from the American public regarding additional ways AIDS can be spread. Definitive information, with little qualification, is publicized freely, as if to condone illicit protected sex minus consequence.

Although we have failed to enact laws protecting Americans from unknowingly coming into contact with HIV/AIDS (See Death Culture), most states have adopted policies to prevent discrimination against the infected. Americans are spending billions on AIDS, the first politically protected disease. When compared to heart disease and cancer, AIDS gets the highest tax-dollars-per-death. (Ray Brubaker. *Cunanan's Path* . . . [St. Petersburg: God's News Behind the News, 1997]. 4). That AIDS merits what is deemed to be disproportionate attention demonstrates the extraordinary power of the politically correct gay rights lobby.

Biblical Perspective

Although the best manuscripts omit the word "pestilence" in the Matthew 24 account, Luke 21:11 does include it as characterizing end-times. The Greek word used is *loimos,* which means literally, a disease, and figuratively, a pest. Accordingly, new diseases as ebola, lyme's and legionaire's diseases, toxic shock syndrome, and flesh-eating bacteria have emerged.

Though not exclusively so, AIDS can be linked to lifestyle choices at odds with the Judeo-Christian mandate (Rom. 1:24-32). God's Word makes it clear that any rebellion may result in a plague seven times as severe as the sin itself (Lev. 26:21). Many prone to debate (Rom. 1:29) have wantonly violated His precepts, and others give "hearty approval" (NAS, Rom. 1:32); therefore, God has appointed a "sudden terror, consumption, and fever that will waste away the eyes and cause the soul to pine away" (Lev. 26:15-26, NAS).

Amnesty International

A human-rights organization, Amnesty International monitors Human Rights Day (December 10), commemorating the adoption of the Universal Declaration of Human Rights by the United Nations General Assembly. Established in the United Kingdom in 1961, its purpose is to campaign for the release of political prisoners worldwide.

Unqualified unification for such a noble cause is considered by many experts to be but one more step toward globalism. The World Constitution and Parliament Association (WCPA) networks extensively in its push for world government. Its director, Philip Isely, who is a prominent figure in the one world movement, is a notable member of Amnesty International, which today has over 700,000 members and section offices in some forty-three countries.

Swedish chemist Alfred Nobel's endowment fund is known to generate free publicity for "one worldism." A high percentage of these prizes is awarded to people recognized for global views. Although politically unaligned, Amnesty International was awarded the Nobel Peace Prize in 1977.

Biblical Perspective

Freedom from imprisonment is a recurring theme in Scripture. The spirit of Yahweh was upon Christ, His Anointed, "to preach deliverance to the captives" (Luke 4:18). While walking in the footsteps of the Master, believers share this meritorious mission. Their message is this: "If, therefore, the Son shall make you free, you shall be free indeed" (John 8:36).

Godly liberty, as ministered by Christ Jesus, is not to be confused with man's efforts, noble as they seem. The global oneness to which our Savior referred (John 17:21-23) is separate from, and diametrically opposed to, the empty promises of unity, harmony, and pseudo-peace associated with a forthcoming New World Order and endorsed by some notable associates of Amnesty International.

Ancient Mystery Religions

(Freemasonry/Witchcraft/New Age)

Ancient Persia had its Mithraic Mysteries, or Zoroastrianism; Egypt and Babylon, their mysteries of Osiris and Semiramis, respectively. Assyrian and Phoenician mysteries included Baal worship, and Greece and Rome birthed mysteries of Eleusis. At the base of all of these mysteries is pantheism, which proclaims all life to be God, or part of God.

Since the beginning of time, God's truths have invariably been attacked. Even today, ancient mystery religions tarry in crafts of Freemasonry and witchcraft, as well as in the swelling New Age Movement. Astonishing similarities expose their demonized core.

Counterfeit Secrecy (Biblical Truth: "Great is the mystery of godliness," 1 Tim. 3:16)

The word "occult" comes from the Latin, meaning "to cover and conceal from 'profane' public scrutiny." As in ancient mystery religions, witchcraft, Freemasonry, and New Age occultism trace back to Babylon, cradle of civilization. Contemporary Freemasonry, for example, is said to be "guardian of ancient knowledge." Each of the three is secret to all except their initiated.

Counterfeit Self-god (Biblical Truth: "There is one God, . . . one mediator, Christ Jesus," 1 Tim. 2:5; 1 Cor. 12:12)

To the Mason, any god will do as "the master architect." In witchcraft, there are many so-called mighty ones (ancient gods and goddesses), but only one initiator (Lucifer). The New Ager speaks of the god-force and holds Lord Maitreya as its New Age Messiah. In each case, there is no personal god to whom one is accountable; rather, self-god reigns.

Counterfeit Becoming God (Biblical Truth: Believers are "partakers of the Divine nature," but always distinct from God, 1 Pet. 1:4 and Matt. 16:17)

For each modern mystery religion, the promised expectation is "life beyond the grave" by becoming god. To the Freemason, rediscovering "the Lost Word" is to possess the divine self, or Christ-state. Moreover, it is to wield "the key of the phenomena of nature," which is a classic witchcraft definition. The New Ager likewise attains to christ-, cosmos-, or group-consciousness—becoming one with the universe and, hence, with God—through a mass planetary quantum leap via Luciferic Initiation, which promises to usher in an anticipated Age of Aquarius.

Counterfeit Fertility Ritual (Biblical Truth: Marital union, type of Christ and the Church, Eph. 5:31–32)

Ancient mysteries usually enact fertility rituals. Even today, the ceremonial Masonic apron covers the male groin, Freemasonry's so-called "Holy of Holies." Based on ancient fertility cults, witchcraft likewise venerates forces of reproduction.

Counterfeit Death and Rebirth Ritual (Biblical Truth: Crucified with Christ, believers yet live, Gal. 2:20)

Even as a deity undergoes death and resurrection in the ancient mysteries, the Third Degree Master Mason ritual reenacts the Epic of Osiris, symbolized in the murder, burial, and resurrection of Hiran of Tyre. For both witchcraft and New Age, belief in reincarnation provides the demi-gods' death-resurrection component. In death and rebirth rituals, witchcraft candidates for initiation act out the part of a hero or heroine of the craft.

Counterfeit Feeding on Flesh and Blood (Biblical Truth: "Unless you eat the Son's flesh and drink His blood, you have no life in you," John 6:47-53)

To obtain communion with the divine, initiates in ancient mystery religions fed on flesh and blood. Reflecting this atrocity, the Fifth Libation of the Masonic York Rite includes drinking wine, as a symbol of blood, from a human skull. In witchcraft, bloody sacrifices (human preferred) coincide with the Supreme Great Invocation.

Counterfeit Degrees of Initiation (Biblical Truth: With unveiled faces, reflecting as in a mirror the glory of the Lord, believers are changed into the same image "from glory to glory," 2 Cor. 3:18)

As with the ancient mysteries, witchcraft, Freemasonry, and New Age occultism retain outer and inner circles while bestowing degrees of initiation toward supreme enlightenment. For example, outer circles comprise the admittedly misled Blue Degrees of speculative or social Masonry. In contrast, inner circles of "adepts," "princes," and "the elect" of the Masonic Royal Arch exercise spiritual or mystical Masonry. In like manner, inner-circle witches are known as Esoteric Adepts; inner circle New Agers are called Initiated Adepts. Witchcraft and Freemasonry alike assume a foundational system of three degrees, with up to thirty-three possible in Freemasonry.

Counterfeit Rituals (Biblical Truth: God looks more at the inward than the outward; the spirit than the letter; "the good things to come" than the shadows, or types of them—1 Sam. 16:7; Rom. 2:28; Heb. 10:1)

Outward ritualism invariably leans toward the occult. This tendency was nowhere seen more clearly than with the ancient mystery religions, in which a mystical catalyst inspirited the rankest of magical ceremonies.

Godless ritual is repeated in today's mystery religions. For example, as the compass pierces the bare chest of a Master Mason candidate, a sword pierces the bare chest of an up-and-coming witch. Freemasonic ritual in its highest degrees exercises astral projection (out-of-body experience), which is also practiced in witchcraft and New Age occultism. Spinning and jostling candidates in witchcraft and Freemasonry parallel New Age states of altered consciousness. Christians are forbidden to pray as the heathen with their "vain repetitions" (Matt. 6:7); however, rhythm and ritual are common among witches, Freemasons, and New Agers.

Counterfeit Symbols—Light and Goat Motifs: The Nimrod-Lucifer Connection

(Biblical Truth: God is the true light, 1 John 1:5; goats are separated from sheep, who hear and follow the Great Shepherd's voice, Matt. 25:32-33 and John 10:27)

All the more revealing is the indisputable link with ancient Babylon's Nimrod. This chief god of Babylon and Ninevah represented the sun, or light. "Jaobulon," chanted by three Masons, represents these three: Jah (for god of the gnostics or Jehovah, a distortion of the tetragrammaton, YHWH), Bul (for Baal, or Nimrod), and On (for the ancient Egyptian sun-god, Osiris).

In Latin, Lucifer means "Bearer of Light." To the mystic Mason, Lucifer is "the Light" while the true God is no more than "the shade." The Eye of Lucifer symbolizes witchcraft enlightenment, and planetary light-bearers usher in New Age mass planetary Luciferic Initiation. All three religions employ candles in their rituals, as did the ancients, to typify this counterfeit light.

That Lucifer is the heart of ancient mysteries, witchcraft, Freemasonry, and New Age occultism is further evidenced in the recurring goat motif. In Greek mythology, Pan is depicted as a man, but with the horns and hoofed legs of a goat, playing a shepherd's panpipe. Pantheism, you recall, underlies all mystery religions.

Similarly, the Satyr is a lascivious deity which is also half-man and half-goat. It is no surprise, then, that the Goat of Mendes is preeminent in both Freemasonry and witchcraft. A torch between the horns of the goatlike Masonic Baphomet distinguishes it as the Light-Bearer, or Lucifer himself. A secret, sacred word of the Masonic Scottish Rite, Abaddon ("destroyer," Rev. 9:11), is an indubitable title of Lucifer.

The Satanic Goat with a little star on its forehead likewise denotes Satan. Perhaps the single horn of the New Age's symbolic unicorn portrays that self-aggrandizing "little horn" spring-ing from the world conqueror he-goat of earlier verses in the eighth chapter of the book of Daniel. In the natural, it was Antiochus Epiphanes; spiritually, it was the Antichrist, an em-bodiment of Satan himself.

Additional Secret Symbols

(Biblical Truth: For self-interest, Christians are to abstain from all outward appearance of evil, examining and putting all things to the test, 1 Th. 5:21-22)

Parallel secret codes and symbols betray oneness with ancient mysteries. For example, the all-seeing eye and trapezoid (unfin-ished pyramid) symbolize New Age occultism, Freemasonry, and witchcraft. Similarly, the blazing star of Freemasonry bears strik-ing resemblance to witchcraft's five-pointed star (Pentagram/Pentacle). Generative organs are pictured in the wand, daggers, goblets, and cauldrons of witchcraft, as well as in the square-and-compass motif of Freemasonry.

Used ceremonially in witchcraft, the Hexagram, or Seal of Solomon, has found its way into the ritual of the Masonic Golden Dawn. The signature crescent moon of Freemasonry represents the moon goddess, Diana, in witchcraft. When adorned with a small star, the same depicts Lucifer. Curiously, this symbol is also associated with Islamic Fundamentalism.

The Counterfeit "Great Work"

(Biblical Truth: "This is the work of God, that ye believe on Him whom He hath sent," John 6:29)

An occult priesthood affects "The Great Work" (universal term for witchcraft, used also by Freemasonry), or "The Seven-Branched Plan" of New Age occultism. This priesthood's focus is "higher knowledge." In ancient civilizations, an occult priest-king served alongside the priest, not unlike the prophetic cou-pling of Antichrist with his False Prophet. In like manner, Free-masonry has its Worshipful Master with underlings; New Agers look to the likes of the Tibetan Djwhal Khul, Master of Wisdom (See Bailey, Alice). In turn, witch covens undertake their work under a male "Magister," a female "Lady," and a third "Officer."

Counterfeit Obligatory Sworn Oaths

(Biblical Truth: Christians confess the Lord, but swear by no oath, Rom. 10:9 and Matt. 5:34)

Curiously, the witch's pact does not compare in gore with the irrevocable blood oaths of Freemasonry. Violators are assured grave and brutal consequences, as discharged in the 1840s to Captain William Morgan of New York. His brutal murder at the hands of Mason "brothers" prompted defection of no less than forty-five thousand Freemasons justifiably aghast over the incident.

Inauspicious Associations

(Biblical Truth: Evil Companions Corrupt," 1 Cor. 15:33)

To be a member of the Rosicrucian Society, one must be a Master Mason with interest in Masonic symbolism and the occult, Kabbalism especially. Birthed in 1888 by Rosicrucian Freemasons, the Golden Dawn is known to be one of the most secretive and influential of all occult orders.

A sex-magic cult founded by an Australian Freemason, the O.T.O. (*Ordo Templi Orientis*) claims illumination to all Masonic secrets. Aleister Crowley, a thirty-third degree Mason who called himself "the Beast 666," later headed this surreptitious organization. It was he who shaped Wicca (modern witchcraft).

Adam Weishaupt's Bavarian Illuminati forged the political power base for Freemasonry. Its agenda corresponds to that of the New Age, whose blueprint contrives a New World Order with one world governmental and religious congruity. Helena Petrovna Blavatsky's Theosophical Society filled all key offices with Masons at its inception. Subsequent occult leader of the Society, Annie Besant, was a co-Masonic hierarch, as were Madame Blavatsky and Alice Bailey, founder of Lucis (formerly Lucifer) Trust. Alice's husband, Foster, a thirty-third degree Mason, spoke of Masonry as "the universal religion."

A veritable trinity of Luciferic occultists were also conspicuous Masons. Occultist Albert Pike, for example, is lauded as the chief Masonic authority and writer. Next, Albert G. Mackey wrote the definitive book on Freemasonry; thirdly, Manley P.

Hall is known as Freemasonry's greatest philosopher. Hall praised Adolf Hitler, who was a disciple of New Age occultist Madame Blavatsky.

Moreover, Master Mason S. L. MacGregor Mathers was a powerful occult practitioner. Not surprisingly, Mathers was among the founding fathers of the occult Masonic order of the Golden Dawn. One of the greatest Masonic authorities of all time, Arthur Edward Waite was initiated into the Golden Dawn while in Mathers' home. Mathers boasts the dubious honor of having coached Aleister Crowley, who later went on to father modern Satanism.

The late Anton LaVey, high priest of the Church of Satan, credits the Golden Dawn as a source of Satanic invocations found in the Satanic Bible he authored. His extraordinary admission reveals that essentially every occult order has many Masonic roots (Anton Szandor LaVey. *The Satanic Rituals* [New York: Avon Books, 1972], 78).

Founder of the modern white witchcraft revival, Gerald B. Gardner is a Freemason. The same holds true for Alex Sanders, self-styled "king of the witches" in London, and one of the most influential leaders of Wicca after Gardner. World renowned witches Janet and Stewart Farrar give credit to the Freemasons of the Golden Dawn for today's cult explosion.

Joseph Smith was also a Mason. Mormon ritual and symbolism coincide neatly with that of Freemasonry. Its roots? Ancient mystery religions.

Biblical Perspective

There is a way that seems right to humans, but it leads nevertheless to deception by the corruption of evil associations (1 Cor. 15:33) and to death (Prov. 14:12). For this reason, the Word of God cautions believers to allow no one to deceive them (1 John 3:7). Nor are they to be partakers with children of disobedience (Eph. 5:6-7), who give way to Antichrist's global schemes.

Counterfeits by definition are not easily detected, but spiritual men/women are equipped to discern them (1 Cor. 1:14) as they rightly exercise the plumb line of God's inerrant Word (2 Tim. 3:15-17) under guidance of the Holy Spirit (John 16:13).

(See Authenticity of Scriptures and Holy Spirit Imparted.)

Truth re: "Mystery" (See Esoteric Philosophy.)

Truth re: Secrecy; Death and Resurrection; Feeding on Flesh, Blood

Paul spoke of "sacred secrets" (Greek for "mystery" in Eph. 3:25), imparted exclusively to those initiated in spirit. Furthermore, he pictured symbolic "burial" with Christ in baptism only to "arise again" in newness of life (Rom. 6:3-11). Jesus Himself told us to "take, eat" and "drink" of his Body and Blood (Matt. 26:26-27). In partaking of this figurative memorial of Christ's life, death, and resurrection, we commune with Him and His Body. Our unshaken hope is certain victory beyond the grave (1 Cor. 15:54-58).

Despite apparent similarities with ancient mystery beliefs and practices, no counterfeit could sufficiently facsimile the "secret doctrine" of the glorious depth of the riches both of the wisdom and knowledge of our God to which Spirit enlightened Christians alone are privy (Rom. 11:33-36).

Truth re: Inner Circle; Degrees of Initiation; Plan/Work toward Enlightenment

Christ Himself had an "inner circle" of associates in Peter, James, and John; but Scriptures clearly invite "whosoever will" to be part of it (Mark 8:34)—this, through "degrees" of initiation. First, one must be "born from above" (John 3:3) and subsequently baptized in water and the Holy Spirit. By degrees, "from glory to glory" (2 Cor. 3:18), the believer is ultimately sanctified as a Bride without spot, wrinkle, or any such thing (Eph. 5:27). Rhythms, rituals, and oaths are forbidden. It is God—not self-god—at work within, ensuring that believers might will, and then do, His good pleasure (Phil. 2:13).

For the true Christian, the end of the matter is to "know as [s]he is known" (1 Cor. 13:12; Eph. 3:10). God's Plan, His Work, is for believers to be one with the Son, as the Father and Son are one (John 17:11).

The Bride of Christ is to partake of the Divine nature (2 Pet. 1:4), while remaining distinctly separate from the blessed and only Potentate, the King of kings and Lord of lords. Only Jesus has immortality, dwelling in the light which no man can approach (1 Tim. 6:15-16)—not Pan, not Buddha, not Lord Maitreya, not the illumined Mason.

Counterfeits Exposed

In ancient mystery religions revived today, Jesus Christ is not given His rightful place as the only way, the only truth, and the only source of life (John 14:6). God's glory is erroneously transferred to others (Isa. 42:8) when it is due to Jesus alone (Phil. 2:9-11). Not some goatlike, or human planetary "light-bearer," but Jesus only is the true Light (John 1:9). Following Him is not stumbling in darkness, as Master Masons in search of the "Lost Word;" instead, it is in the "light of life" (John 8:12). At the brightness of Christ's coming, that Wicked One, Satan, and his cunning cohorts will be destroyed; with the spirit of His mouth, they shall be utterly consumed (2 Thess. 2:8).

God is not some distant "master architect" or "god-force" common to all of life, nor is he chief among many gods and goddesses. Jesus is the Alpha and Omega, the beginning and the end (Rev. 1:8). All authority in heaven and earth is His (Matt. 28:18). He stands alone as Creator (Heb. 1:8-12), Savior (Titus 2:10; 13-14), Shepherd (John 10:11), King of kings (1 Tim. 6:15), and soon-coming Heavenly Bridegroom (2 Cor. 11:2). Whatsoever we do in word or deed, we are to do all in the wonderful Name of Jesus, giving thanks to the Father by Him (Col. 3:17).

In assessing the worth of any belief system, one principle prevails—let God be true, and every opposing man (or demon spirit), a liar (Rom. 3:4). As Christians, we must touch no unclean thing; instead, we are admonished to come out in holy separation from among those who contravene the one living God (Isa. 52:11) and His holy, inerrant Word (Matt. 24:35).

Antichrist and False Prophet

Biblical Perspective

"Antichrist" refers to a literal man present in type, or picture, throughout history (e.g., in Nebuchadnezzar, Antiochus Epiphanes, Nero, Napoleon Bonaparte, Hitler, Lenin, Stalin, and Hussein). Both John's and Paul's references to the Antichrist show that his tradition was well known to their contemporaries (1 John 4:3 "ye have heard"; 2 Thess. 2:6 "ye know").

A latter-day visionary, the Antichrist will become the greatest dictator the world has ever known. In time, he will demand the loyalty, and eventually the worship, of earth's well-conditioned inhabitants (Rev. 7:14; Rev. 13:7b-8).

Spirit of the Beast

The term, "antichrist," refers to one who stands in opposition to all that Jesus Christ represents (1 John 2:18, 22; 4:3; 2 John 7). In 1 John 2:18, Antichrist can be interpreted "in place of Christ," or "a substitute for" Him. It can also mean "against" or "opposed to" Christ. Antichrist will oppose Christ while pretending to be Christ. In so doing, the Antichrist may claim to be the latest reincarnation of the New Age "Christ spirit" that was allegedly in Krishna, Buddha, Jesus, Mohammed, and others.

Having existed throughout the course of history (1 John 4:3), antichrist spirit is paired with love of the world and the things therein, denial of the Father and Son, and hindrance to true worship (1 John 2:15-18, 22; 2 Thess. 2:4).

Biblical Titles of the Beast

The term, "antichrist," is used in the New Testament only in the writings of John (1 John 2:18, 22; 4:3; 2 John 7). There are, however, thirty-three titles for Antichrist in the Old Testament; thirteen in the New. The Antichrist is known as the "Lawless One," or the "Man of Sin" and "Son of Perdition" (2 Thess. 2:3); the "Beast" (Rev. 13:2); the "Little Horn" (Dan. 7:8); the "Abomination that Causes Desolation" (Matt. 24:15); and the "Prince that Shall Come" (Dan. 9:26-27).

Reign of the Beast

In the account of the "Little Horn" (Dan. 7:8), we learn that Antichrist's power will differ from his predecessors (verse 24) in that he will speak great blasphemies, claiming to be God (Rev. 13:5). As her persecutor, he will weary the true Church (Rev. 13:7), thinking to change sacred times and laws (Dan. 7:25) for self-interest. The duration of Antichrist's reign is identified as "time and times and the dividing of time," or three and one-half years (verse 25, with Rev. 12:14, coinciding with Great Tribulation).

The Abomination of Desolation

The Seleucid ruler Antiochus IV adopted the label "Epiphanes" or "Coming One." In his commitment to crush Judaism, he had a sow sacrificed on the sacred altar of the Temple in Jerusalem. Even worse, he placed an idol to Zeus inside the *naos,* or Holy of Holies. Such desecration is known specifically as "The Abomination of Desolation."

The people of this "Prince that Shall Come" would destroy the city of Jerusalem and her sanctuary. Historically, this happened with the Roman legions under Titus Vespasian in A.D. 70. No opportunity to date, however, has fully established the desecration fitting Biblical specifications (Matt. 24-25; Mark 13-14; Luke 21-22). One can only suppose a future similar desecration will occur under Antichrist.

Sources of the Beasts: Earth and Sea

Revelation 13 identifies two Beasts—one emerging from the stable religious element of the earth, the other from the more variable political element of the sea. The former acts as False Prophet for the latter, who is Antichrist himself.

In wielding power over all nations, the Antichrist will speak peace while warring specifically against believers (Dan. 8:25). This future charismatic world leader will emerge from, and then lead, the global community of "peoples, nations, multitudes, and tongues" (Rev. 17:15). Psalm 2 pictures the rebellion of the world kingdoms, united under Antichrist, against Yahweh and His Messiah (verse 2).

Serving as head of the one world false religious system, the False Prophet is identified in Revelation 17 with "Mystery Babylon, the Great, the Mother of Harlots and Abominations of the Earth." Known for evil excess (verse 6), she sits as a great whore on the many waters of "peoples, multitudes, nations, and tongues" (Rev. 17:1,15). Similarly, she sits on the seven hills of the Revived Roman Empire (verse 9), reigning over kings of earth (verse 18). Yet her future is finite; her destiny, dire (verses 16-17).

Mark of the Beast

The False Prophet causes all to receive a mark on the right hand or the forehead. A more literal translation of the Greek is a "stamp" or "brand," referring to the ancient custom of a master's branding his slaves, attesting to ownership and subservience. Despite socioeconomic standing, each one must be branded with this Mark of the Beast in order to buy or sell in Antichrist's New World Order (Rev. 13:4-18).

The most fearful punishment found anywhere in Scripture is related to this mark: "If any man worship the Beast and his image, and receive his mark in his forehead, or in his hand, the same shall drink of the wine of the wrath of God, which is poured out without mixture into the cup of his indignation. And he shall be tormented with fire and brimstone in the presence of the holy angels, and in the presence of the Lamb" (Rev. 14:9, 10).

Number of the Beast: 666

The numeral 666 is said to be the number of Antichrist, as well as the number of his mark. Significantly, six is the Biblical number of humankind; it embodies the godless religion of Secular Humanism. Each of the three sixes may be said to represent a key aspect of Antichrist's control—economic, political, and religious.

Nature of the Beast

Destined to "be revealed in his time" as a diabolical despot, a mystical humanist of sorts, Antichrist most likely will be of Hebrew descent. After all, he claims Messiahship and, as such, appears in the very *naos,* the Holy of Holies, of the rebuilt Temple of Ezekiel. Were he Gentile, that would not be likely. When the Antichrist claims to be God (2 Thess. 2:4), he will take away the daily sacrifice, deemed necessary no longer (Dan. 12:11).

Work of the Beast: Mystery of Iniquity

The joint work of Antichrist and his False Prophet is called "the mystery of iniquity" (2 Thess. 2:3-10), which began in the Garden of Eden (Gen. 3) and will continue until its end-time culmination. Through the yielded vessel of Antichrist (2 Cor. 11:14, 15), Satan will be transformed into "an angel of light." This impostor (John 5:43) will be the closest counterfeit of Christ that Satan can produce. While standing in direct opposition to the "mystery of godliness" (2 Tim. 3:16), the "mystery of iniquity" will purpose to supplant "Christ within, the hope of glory" (Col. 1:27) with Luciferic Initiation.

Together, Antichrist and his False Prophet promise the world "a more excellent way." Instead will come the red horse of warfare, the black horse of famine, and the pale horse of death. The conquering counterfeit sits with bow in hand on the white horse of his own godless system. That the bow lacks arrows signifies Antichrist's empty promise of peace (Rev. 6:2-8). This deceptively silent weapon of war depicts his shrewd subtlety.

In this picture, the Antichrist imitates the true and infinitely greater White Horseman, called "Faithful and True" (Rev. 19:11). However, instead of delivering peace, plenty, and abundant life, as offered by Christ, Antichrist incites warfare, famine, and death.

Anointing of the Beast: Luciferic Initiation

Counterfeiting baptism in the Holy Spirit (See Holy Spirit Imparted), Luciferic Initiation is demon possession referred to by New Agers as "transformation." Curiously, to avoid talking openly of their plan for godless world government, internationalists use the buzz word "global transformation." Mystics anticipate mass planetary Luciferic Initiation, or pledging of loyalty to Lucifer as "God." According to occultists, Lucifer is the grandest of Ideals (See Adept), an angel proud enough to believe himself to be God and courageous enough to assert his own independence from the one true God.

Arsenal of the Beast

Antichrist is said to be so strong that none can make war with him (Rev. 13:4-7). This lawless one, inspired and empowered by Satan, will lead the final rebellion against God, while displaying "all kinds of counterfeit miracles, signs and wonders" (2 Thess. 2:9, NIV; Matt. 24:24-25). The world's acceptance of occult and New Age philosophies will set the stage for Antichrist's forthcoming "strong delusion" (2 Thess. 2:8-12).

Two Appearances of the Beast

Many scholars believe that the Antichrist will appear once before the Rapture and a second time thereafter. At the latter appearance, the Antichrist will be fully possessed of Satan. As Jesus was Emmanuel ("God with us," Matt. 1:23), Antichrist will be "Satan with us."

Prior to the Rapture, believers effectively restrain Antichrist, disallowing his full manifestation (2 Thess. 2:7). When Christ's Bride is snatched from this earth at the Rapture, the "salt of the earth," acting as preservative, will no longer be present to restrain his corruption (Matt. 5:13); therefore, the Antichrist will be given full reign.

At the Rapture, much of the world will remain dangerously unmanned. Among those instantaneously snatched away will be pilots, surgeons, fire fighters, police officers, and emergency vehicle drivers (Matt. 24:40-42). The Antichrist, therefore, will present a plan of action to address resulting chaos. No doubt he will offer solid rationale for the hair-trigger removal of multitudes (Re. 12:5).

Despite Antichrist's demonstrated competencies, the Rapture most assuredly will wield a fatal blow to his headship (1 Cor. 15:51-57; Rev. 13:3). Some believe he will establish his sovereignty by counterfeiting the closest thing to a resurrection that Satan can produce. Receiving his authority and power from Satan, the Antichrist will make a pact with him—this for but a few months of glory (Rev. 13:4).

Old Testament Prophecies

The work of Satan through the Antichrist is clearly rooted in the prophecies of Daniel. Antichrist will be the sum total of all beasts referred to in Revelation 13:1-4 and Daniel 7.

New Testament Prophecies

The brightness of Christ's Second Coming will spell Antichrist's doom of consummation and destruction (2 Th. 2:8). Those who worship the Antichrist will also experience certain wrath of God for participating in blasphemy (Rev. 14: 9-11). Having warred against Christ and His army, the Antichrist will eventually be "cast alive into the lake of fire burning with brimstone" (Rev. 19:20). There, he will be joined by Lucifer, and together they "will be tormented day and night forever and ever" (Rev. 20:10).

Antichrist and the Great Apostasy

Although the apostle Paul does not use the term, he surely had Antichrist in mind when he wrote of the coming Great Apostasy, or falling away, which will occur before the return of

Christ (2 Thess. 2:1-12). To "fall away" presupposes previous right standing with God. That is to say, believers who have known and loved the Savior will believe "the lie" of Antichrist and will fall from grace. They will be as wells without water, or clouds carried with a tempest, when they turn, as dogs, to their own vomit, or sin (2 Pet. 2:17; 20-22).

Jesus warned that "if it were possible" the Master of Deception would deceive even the very elect of God (Matt. 24:24). For this reason, believers are warned to be watchful (2 Cor. 10:12 and 1 Pet. 5:8). Those who do not believe the lie of Antichrist are identified as Philadelphia saints commended by God for having kept God's Word without denying His Name (Rev. 3:8). Truly, the victory that overcomes Antichrist and his diabolical spirit is "even our faith" (1 John 5:4).

Antichrist and the Christian

The main reason the Bible discusses the Antichrist is not to encourage idle speculation, but to warn believers not to be misled by his deceit (Matt. 24:4-5; 23-24).

Armageddon

Biblical Perspective

The term "Armageddon" is found only in Revelation 16:16; it literally refers to a "mound" or "hill of assembly." A Greek word (from the Hebrew, *har mègiddô, mègiddon*), Armageddon refers to the mountain region of Megiddo, scene of many ancient battles in the history of Israel (Judges 5:19; 2 Chron. 35:22-24).

Appropriately, "Armageddon" comes from a Hebrew root meaning "to cut off" or "to slay." It was here that David overcame Goliath. Armageddon is also called the "Valley of Decision." It signifies a time of God's pronouncing and executing judgment (Joel 3:14-16). Known as the Valley of Jezreel, or Jehoshaphat, meaning "God has judged," Armageddon is sometimes referred to as the Plain of Esdraelon (Joel 3:2). Generally, Armageddon speaks of a decisive, catastrophic conflict. Specifically, it is the scene of a final war of several huge battles between the allied forces of evil and Israel, both national and spiritual.

Time Frame

Nearing the end of the Seventieth Week of Daniel (Rev. 16:12-16), after the sixth bowl is poured out, Armageddon parallels in time the Second Coming of Christ (Zech. 12:9-12, 14:1-5; Jude 14-15; Rev. 1:7, 19:11-21). Its outcome establishes on earth the Prince of Peace's intended world order for one thousand years (See Millennium; Ezek. 39:6, 7, 21, 22, 29; Zech. 14:4, 9, 11).

Location

The crossroads of two ancient trade routes, this Valley of Megiddo was a strategic military site. Scholars disagree about its exact location. Most likely it is the valley between Mount Carmel and the city of Jezreel. Various names denoting its location all encircle Jerusalem. In view of Isaiah 34:6-8 and 63:1-6, it is likely that a line of encamped forces will extend from Bozrah on the southeast to Megiddo on the northwest.

Impact

Some authorities claim that there are more warnings in Scripture about the Final Battle of the war of Armageddon than anything else. At that time, "the cup of the wine of the fierceness of [God's] wrath" (Rev. 16:19) will be poured out, for "the press is full, and the vats overflow" with the greatness of the heathen's wickedness (Joel 3:13). At Armageddon, God will destroy the collaborating armies of Satan and cast him into "the bottomless pit" (Rev. 16:16; 20:1-3, 7-10).

Jesus Christ and His Bride (Rev. 19:13-14) will prevail against allied evil powers gathered together (19:19). Under God's direction and anointing, even feeble inhabitants of Jerusalem will be as David, the foremost man of war in Biblical history (Zech. 12:8).

Those not killed among God's enemies will stubbornly refuse to repent (Rev. 9: 20-21), and ultimately will be slain (Rev. 19:21); therefore, they will lament Christ's coming with His saints (Rev. 1:7). Bloodshed and death define Armageddon (Rev. 19: 15, 18). So great will be the devastation that it will take seven months for all remaining to undertake burial of the dead (Ezek. 39:1-19, 20). Thereafter, professionals will likely wrap up the job.

Key Players (Rev. 16:14)

It is clearly for military purposes that "the whole inhabited earth" is impelled to gather together, seduced by unclean demon spirits under Lucifer, Antichrist, and his False Prophet. Some believe the phrase, "the whole inhabited earth," is used hyperbolically. Its additional use with regard to the Great Tribulation (Rev. 3:10) and universal preaching of the Gospel (Matt 24:14) leads others to accept a more literal interpretation.

This imposing gathering of the host of Antichrist into the wine-press of judgment, and the treading of it by the King of kings and Lord of lords, is described in the latter parts of Chapters 16 and 19 of Revelation, and also in Isaiah 63:3. With chilling vehemence, the wrath and displeasure of God and His Anointed will pour out on godless Gentile rulers and their armies (Ps. 2:5, 12).

Tenor

Terms of woe—utter destruction, killing, wailing, vengeance—describe Armageddon, which will culminate in the Second Coming of Christ (Isa. 34:2-3; 9:17-18; 63:4). It will be a time of darkness and gloominess, a day of clouds and thick darkness (Joel 2:2).

Israel's Involvement

Despite the fact that her Jewish population is roughly the same size as the population of Iowa, and her more than 140 million enemies cover a surrounding land mass exceeding that of the entire U.S., national Israel will "live securely" after returning from many nations (Ezek. 38:8). Following this short-lived period of pseudo-peace, Armageddon will be inflamed by the age-old dispute over Jerusalem. "A cup of staggering" and "a burdensome stone" to surrounding nations (Zech. 12:2-3), Israel will be shaken by multiple all out nuclear exchanges (Ezek. 39:9-12). This war of the Great Day of God Almighty (Rev. 16:14-16; Zech. 12:2-3) will prove to be the greatest holocaust in history, but Israel shall be spared total annihilation.

Israel's Enemies

According to the prophets Ezekiel, Daniel, and John the Revelator, four spheres of political power will come against na-

tional Israel. These include the "King of the South" Arab Con-
federacy; Northern Confederacy, headed by Russia; "Kings of the
East" Asian Confederacy; and the Revived Roman Empire of the
United States of Europe.

"King of the South" Arab Confederacy (Ezek. 38:5, 6, 8, 9, 19, 21, 23):

The Islamic Coalition is a force to reckon with. Today's
leader of the New Islamic World Order, Iran, seeks to exert her
military authority in the region and, concurrently, her spiritual
authority over the entire Muslim world. Iran's former President,
Akbar (meaning "the greatest") Hashemi Rafsanjani explained
Islamic Fundamentalism's "Grand Design" as follows. In uniting
all Islamic nations under the leadership of a coalition led by Iran
and Syria, the West, first, must be driven out of the Middle East,
thus "liberating" Palestine. Next, the Judeo-Christian World Order
must be supplanted with an Islamic one.

Northern Confederacy, Headed by Russia (Ezek. 38:2, 3, 4, 8, 9, 13-23):

Gog (chief prince of the land of Magog), Magog (Scythian
Mountains in Russia), Meshech (Moscow), and Tubal (Toblask)
most likely identify the Northern Confederacy as Russia. Theirs
is a imperialist role, as demonstrated later in Scriptures during a
short season at the wrap-up of the Millennium (Rev. 20: 8).
Even the Koran represents this conglomerate as barbarians of the
North who swarm the South in predatory irruption against the
Holy Land.

"Kings of the East" Asian Confederacy (Re. 16:12-21):

Kings of the East, or "of the rising sun," play a vital role in
"the battle of that great day of God Almighty" (verse 14). Their
armies number an impressive two hundred million (Rev. 9:16).
To prepare their way, the great River Euphrates will be dried up
(See also Isa. 11:15). This could be a supernatural act of God, or
a repeat of Turkey's 1990 cutting off of the Euphrates' flow by
means of the Ataturk Dam. At any rate, some authorities see the
Hill of Megiddo as a vital link between Asia and the oil reserves
of the Middle East. A decidedly opportunistic tactical decision
will land Asia in the midst of this unmatched conflagration.

Revived Roman Empire of the United States of Europe:

According to Biblical prophecy, ancient Rome will revive in
the end-times as a worldwide empire ruled by Antichrist. Known
for "devouring and breaking in pieces" (Dan. 7:19), this revived
colossus is actually unified Europe, a foundation stone for what
will become the United States of the World. As with ancient
Rome, the glue binding this political, economic, and military
entity will be religion, the core of which is pantheism and the
source of which is Babylon (Rev. 17:5). In response to this flood
of spiritual error, God will make Himself gloriously known in
the eyes of many nations (Ezek. 38:23).

Twentieth-Century Weaponry

The "great sword" of Revelation 6:4 speaks more literally of
a "tremendous arsenal of weapons." From the atomic bomb, to
the hydrogen bomb, to the neutron bomb, to current methods of
attack, nuclear capacity has expanded in capability and accessibil-
ity beyond the superpowers of America, Britain, France, Russia,
and China. Furthermore, nuclear methods now include aircraft
bombs, rocket-propelled missiles with nuclear warheads, depth
charges, and high-powered land mines. Remember that nuclear
warheads have limited shelf life (about seven years). This means
use them or lose them.

Not surprisingly, Scripture depicts with remarkable accuracy
what appears to be forthcoming full-scale nuclear exchange. Six
centuries before Christ, Holy Writ described torrential rains of
hailstorms, fire, and melted earth, all precise results of nuclear
holocaust. Mid-air hydrogen bomb tests have resulted in hun-
dred-pound hailstones' hitting top sides of armored ships. Revelation 16:21 describes such hailstones falling out of heaven.
Measuring two feet in diameter and weighing about one-hun-
dred pounds each, these formidable stones will shower horror-
struck victims.

The sixth chapter of Revelation describes what is known as
nuclear winter, the expected long-term effect of widespread nuclear
war. Atmospheric pollution could effectively block the sun's rays.
Accordingly, John, the Revelator, aptly describes the sun becoming black (6:12). In Ezekiel 39:15, methods for handling bones
of victims follow guidelines issued by our own Department of
Defense following the use of nuclear weaponry.

Twenty-first Century Weaponry

Trilateralists have studied effective geophysical tactics of weather modification with intent to subjugate. The founding director of David Rockefeller's Trilateral Commission, Zbigniew Brzezinski included discussion of weather-war strategies in his 1970 paperback, *Between Two Ages*.

Other contemporary weapons could include, but are not limited to, cyberspace sabotage, USSR psycho-warfare techniques, and Global Magnetic Warfare by means of the Tesla Magnifying Transmitter, which would electronically incite large populations to unstable behavior.

Conclusion

Armageddon will be Satan's ultimate, but unsuccessful, challenge to Christ's right to take tenant possession of earth and thereby rule it (Ps. 2:1-3). With the final battle, the strength of antichrist forces will be brought down (Isa. 63:6) with utter destruction (Isa. 34:2-3), and at long last the Plan of God will be realized.

Ascended Master/Master

Sr. Master of Wisdom

See Adept/Initiated Adept.

Aspen Institute for Humanistic Studies

The Aspen Institute for Humanistic Studies grew out of a global meeting planned by three Chicago men in Aspen in 1949. The Institute is a private, nonprofit organization and is international in scope. Heavily funded by the Ford and Rockefeller Foundations, it is a sister organization to the Council on Foreign Relations and the Bilderbergers.

Headed for many years by Robert O. Anderson, the Institute has been aptly described as "a training and orientation school for prospective world government administrators." Leading officials of the Trilateral Commission, the White House, and the Rockefeller Foundation attend advanced seminars in global ideology at this prestigious Colorado establishment.

Along with the Council on Foreign Relations, the Trilateral Commission, the Royal Institute of International Affairs, Dartmouth Conference, the Atlantic Institute, and the Bilderberger group, the Aspen Institute is within the stalwart Eastern Liberal Establishment of Insiders, serving to coordinate and disseminate plans for the coming New World Order. The sway of these groups spans powerful business, financial, and official circles.

The Aspen Institute's imprint of secular humanism on education is especially dramatic (See Public Education and Outcome-Based Education). Former California state superintendent of schools Dr. Max Rafferty warned, "Somebody or something is fooling around the children's books these days." By admission of the Institute's own Joseph Slater, "Most of the materials which we develop [at the Institute] sooner or later find their way into [the nation's] textbooks." (See Textbook Conspiracy.)

Biblical Perspective

See Insiders/Eastern Liberal Establishment.

Atlantis/Atlantis Project

According to tradition, Atlantis was a city (or island), which contained elements of democracy and existed at the helm of a world government based on ten geo-political regions. Some pair Atlantis with the 4,000-year-old Minoan ruins at Akrotiri on the Greek Isle of Santorini. Others couple Atlantis with the biblical account of the Great Flood of Noah's time. Because of rampant human preoccupation with the occult, demons were said to be empowered to manifest themselves physically. They then engaged in sex with human women. Some Christians believe this highly unlikely scenario is supported in Genesis 6:4 by mention of the "giants," or "giant demi-gods," who were supposedly the unnatural offspring of women and fallen angels.

Most authorities agree that Atlantis existed only in the minds of those prone to imagine an ancient utopia as source for occult teachings. The only historical sources for Atlantis were described by Egyptian papyrus thousands of years ago, and later supported by two dialogues of Plato. Regarding Atlantis, C.S. Lewis commented in his journal, ". . . nobody seems to realize that a Platonic myth is fiction, not legend, and therefore no basis for speculation."

Nonetheless, the pyramid symbol on the one-dollar bill is said to be rooted in the legend of Atlantis, and thirty-third degree Mason Manly Hall claims that Freemasonry originated in Atlantis. It was the Atlanteans, he says, who devised a "Great Plan" whereby the world would be directed toward global government. This plan allegedly included an enigmatic blueprint of what was subsequently to become America. Creation of a New Atlantis in North America is what Hall identified as the unifying goal of secret societies. Author William T. Still documents involvement of secret societies for a New World Order as being instrumental in British colonization of America.

Even today, many Masons and New Agers give serious attention to the idea of a New Atlantis in the Caribbean—a floating city complete with parks, theaters, shopping, sports facilities, and ports for aircraft. One organization is actively recruiting "freedom-loving citizens" with promise of this project, first of a new sovereign nation to be called Oceania.

Biblical Perspective

In Paul's second epistle to the church at Thessalonica, he speaks of the "sacred secret" of lawlessness already inwardly working itself (2:7). Occultists are not new, but have worked their lawless deeds since the beginning of time. Indeed, a master plan promising a New Order of the Ages was concealed in the entrance of the King's Chamber within the Great Pyramid of Gizeh. Christians are admonished not to be quickly disconcerted or alarmed (2:2) by such fanciful thoughts or wayward ways. The bottom line is this: "Except the Lord build the house, they labor in vain that build it" (Ps. 127:1).

Authenticity of Scriptures

Biblical Perspective

The Biblical position of verbal plenary holds that in its original language (Hebrew and Chaldeac, Old Testament; Greek and Aramaic, New Testament) all of the Bible, Genesis to Revelation, is fully "God-breathed" to the slightest stroke of the smallest alphabet letter (Matt. 5:18). Scriptures seem, claim, and prove to be fully inspired.

Scriptures Seem to be Inspired

Written over an extended period of some sixteen hundred years by over forty penmen of varied trades (from tentmaker to king), the Bible still remains one book with one universal theme, that of redemption by blood. Certainly by its origin, the Bible seems to be inspired.

Although the Bible is ancient, it is nonetheless altogether modern. Last-day prophecy, as found in Paul's second letter to Timothy, reads like today's news. By its very nature, the Bible seems to be inspired.

For being ancient, the Bible consists of an overwhelming number of preserved ancient manuscripts. The New Testament alone has nearly 8,000 manuscripts and fragments of manuscripts validating its authenticity. There is more evidence to support the life of Christ than that of Alexander the Great, yet no one doubts Alexander's role in history. Despite repeated copies and translations, Dead Sea Scrolls demonstrate that the 125 B.C. book of Isaiah matches perfectly that of A.D. 916. Given manuscript evidence, the Bible indeed seems to be inspired.

The Bible has been studied and questioned more than any other book. Despite relentless persecution against it and its adherents, the Bible remains the all-time best seller with a couple billion copies (in a couple thousand languages) in print. If this Book of books were fraudulent, it would have fallen by the wayside long ago. Even by its circulation, the Bible most assuredly seems to be inspired.

For several months, the founder of the Harvard Graduate School of Law examined claims of Jesus on the basis of legal evidence. His conclusion? There is no doubt that Jesus is who He claimed to be. By laws of evidence, as presentable in a court of law, the Bible seems to be inspired.

Scriptures Claim to be Inspired

In a number of specific passages, the Bible without excuse claims to be fully inspired. The telling phrase "thus saith the Lord" is found 700 times in the Pentateuch, 400 times in the historical books, and 1300 times in the prophetic books. "By the Holy Spirit being borne along (literal Greek)," the Bible's forty penmen "spoke from God" (2 Pet. 1:20-21), not as men with "cunningly devised fables" (2 Pet. 1:16). (Russell MacKenzie. *Authenticity of Scriptures* [Seattle: Pacific School of Theology, 1976]. p. 530).

The most credible witness of all, Jesus Himself, affirmed that "Scripture cannot be broken" (John 10:35) and "the Law will never pass away" (Matt. 5:18). He recognized Divine inspiration of the Word, Himself being the Word made flesh. The three Greek words of 2 Timothy 3:16 tell it all: "All Scripture God-breathed."

Scriptures Prove to be Inspired

Even more convincingly, the Bible proves to be inspired, not only by its credibility in the lives of numberless Christians throughout the ages, but also historically, scientifically, medically, theoretically, and prophetically.

Historically

Historically, there are some twenty-nine ancient kings of Egypt, Israel, Moab, Damascus, Tyre, Babylon, Assyria, and Persia whose names are mentioned both in the Bible and also on monuments of their own time. Some date back four thousand years. This accuracy far surpasses that of other records (Ptolemy's, for example).

Daniel's image (Chapter 2) is thrillingly true to history. Dated at the time of Babylonian Captivity, this account was written prior to the last two world empires to which it refers. Another stunning Biblical prophecy is the fact that Cyrus, the Mede, was actually identified and named by Isaiah some one hundred and seventy-six years before Cyrus was even born (Isa. 44:28).

That the descendants of Jacob could be scattered throughout the world for twenty-five hundred years, but still remain an identifiable ethnic group since their Babylonian captivity, is of itself a miracle. That they then returned to their own land, established once again as a nation, as the Bible prophesied, is stunning indeed.

In 1881, Sir William Ramsey planned an expedition to follow Paul's travels and, in so doing, disprove the Bible. After he had investigated for some fifteen years, the unexpected happened. Ramsey met the Lord Jesus as personal Savior. For the next twenty years of research, Sir William Ramsey wrote tirelessly of the exact preciseness of Biblical accounts, as affirmed by sound archaeological evidence.

Scientifically

Some of the most fascinating proof of the Bible's authenticity was undertaken by former Princeton professor Robert D. Wilson. His book, *Scientific Investigation of the Old Testament*, is a classic. In it he affirms, "There is not a page of the Old Testament concerning which we need have any doubt."

A number of scientific facts anticipated in the Bible further affirm its Divine inspiration. Job 26:7 refers to "the empty place," which today can be discerned by pointing a telescope into the sky near the North Star. The dictionary defines "dust" as the "earthly remains of a human body." From the very beginning of time, the Bible rightly called man "dust," and this is now confirmed by scientific know-how (Gen. 2:7).

Whereas the hydrological process was not understood with accuracy until fifteen hundred years after Christ, it was described in the oldest book of the Bible (Job 36:26-28) some fifteen hundred years before Christ. Furthermore, Ecclesiastes 1:6-7 provides a scientifically accurate description of the meteorological wind cycle, moving South to North.

That the earth is spherical was conceptualized by innovative scientists in 1519, but even then the notion was resisted. About twenty-two hundred years earlier, the Bible first alluded to earth's circle ("compass," "globe," "sphere" in the Hebrew, Isa. 40:22).

Evidence is overwhelming in favor of a young earth and Noah's Flood, as recounted in the Bible. The earth's constantly decreasing magnetic field indicates its age as being no more than ten thousand years old. Widespread global distribution of sediment and the abundance of fossils, indicating rapid deposition, further argue in favor of the Bible account.

Medically

Blood-letting was a common medical practice even in the earlier years of America's history, but the Bible lets us know that "life itself is in the blood" (Lev. 17:11). Had physicians believed this, they would have avoided this imprudent treatment. Contemporary medical knowledge places the maximum peak for clotting after eight days, exactly when God commanded Hebrew males to be circumcised.

The Pentateuch listed advanced hygienic laws that did not come to light in the medical community until much later. For example, Leviticus teaches washing hands with soap and hot water. Not until the 1900s and the study of germs was this practice shown to be medically sound.

Theoretically

The creation account in the Book of Genesis is not unlike the opposing view of evolution in that belief in either requires a leap of faith. A tornado ravaging a junkyard can no more produce the Boeing 777 aircraft than a random combination of time and elements can give rise to the universe. It is easier, and infinitely more logical, to embrace the established principle of cause and effect. That is to say, the creation's symbiotic complexity demands no less than the intellect and skill of a Master Designer.

Prophetically

About one-third of the Bible is prophecy. Already-fulfilled prophecies have proved to be one hundred percent accurate. For example, despite astronomical odds, about three hundred prophecies surrounding the birth, death, and resurrection of Jesus were fulfilled to the detail. Remarkably, Daniel's prophecy of Seventy Weeks foretold the exact month, day, and year (6 April A.D. 32) Jesus would present Himself as Messiah (on what we call Palm Sunday today).

Conclusion

In conclusion, the Bible seems, claims, and proves to be fully inspired. The Bible's last-day prophecies can be trusted and must be heeded.

B

Baer, Randall

For about fifteen years, Randall Baer and his wife, Vickie, were recognized globally as New Age experts; moreover, Randall was one of the movement's leading spokespersons. A naturopathic doctor, Randall authored two national best-sellers on "crystal power" and "sacred science." As his popularity grew, Randall became a favorite seminar speaker on occult-based practices, and he appeared on many national television programs.

Randall and Vickie both had a change of heart when each met the Lord Jesus as personal Savior. A zealous new Christian, Baer then committed to the task of exposing Antichrist workings of the burgeoning New Age Movement. As a Christian, Baer authored *Inside the New Age Nightmare* with intent to expose clandestine plans to overtake America's political institutions. On the very day his book was released, Baer died suspiciously in Colorado. Three investigations suggest that he may have been murdered.

Biblical Perspective

The Bible prophesies of great spiritual revival prior to the Rapture of Christ's Church (See Holy Spirit Imparted). Even those caught up in New Age occultism and sin are candidates for salvation (1 Tim. 1:15) and, subsequently, persecution (2 Tim. 3:12).

Jesus spoke of a time when killers of committed Christians will think that they are doing God's service (John 16:2). Truly, the servant is not greater than his master. If Jesus Christ Himself was unfairly persecuted, so it will be for those who follow closely in His footsteps (John 15:20). Nina Shea, author of *In the Lion's Den*, writes that in this century more Christians have died for their faith than in the first nineteen centuries after the birth of Christ. To share in Christ's sufferings is ultimately to share His glory. Therefore, in the Beatitudes Jesus describes believers as "blessed," or "happy," when persecuted for His Name's sake (Matt. 5:11).

Bailey, Alice (1880-1949)

Born in England in 1880, Alice Bailey is probably the most notable founder of today's New Age Movement. In her early years, she labored long and hard in Christian ministry; nevertheless, following an abusive marriage, coupled with work burn-out, Alice became an extraordinarily receptive channel of demonic influence.

Both Madam Blavatsky and Alice Bailey were notable female leaders of Theosophy, as well as co-Masonic hierarchs. It was Bailey who established Lucifer Press (1920), which was later softened to Lucis Press, Ltd. Until recently, the parent organization, Lucis Trust, was headquartered at the United Nations Plaza in New York. Occult concepts of the powerful Lucis Trust continue to influence key members of the United Nations and the Council on Foreign Relations.

Alice Bailey is credited with having established World Goodwill in 1933. Composed of the "New Group of World Servers," it distributed literature globally. The intent was to destroy Judaism and Christianity while promoting Theosophy's Luciferic views. In 1961 this group linked with World Union. Along with Lucis Trust, World Union feeds directly into the World Constitution and Parliament Association, charged with the task of ushering in the New World Order. Key figures of the WCPA and World Union, A. B. Patel and Philip Isely further demonstrate indisputable link between one worldism and New Age mysticism.

Triangles was one of the organizations established by Bailey to promote "the science" of Transcendental Meditation. A triangle is a group of three people who link in thought for a few minutes each day. By visualizing energy as circulating through the three points of each triangle and pouring out through the network of triangles surrounding the planet, participants believe they are invoking the energies of light and goodwill (See Pantheism). Many of the hundreds of participants from different countries repeat the Great Invocation for the return of Christ (Antichrist in actuality). This is done to promote the New World Order. Curiously, Triangles is the name given to the Masonic

Palladian Lodges, started by occultist Albert Pike. Alice's husband, Foster, spoke of Freemasonry as "the universal religion."

Bailey is credited further with the Arcane Schools of New York, London, Geneva, and Buenos Aires. These provide special training in ancient mysteries and high-level networking of the New Age Movement.

Working from the Himalayan retreat of her spirit guide, Tibetan Djwhal Khul, Alice Bailey wrote twenty books, not least of which were *Education in the New Age* and her 1934 classic, *The Externalization of the Hierarchy*. In it, Bailey falsely identifies Jews and true Christians as "forces of darkness."

Considered to have attained "christ-consciousness," or "christhood," the Tibetan was official head of the Hierarchy. Just thirty days after the Tibetan had finished writing through her, Alice Bailey died in 1949.

Biblical Perspective

See Ancient Mystery Religions.

Believers in Jesus have been called out of darkness into Christ's marvelous light (1 Pet. 2:9). In contrast, the likes of Alice Bailey and Djwhal Khul were enamored with darkness. Having fallen prey to the spirit of Antichrist (2 Thess. 2:11), they believed not the truth, but instead had pleasure in unrighteousness (verse 12).

Referring to signs of the Second Coming, Jesus warned believers to take heed lest anyone deceive them (Matt. 24:4), for many in these last days will come claiming to have attained "christhood" (verse 5).

Besant, Dr. Annie Wood (1847-1933)

As the daughter of an Anglican clergyman and ex-wife of another, Annie Wood Besant most likely heard, but ultimately rejected, Biblical truth. As early as 1889, Dr. Besant became a devout disciple of Helena Petrovna Blavatsky. In New York in 1875, Madam Blavatsky and Besant started the Theosophical Society of "ancient wisdom," representing a pantheistic form of Gnosticism.

Dr. Besant is listed in the *Dictionary of Mysticism and the Occult* by Nevill Drury as an English Theosophist and social reformer who in 1891 became international president of the

Theosophical Society. Looking toward a global federation by the century's end, Dr. Besant founded the Fabian Parliamentary League. Its membership included dramatist and novelist George Bernard Shaw, an early member of the Socialist Fabian Society.

Dr. Besant was the disciple of Tibetan Mahatma Master Morya, one of Madam Blavatsky's masters. A notable leader in the Co-Masonic Movement, Dr. Besant was a prolific writer. She wrote *Seven Principles of Man, Esoteric Christianity,* and *Ancient Wisdom,* published in London (1897). Besant's prolific writings both mirror and laud Blavatsky.

A prominent luminary, Dr. Besant founded the Central Hindu College at Benares, India (1898), and also the Indian Home Rule League (1916). Regarded as a powerful figure in Indian politics, she was elected president of the Indian National Congress in 1917.

Mrs. Besant declared, "Man is a spiritual intelligence, a fragment of divinity clothed in matter" (*Man's Life in Three Worlds*). In *Is Theosophy Anti-Christian?* she claimed further that "in time all men become christs." Her writings make extensive reference to the Theosophical dogma of concurrent reincarnations. In 1925, Dr. Besant claimed for her adopted son Krishnamurti, an Indian mystic, the title of "Messianic Leader and Reincarnation of the World Teacher." Her son once suggested, "You must dig deep down into yourself to find the God within you, and listen to his voice, which is your voice."

After Dr. Besant's death in 1933, George Arundale and C. Jinara Jodosa succeeded to the presidency of the Theosophical Society.

Biblical Perspective

Dr. Besant's life reflected last-day heresy as depicted in 2 Timothy 3. Her New Age form of godliness denied its true power (verse 5), and opposition to biblical Christianity exposed her as a despiser of those that are good (verse 3). In her quest for "higher self," she was both heady and high-minded (verse 4). Ever learning, she never came to the knowledge of truth (verse 7); rather she engaged in deceiving, and being deceived (verse 13).

Bilderbergers

The Council on Foreign Relations is at the center of insider power and planning; in fact, it is the glue that holds together the Rockefeller Eastern Liberal Establishment. Its influence is concentrated in the executive branch of the federal government. State, Treasury, and Defense Departments are particularly hard hit by the council's undisguised aim to supplant national sovereignty with globalism. Whereas the CFR is the "brain" of globalism, CFR spin-off groups wield three arms of power: economic (Bilderbergers), spiritual (Club of Rome), and political (Trilateral Commission).

Founded by Prince Bernhard of the Netherlands in 1954, the Bilderbergers are a sort of international Council on Foreign Relations. Bilderbergers in powerful circles coordinate and disseminate plans for the New World Order. A number of prominent one world institutions, including the Ford and Rockefeller Foundations, fund the society.

The public name for the Bilderberger group comes from the Bilderberg Hotel in Oosterbeek, Holland, where the association first met. Its membership of approximately one hundred of the world's elite men and women of politics, business, banking, and labor (all from the member nations of the North Atlantic Treaty Organization) meets once yearly, ostensibly unnoticed by the mainstream media. Meetings are closed to reporters, and their resolutions are not given to the press. However, representatives from *Look, Time,* and the *Washington Post* are known to attend, but elect not to write about it. This is despite the fact that over one thousand troops surround their meeting place, and attendees arrive in bulletproof limousines encased by escort vehicles of bodyguards with submachine guns.

Among America's prominent Bilderbergers are David and Nelson Rockefeller, Henry Kissinger, Robert McNamara, former president of the World Bank, former President Ford, and President Clinton. Every American Bilderberger is a current or former member of the CFR. The Bilderbergers also have heavy cross-membership with the Trilateral Commission.

The Treaty of Rome, which brought the Common Market into being, and the European Economic Community (EEC), were nurtured at Bilderberger meetings. The society's responsibility for Europe's economic integration enables the Trilateral Commission to proceed with its avowed purpose of administering world government politically and on a regional basis.

Biblical Perspective

See Council on Foreign Relations.

Blavatsky, Madam Helena Petrovna (1831-1891)

Granddaughter of a German noble, Helena Petrovna was Russian-born (1831). From an early age, Helena demonstrated the ability of a medium. To spite her governess, seventeen-year-old Helena married an elderly Czarist general; not surprisingly, the union with Blavatsky lasted no more than three months.

After her divorce, Helena traveled extensively to pursue a longtime interest in mysticism. During her travels in India and England, Blavatsky met Annie Wood Besant. A devout pupil and disciple of Madam, Besant carried on Blavatsky's work after her London death in 1891.

With Colonel H. S. Olcott and W. Q. Judge, also fervent devotees, Blavatsky founded the Theosophical Society in New York in 1875. At its inception, this occult society filled all key offices with Freemasons; Blavatsky herself was a co-Masonic hierarch. Madam Blavatsky also founded the Esoteric School of Theosophy in London in 1888.

Blavatsky is perhaps best known for her occult classic, *The Secret Doctrine,* allegedly dictated to Blavatsky through her masters Koot, Hoomi, Morya, and "The Ascended Masters of Wisdom." Apollonius and Eliphos are apparently Initiated Adepts through whom Blavatsky received her directives.

Regarded by Theosophists as divinely inspired, *The Secret Doctrine* calls Lucifer the "grandest of Ideals." Blavatsky saw "ascended master" Satan as a blameless victim of God's wanton wrath. Blavatsky later published a short-lived magazine, *Lucifer.* Many of her beliefs are found in the two thick volumes of *Isis Unveiled.*

Known as the spiritual godmother of today's New Age Movement, Madam Blavatsky's influence on contemporary history is apparent. Adolf Hitler, for example, kept a copy of *The Secret Doctrine* at his bedside; and, compliments of Madam Blavatsky, the Nazis incorporated a Tibetan symbol, the swastika.

Shortly after the murder of Senator Robert Kennedy, Sirhan Sirhan requested a copy of Blavatsky's *Manual for Revolution* from his jail cell. In this book, she calls for the assassination of national leaders.

Biblical Perspective

Madam Blavatsky's life reflected the last-day attributes depicted in 2 Timothy 3. As a child, she was disobedient to her parents (verse 2). In marrying out of spite, and in calling for assassination of national leaders, Helena might be said to have lacked natural affection (verse 3).

Her New Age form of godliness denied its true power (verse 5), and opposition to biblical Christianity exposed her as a despiser of those who are good (verse 3). In her absorption with "higher self," she was both heady and high-minded (verse 4); moreover, her mind was corrupted (verse 8). Ever learning, she never came to the knowledge of the truth (verse 7); rather she engaged in deceiving, and being deceived (verse 13).

Enamored with Lucifer, Blavatsky fell prey to the spirit of Antichrist (2 Thess. 2:11) that she might be damned (literally, "judged"). She believed not the truth, but instead had pleasure in unrighteousness (verse 12).

Buddha (Siddhartha Gautama of Sakyas)

Biblical Perspective

Tibetan Buddhism is among many pagan religions broadly accepted today even in the West. The exiled Dalai Lama is warmly embraced worldwide by more than one hundred diverse faiths united in their quest for a global ethic in the emerging New World Order. Among numbers of celebrities known for their Buddhist beliefs are Richard Gere, Steven Seagal, and Tina Turner.

To the New Age mystic, Buddha's enlightenment supposedly exceeded that of Christ, but comparisons prove otherwise.

While Buddha remains dead and buried, Christ lives today in the hearts of millions called by His Name (Gal. 2:20; Eph. 3:17). Buddha's life was encased in legend, but there are 800 Old Testament and 4,800 New Testament manuscripts indisputably substantiating the life, death, and resurrection of Christ (See Authenticity of Scriptures). Despite Buddha's title, Tathagata, or "truth-winner," Jesus is Truth personified (John 14:6).

Whereas Buddha was son of a feudal-lord, Jesus was the son of the living God, conceived miraculously by the Holy Spirit (Matt. 1:20). To determine his heir's unknown future, Buddha's father summoned fortune-tellers at his birth. Christ's mission was foretold thousands of years prior to his birth, as early as Genesis 3:15; He came with purpose at the fullness of time (Gal. 4:4). In fact, in Jesus were all things created (Col. 1:16); He needed no fortune-teller.

Buddha's awakening presupposes previous non-enlightenment. Indeed, Buddha never admitted to being "God." In contrast, Jesus needed no awakening. As Emmanuel (God with us), Jesus bears a Name above every name (Phil. 2:9-11). He claimed, and proved, to be the I AM of Exodus 3:13-14 (John 18:1-8; 8:24, 28, 58). Having originated with man, Buddha's religion was devoid of the supernatural; in contrast, the Spirit of the Lord was upon Jesus to heal, deliver, and restore (Luke 4:18).

For six years, Buddha searched and learned from Hindu Masters, aesthetics, and mystics, until finally he was enlightened under a Bo, or fig tree. Jesus, instead, enjoyed unbroken communion with the Father. He had no need to search for answers or personal identity (John 17:21-25). Nonetheless, Buddha felt elevated above his peers, while Jesus took on the intrinsic character of a slave (Phil. 2:7).

Buddha's Four Noble Truths begin with suffering, caused by desire and overcome by an eightfold path of right knowledge, effort, aspiration, speech, behavior, livelihood, mindfulness, and absorption.

Disciples of Christ likewise suffer, but then they reign (2 Tim. 2:12). To overcome craving is not within carnal man (Rom. 7), for the best of man's righteousness is as filthy rags before the holiness of God (Isa. 64:6). Christ's righteousness in and through the believer is man's only hope of glory; furthermore, His yoke is easy, never involving burdensome self-effort (Matt. 11:28-30).

In his twenties, Buddha was discontented with his well-born family and marriage, and thus broke from his wealthy estate. Never did Jesus waver in discontentment although (unlike Buddha) He was uncomely (Isa. 53:2), a poor carpenter's stepson of lowly birth (Matt. 1:20), single, and homeless (Luke 9:58). For the joy set before him, Jesus endured the Cross (Heb. 12:2). He knew the present sufferings were not worthy to be compared to forthcoming glory (Rom. 8:18). Whereas Buddha relied on self, Jesus relied solely on His Heavenly Father.

While Buddha admitted to indulging his flesh, Jesus never sinned, neither was guile found in His mouth (1 Pet. 2:22). He was as a lamb without spot or blemish (1 Pet. 1:19). Unlike Buddha, who abandoned his wife and son at his Great Going Forth, Jesus never broke sacred vows (John 14:6).

Buddha died a rather inglorious accidental death by food poisoning, but Jesus' death and resurrection were of supreme consequence. Today He lives in the hearts of believers as the "blessed and only potentate" (1 Tim. 6:15), Who alone has immortality (v. 16). Buddha taught Nirvana, which literally means, "extinction," as the human spirit's highest destiny. To Buddha, there was no life after death as Christians know it. Jesus spoke of a far more exceeding and eternal weight of glory (2 Cor. 4:17) in Paradise (Luke 23:43) with Him (John 14:3; 2 Cor. 5:8). He alone has the keys of death and hell (Rev. 1:18).

Buddha may be considered one of the greatest rationalists of all time, but no man spoke as Jesus did, for His Word was with power (Luke 4:32). Whereas Buddha preached a religion devoid of authority, Jesus claimed "all authority" in heaven and earth (Matt. 28:18). It is not Buddha's *skandas* (or *skeins*) that hold life together, for of Jesus, and through Him, and to Him, are all things, to Whom be the glory forever (Rom. 11:36).

Finally, three angles within Buddhism (Little Raft, Big Raft, Zen) differ so drastically that it is impossible to consider them aspects of a single religion. In Christianity, however, there is one hope, one Lord, one faith, one baptism (Eph. 4:3-6). Jesus is not an "ascended master," as Buddha is claimed to be, but rather the Master. It is Jesus Who stands incontrovertibly alone.

C

Certificate of Initial Mastery (CIM)

High School Diploma of the Future

(See Outcome-Based Education.)

Resulting from efforts of Goals 2000, the Certificate of Initial Mastery is a constantly upgraded portable document. It is, in effect, the high school diploma of the future, supplanting higher academic standards with new ones emphasizing vocational skills and social engineering. The CIM is a prerequisite for pursuit of higher education, as well as employment, for anyone and everyone at or beyond the tenth grade level.

Serving as technical advisor to states on the CIM and the national human resource system, the National Center on Education and Economy (NCEE) proposed creation of mastery certificates. The assessment-based series of specific certificates includes the Occupational Skills Certificate, as well as Certificates of Initial and Advanced Mastery to insure cradle-to-grave, lifelong learning. Oregon already distributes such certificates.

Work Permit of the Future

To obtain or keep a job, everyone over the age of sixteen will be required to have the CIM, tantamount to a government "work permit," allowing little flexibility, not to mention lifelong monitoring by the state. To take a new career path, a new skill Certificate of Mastery is required.

Departments of Education and Labor intend to supplant the high school diploma, driver's license, social security/healthcare cards, resumé, and official transcript with this certificate; in fact, they are colliding to develop student data banks through a central computer system already in use. Since 1978, the Institute of Electrical and Electronic Engineers has warned that, in so doing, the Department of Education and the National Center for Education Statistics are violating federal and state privacy statutes.

Nonetheless, almost every state has introduced legislation to tie drivers licenses, health care, and job permits to graduation.

National Identification Card of the Future

The Certificate of Initial Mastery will store medical, educational, financial, voting, marriage, and driving records in a single micro-chip placed on the certificate, much like a credit card, or perhaps even under the skin. The CIM will be required in order to drive, work, marry, or vote. The idea, of course, is a national identification card replete with personal biographical information that can be accessed by doctors, police, potential employers, and government agents. Adults changing jobs will need vocational retraining to qualify for these mandated work certificates. Skills transferable from job to job, as determined by the Secretary of Labor's Commission, SCANS, are higher-order, critical thinking skills often referred to as "political correctness."

Biblical Perspective

See Mark of the Beast: 666 and Related Technology.

Change Agents

Secular Realm

The Father of Progressive Education, John Dewey, said, "Things are to be understood without intrusion of supernatural consideration." He saw education as life adjustment, with no concern for the "hereafter," and schools as agents of social change. These perspectives underlie Dewey's contribution as professor of philosophy at New York's Teachers College, Columbia University, which became the model for teacher training at colleges and universities across America. Progressive perspective virtually controlled American Public Education for the fifty years Dewey served at Columbia; moreover, his influence today is no less felt.

Mystical Realm

The goal of American public education has increasingly become to develop a society in which people can more comfortably live with political and economic change, in preparation for the New World Order with its New Age of spiritual enlightenment.

Be assured that all members of the Design Teams for the United Nation's Global Education Project are activists for globalism and New Age philosophy (See Public Education: Christian to Secular to Mystical).

Dr. John Goodland of the National Education Association wrote a report entitled "Schooling for the Future" in which he applauded behavioral change (resocialization), not academic pursuit, as education's paramount goal. In 1956 psychologist Benjamin Bloom published his famed *Taxonomy of Educational Objectives*, which forms the basis for today's Outcome-Based Education (OBE). The idea is to foster higher-order thinking skills and invade the domain of emotions, beliefs, and values (See Values [Affective] Education). Through this model, the public school system purposes to change student thoughts, feelings, and actions to conform with global interdependence and pantheism.

Take for example the Educational Kinesiology program called "Brain Gym," intended to ease change from old to new beliefs and behaviors. Selected by the National Learning Foundation as a top educational technology for the 1990s, "Edu-K" promises to minimize or even eliminate learning problems such as dyslexia and hyperactivity. Among "Edu-K's" components are self-affirmation, high-level thinking skills, and energy balancing (See Pantheism ["All is Energy"]). Its literature is strewn with New Age buzz words like "higher source," "full human potential," "self-affirmation," "transformation," "balance of energy," and "integration." Educational kinesiology supposedly allows physical, emotional, mental, and spiritual aspects of the individual to function harmoniously.

Biblical Perspective

Change itself is a scriptural concept. Agents of change work for God's good or for the cause of corruption. For example, Christ came to replace the old covenant with a new covenant, so that believers are empowered to change their sinful natures to Christ-likeness and their citizenship and eternal destiny to Heaven (Matt. 5:17; 2 Cor. 5:17, 21; Col. 1:5). In contrast, Satan seeks to replace the old Judeo-Christian world order with a New World Order. In it believers are empowered to change their nature to mystical "christhood," their citizenship to the global village, and their eternal destiny to perdition (Matt. 24:5; Rev. 13:1, 7, 11-12; Rev. 20:12-15).

In God's economy, change takes place under His orchestration and through His Spirit dispensed to humankind (See Holy Spirit Imparted). With angelic messengers given charge over them, born from above believers work with Jesus to bring about the Plan of God (Acts 1:8, Col. 1:27; Heb. 1:7, 14; John 3:3; Gen. 1:26 with John 5:17 and John 9:4 [lit., "we" must work]). In Satan's economy, change takes place under Lucifer's orchestration, through legions of demons. "Enlightened" believers work with "powers and principalities in high places" to effect mass planetary Luciferic Initiation (1 Cor. 10:20-21; 1 Tim. 4:1; Rev. 9:20; 2 Cor. 4:4 with Gen. 3:5; Jude 15; Rom. 1:25; Eph. 6:12).

Once they have reached full maturity, mortal believers will put on immortality (1 Cor. 15:53). At the Rapture they will be changed in the split second of the last trump to suit their new environment. Their mass exodus will render a death blow to the headship of Satan (Rom. 8:19; 1 Cor. 15:51-52; Rev. 13:3) and his emissary, Antichrist, whose empty promise of peace will alternately result in Great Tribulation, plagues, and finally Armageddon (Matt. 24: 6, 7, 8, 11, 29; Rev. 13:1,11; 2 Thess. 2:7-8; Rev. 6:2-11; Rev. 8, 9, 19; Rev. 16:12-21 and 19:11-21) .

Despite Armageddon's ineffable havoc, the Lord's ultimate plan for change on earth will prevail when, at the Second Coming, Christ Jesus will return to establish a Millennium of peace under His apt rule. Global change does not cease at the close of Christ's Millennial Reign, for at its conclusion, the earth as we know it will roll up as a scroll to prepare for a new heaven and earth (Rev. 6:2-11; Jude 14; Rev. 1:7; 19:1-16; Rev. 20:2-7; Rev. 6:14).

While Christians cry out, "Even so, come, Lord Jesus," at the prospect of a glorious transfer of residency in the presence of Almighty God, the formerly deceived and destined-to-be-damned will lament their future, an eternity with Lucifer and his lecherous legions in the Lake of Fire (Rev. 22:20; Matt. 13:42, 50; Rev. 20:14-15).

de Chardin, Pierre Teilhard (1881-1955)

Marilyn Ferguson authored a best-selling book, *The Aquarian Conspiracy*, which serves as blueprint for today's New Age Movement. Having surveyed practices and beliefs of the movement, Ferguson asked leading New Age proponents for names of those whose ideas influenced them most. Pierre Teilhard de Chardin and Carl Jung were the two most frequently mentioned. Ferguson herself credits Teilhard for inspiring the name "Aquarian Conspiracy."

Known as the patron saint of the New Age, Teilhard is frequently quoted by leading occultists. According to *Harper's Encyclopedia of Mystical and Paranormal Experience*, Teilhard's blend of pantheism and Christianity stands out among his greatest contributions. Perceiving humanity as evolving unceasingly toward a perfect spiritual state, he compelled millions to join lovingly in spirit toward mass global transformation, a New Age term for demon possession (See Luciferic Intitiation).

A French Jesuit, Teilhard's academic interests were varied, and his followers were also highly educated. A devoted student of Teilhard and a noted Club of Rome leader, Aurelio Peccei is best known as author of *Mankind at the Turning Point*, which discusses humankind's communion with nature in New Age, pantheistic terms. In referring to the collective field of human intelligence, Peccei borrows Teilhard's occult term, "noosphere."

Besides being a theologian of distinction, Teilhard was a paleontologist and philosopher. He participated in excavations of the Peking and Piltdown men, both found to be frauds; his views, as expressed in *The Phenomenon of Man*, were peremptorily unorthodox. Charles Darwin was Teilhard's hero. The theory of evolution was the foundation upon which all his beliefs stood.

Deeply influenced by Pierre Teilhard de Chardin, Thomas Berry is a New Age Catholic priest who served as president of the American Teilhard Association. A "geologian" (theologian of the Earth), Berry blames Christians for environmental ills (See Radical Environmentalism). His idea for "cosmic interdependence" would mandate "biocracy" (self-governing bioregions to replace democracy), exactly in line with Council on Foreign Relations global plans for the New World Order in an enlightened New

Age. The UN's "Prophet of Hope," Robert Muller likewise extols Theilhardian enlightenments in his book, *New Genesis*.

Biblical Perspective

Pierre Teilhard de Chardin falls in the category of those in the last days whose primary pursuit is knowledge. According to the Rotherham translation, such ones, though ever learning, are "never unto a personal knowledge of truth able to come" (2 Tim. 3:7).

Jesus warned His own to take heed lest anyone deceive them (Matt. 24:4), for many in the days preceding Christ's coming will claim falsely to have evolved to godlike perfection (verse 5), as espoused by Teilhard's "new faith for the future." From beliefs as his, Christians are to separate themselves.

Club of Rome (COR)

At the center of Eastern Liberal Establishment power, the Council on Foreign Relations purposes to abolish national sovereignty for globalism.

Whereas the Council on Foreign Relations is the "brain" behind the one world movement, CFR spin-off groups wield three arms of power: economic (Bilderbergers), political (Trilateral Commission), and spiritual (Club of Rome). Most of the planning directives for world government come from the COR. In the early nineties, it first envisioned an unified Europe. In fact, the COR's 1972 report, *The Limits of Growth*, served as blueprint for today's bold new economic, military, and political union in Europe.

A cabal called "The Inquiry" was a small group of one hundred social engineers. Chief architect of the Council on Foreign Relations, Colonel Edward Mandell House, was a member. A spin-off of the CFR, the Club of Rome was founded in 1968. It likewise has a small membership of about one hundred. Approximately twenty-five CFR members belong to the Club of Rome's American Association. The COR pledges worldwide peace and prosperity at the expense of national sovereignty; it further envisions a cashless society not unlike the scriptural account of the Mark of the Beast.

As was "The Inquiry," the Club of Rome is unmistakably spiritually driven. Its founder, Italian industrialist Aurelio Peccei, is a close associate of the Bilderbergers. Peccei discloses his pantheistic New Age beliefs by using Pierre Teilhard de Chardin's occult term, "noosphere," in *Mankind at the Turning Point* (1974).

Biblical Perspective

(See Council on Foreign Relations.)

The COR calls for a "brave new world" with a new Caesar (actually Antichrist). As such, it has been charged with the task of overseeing the regionalization and unification of the entire world. In fact, the September 1973 document "Regionalized and Adaptive Model of the Global World System" reveals that the Club of Rome has already divided the world into ten political/economic regions, referred to as "kingdoms" (Dan. 7:15-28; Rev. 13).

Council on Foreign Relations (CFR)/"The Establishment"

To continue its work in the U.S., the Bavarian founded Order of the Illuminati, a secret society of New World Order "enlightened ones," took on a more agreeable name, the Council on Foreign Relations. Colonel Edward Mandell House and Bernard Baruch formed the CFR in 1921. Its founding president was John W. Davis, J.P. Morgan's attorney.

The CFR's original hierarchy consisted of Illuminists whose names were changed to more American sounding ones. As with the Illuminati, CFR members can be dropped if they fail to adhere to vows of secrecy. Moreover, the CFR journal, *Foreign Affairs,* is inscribed with cabalistic symbolism (See Kabbalism).

Headquartered at the Harold Pratt House, New York City, the council is America's preeminent non-governmental foreign affairs organization. From its conception, the council has demonstrated open intent to consolidate power. Following World War I, subsidiaries, such as Americans for Democratic Action, were set up quickly; the council's membership today boasts America's top political figures. The CFR embodies what is said to be "the Establishment." In other countries, the CFR is found under different names, such as the British Institute of International Affairs.

The Council's Financial Backing

Created by tenacious efforts of illumined Freemasonry, the CFR eventually was financed by Federal Reserve moneys. Starting in 1927, monetary backing from Rockefeller, Carnegie, and Ford foundations poured into the CFR.

The Council's Aim

In 1953, the congressional Reece Committee investigated the CFR and her sister organization, the Institute of Pacific Relations. The committee and Director of Research, Norman Dodd, found that the council "overly propagandizes the globalist concept." Quite plainly, the council's aim is to abolish national sovereignty for globalism. Its two objectives are world government and global banking (See New World Order and Global Economics/Banking). While building a universal community of nations, President Leslie Gelb defined one of the council's major undertakings as finding, nurturing, and placing people in today's one world order.

Toward this end, the CFR acted through the State Department to establish the United Nations just weeks following Pearl Harbor. According to Study No. 7, published by the CFR (25 November 1959), and as witnessed in more recent decades, the council purposes to increase UN authority, albeit gradually.

The Council's Membership

Influence of the Council on Foreign Relations is concentrated in the executive branch and especially State, Treasury, and Defense Departments. The CFR has thirty-eight affiliated organizations and some 2,670 deliberately anonymous members, all from the U.S. Every major department store chain has on its board of directors at least one officer who is a member or partner in CFR international banking chains. Nine out of thirteen CIA directors have been council members.

Furthermore, major book publishers have CFR representatives, many of whom specialize in publishing textbooks (See Textbook Conspiracy). The council is well-connected to the mainstream media. The *New York Times*, *Washington Post*, and *L.A. Times* are CFR-affiliated.

Whereas David Rockefeller is the CFR's most powerful participant, former President Bush is perhaps the most prominent Insider ever to have attained the position of Chief Executive; moreover, he was first to publicly use the term, "New World Order." All of President Clinton's cabinet members belong. For Democrats and Republicans alike, the CFR serves as an employment agency. Indeed, the CFR and Trilateral Commission virtually run our federal government.

The Council's Spin-Offs

Toward establishing a New World Order, the CFR is at the center of Insider Eastern Liberal Establishment power, influence, and planning. The glue that holds the Rockefeller Insiders together, the Council on Foreign Relations, has been dubbed "the invisible government."

Whereas the CFR is the "brain" of globalism, CFR spin-off groups wield three arms of power: economic (Bilderbergers), spiritual (Club of Rome), and political (Trilateral Commission).

Economic • <u>Bilderbergers</u> (founded 1954): The Bilderbergers are a sort of international CFR. The European Economic Community is a product of the Bilderberg Group. Their membership, which consists of the world's elite, meets once a year to coordinate and disseminate plans for the New World Order.

Spiritual • <u>Club of Rome</u> (founded 1968): With less than one hundred members, the occult-driven Club of Rome is charged with the task of overseeing regionalization, then unification, of the entire world. Most of the planning directives for world government come from the Club of Rome.

Political • <u>Trilateral Commission</u> (founded by David Rockefeller, 1973): Members of the Trilateral Commission include leaders from the world's three economic superpowers (North America, Western Europe, and Japan); hence, the term "trilateral." This multinational planning commission seeks to unite superpowers into a one world socialist government, requiring the voluntary demise of American independence.

Biblical Perspective

The notion of one world government on earth is not evil, as some suppose. In fact, the forthcoming Millennium is just that. Keep in mind, however, that apart from Jesus Christ, every historic case of multinational government has resulted in departure from truth, tyranny, and suffering. Examples include Babylon (608-538 B.C.), Medo-Persia (538-330 B.C.), Greece (330-30 B.C.), and Rome (30 B.C.), to which Daniel's prophetic visions allude (Dan. 2; 7). The end-time Revived Roman Empire with Antichrist at its helm is no exception.

The iron of paling totalitarianism mixed with the miry clay of democracy in Daniel's image bears noticeable resemblance to today's European Economic Community. Many experts believe that the ten toes of Daniel's image (Chapter 2) picture ten global mega-regions into which the world will be divided under Antichrist. Not surprisingly, the Constitution for the Federation of Earth proposes an administrative structure of twenty world electoral and administrative regions with ten mega-regions. Others pair the ten toes with ten horns of worldly power, as depicted in Revelation 17. These "kings without kingdoms" willingly submit to Antichrist, but they wield phenomenal global power as mega-magnet international financiers (See Revived Roman Empire; Kings without Kingdoms).

Specific tasks of the one world strategy are assigned to spin-off groups of the Council on Foreign Relations. First, countries are to be divided and subsequently merged into several regions (economically by the Bilderbergers, then politically by the Trilateral Commission). Next, concepts of national sovereignty are to be effectively dissolved as regions unite under the furtive banner of global sustainable development and merge into end-time one world government, as prophesied by scriptures (See Radical Environmentalism and Dan. 4:19-27; 7:2-8; Rev. 12:3; 13:1, 5; 17:9-12).

D

Darwin, Charles Robert (1809-1882)

Unitarian Universalist Charles Robert Darwin (1809-1882) was an English biologist known especially for developing the systematic, codified view of today's prevailing and politically correct theory of evolution. With Alfred R. Wallace, Darwin also proposed the principle of natural selection. In 1859 he published *On the Origin of the Species by Means of Natural Selection or the Preservation of Favored Races in the Struggle for Life,* which explained the evolutionary process through principles of natural and sexual selection.

Despite this publication's global celebrity, Darwin's true claim to fame is his philosophy of historic optimism. Historic optimism contends that apart from God, humankind's thinking, philosophy, and destiny are improving progressively with the passing of time. This theory opposes the Second Law of Thermodynamics, which maintains that all things in the natural realm are in an ongoing state of deterioration and decay.

Based on the work of Charles Darwin and Herbert Spencer, Social Darwinism offers scientific justification for late nineteenth-century *laissez-faire* capitalism. Resting on the principle of unrestricted privilege in commerce, it held that only the strong and innovative can flourish in a free environment. Entrepreneurs such as Andrew Carnegie popularized Social Darwinism, while using it to legitimize competitive individualism in an unregulated market economy.

Political internationalists embrace the related belief that those with special talents and aptitudes have claim to rule the less gifted, who are clearly unaware of what is best for them. Given this perspective, Social Darwinism continues to play into the socialist global agenda of the burgeoning New World Order.

Biblical Perspective

By extrapolation, Darwin somehow felt assured that man's efforts, apart from God, will yield a future utopia in which only the fittest among favored men hold rank, which is contrary to Acts 10:34. Because the Bible clearly teaches that efforts apart from God are but "filthy rags" (Isa. 64:6) and utter vanity (Eccles. 1:2-3), believers are commanded to avoid such "profane, vain babbling, and oppositions of science, falsely so called" (1 Tim. 6: 20).

Be sure that Darwin's godless theories appeal to secularists and mystics alike. Evolution upholds secular humanism by circumventing accountability to God and New Age mysticism by proclaiming self to be God (See Pantheism). Both cling to "the lie" of Antichrist's bogus claim to godhood (2 Thess. 2:4, 11) and, thus, give form to an emerging global ethic significantly at odds with the Judeo-Christian tradition.

Day of the Lord

Biblical Perspective

About one hundred years after Christ, John the Revelator said he was "in the Spirit in the Lord's Day" (Rev. 1:10). Scriptures never call Sunday "the Lord's Day," nor do any Christian writings in this same historical period; therefore, this Lord's Day cannot possibly refer to Sunday. Such is the case elsewhere in scripture where the Day of the Lord is called "that great Day of God Almighty" (Rev. 16:14), "the Day of God" (2 Pet. 3:12), "the great and the terrible Day of the Lord" (Joel 2:31), "the Day of our Lord, Jesus Christ" (1 Cor. 1:8), "the Day of the Lord, Jesus" (1 Cor. 5:5; 2 Cor. 1:14; Phil. 1:10; 2:16), "Day of Jesus Christ" (Phil. 1:6), "that great and notable Day of the Lord" (Acts 2:20), "that day, the great day, the day" (Isa. 2:12).

As recorded in the first chapter of the Book of Revelation, John was caught out of his own time—not necessarily bodily, but rather "in the spirit"—to be positioned just beyond some future occurrence identified as "the Lord's Day." From this new vantage point, John looked back in time to what for him and for us today remains the future. After this remarkable experience, John wrote

his observations under Divine inspiration especially for our benefit, upon whom the ends of the ages are come (1 Cor. 10:11).

Definition

By definition, the Day of the Lord is an eschatological term
referring to God's special intervention to judge His enemies and,
thus, accomplish His Divine purpose of vindicating and delivering His people. It is strongly related to God's rule on earth and,
therefore, to His sovereign design for global history. God's very
being demands a perfect reflection of Himself in creation. For
this reason, despite frenzied efforts of radical environmentalists
with New Age ideals, our tainted earth will one day be dissolved
and the season of world history terminated (Isa. 2:10-22).

The term "Day of the Lord" is mentioned first in Amos
5:18-20, and subsequently some nineteen times in the Old Tes-
tament and three times in the New. Many previous days of the
Lord pointed in type to the primary future and singularly great
Day of the Lord addressed by Isaiah, Joel, Zechariah, Malachi,
Peter, and Paul.

Natural and Supernatural Tools: Gentile and Israelite Involvement

"Indignation" often refers to God's anger with Israel, national and/ or spiritual, because of rebellion and apostasy. The
sage Daniel prophesied of extraordinary indignation to accompany the end-times, aligned with the self-god delusion of Antichrist and his False Prophet (Dan. 11:36; See Pantheism).

Unlike previous days of the Lord, the end-time wrath of
God will visit all nations to recompense the controversy of Zion
(Isa. 34:1-8; Obadiah 15; See Islamic Fundamentalism). This
Great Day of Judgment will demonstrate God's incontestable
sovereignty when the Messiah Himself wars victoriously against
the world's premier armies, who will be militantly postured against
Israel and the city of Jerusalem (Joel 3:1-16; Zech. 14:1-3; 12-
15).

In executing His sovereign purpose against His enemies, God
often uses war coupled with supernatural terrors (Isa. 13; Zeph.).
Intended to remove class distinction and idolatry (Isa. 2:12-21)
and to abolish sin (2 Pet. 3:11-13), the Day of the Lord will
entail social calamities and physical cataclysms (Matt. 24; Luke
21:7-33).

Scope

Most scholars view the Day of the Lord as being expansive in scope; others see it as being constrictive.

Expansive Scope

With the Lord, a day is as a thousand years, and a thousand years as one day (2 Pet. 3:8). This concept is connected with events surrounding the Day of the Lord (verses 3-15), which, consequently, is believed to cover a period of about one thousand years. The prophet Malachi, whose name means "My messenger," described several events that will unfold in that day (Mal. 4:1-6).

Beginning with the Rapture of Christ's bride, that great and dreadful day will unveil Antichrist and unleash the global Tribulation with subsequent plagues, all building toward World War III, or Armageddon. Light is like a laser, used to destroy or heal; thus, Christ's brightness at His Second Coming will devastate the wicked. Concurrently, it will bring life to the righteous through Christ's Millennial Reign and its fitting zenith of the Great White Throne Judgment.

Constrictive Scope

The constrictive view restricts the Day of the Lord to Christ's Second Coming. Although the Lord's return to earth, as described by Joel (2:31) and Malachi (3:2-5), will be the grand climax of the judgment phase of that day, it is more appropriately viewed as part of a larger window of Divine activity, as held by the expansive view. In either perspective, major occurrences characterize the Second Coming of Christ. First, God will expose His enemies (Matt 24:29-30; 25:31 and Rev. 19:11-12, 15). Next, He will release angelic armies against those enemies (Matt. 13:40-42, 49-50; 25:31).

As a result, the rule of Satan and his cohorts will end at what is called the Valley of Decision (Joel 3:14) with their certain eviction from earth (Matt. 13:41-42; 49-50; 25:41, 46; Rev. 19:17 through 20:3). In that day, heaven and earth will be removed from the usurper's power, for Satan and his demons will be bound for one thousand years before being cast into the Lake of Fire (Rev. 20:2-3).

Good News with the Bad

Throughout the Day of the Lord, darkness will attend Divine wrath (Joel 2:1-2; Amos 5:18-20; Zeph. 1:14-15), and light will attend Divine blessing (1 Thess. 5:1-11).

After talking about the Great Tribulation, Jesus warned, "Except those days be shortened, there should no flesh be saved." He continued, "but for the elect's sake, those days shall be shortened" (Matt. 24: 21-22). "Shortened" here means "to terminate" or "to cut off." The verbs in this passage indicate that God has set a time for tribulation to end lest no flesh survive its darkness and wrath.

True, the Day of the Lord is defined by gloom and doom (Amos 5:20); however, it is not stripped entirely of light and life (Zech. 14:1-9). This was foreshadowed in Creation when the "evening" was followed by "day" (Gen. 1:4-6). Within that day, the blinding light of Christ's glorious appearance will attend the Rapture (Tit. 2:13). With the Millennium, the Bright and Morning Star (Rev. 22:16), Jesus Christ Himself, will shine on the righteous as an everlasting light. Finally, inexplicable glory associated with the New Heaven and Earth will splendidly consummate that great and notable Day of the Lord (Isa. 65:17; 66:22; Rev. 21:1).

Death Culture

Given the flood of humanism, which for several decades has increasingly defined public belief, the death culture has revived and thrived with the conviction that absence of any supreme being sanctions freedom from accountability to outside expectations. To the humanist, man is the measure of all things; it is his right to live "the good life" and, at its close, to choose "the good death." In today's humanistic society, death by suicide, abortion, and euthanasia enjoy high profile, big money organizational clout. Among the most visible of pro-death groups are Planned Parenthood and the National Abortion Rights Action League.

In recent years, death has become a subject of great intrigue, and even seduction. Melvin Morse, M.D., and Paul Perry of Seattle recount powerful effects of near-death experiences, not least of which include alleged out-of-body experiences and tunnel adventures augmented by increased paranormal activity. A large number claim such a profound change in their electromagnetic signatures that their watches actually stop. Especially prone to these near-death manifestations, New Age mystics view death as occasion to ascend the evolutionary ladder toward some mystical goal. In the spring of 1997, thirty-nine highly intelligent, computer literate professionals longed for the "next level in human Evolution." These devotees of a flying saucer cult known as Heaven's Gate shed their earthly "vehicles" to acquire new glorified bodies by means of an eerily ritualistic mass suicide in Rancho Santa Fe, California.

Death by Choice

A majority of Americans believe it is appropriate for the elderly or feeble to commit suicide, which is referred to as "self-deliverance" by groups as the Hemlock Society. Even successful men in their prime, such as Nirvana singer Kurt Cobain and Nobel Prize winner Lewis Puller, Jr., are championed for having chosen for themselves "the good death."

The ongoing, albeit controversial, work of Michigan pathologist Jack Kevorkian, known as "Dr. Death," has served to broaden the concept of suicide. In 1994 Oregon became the first state to legalize physician-assisted suicide; and effective 1 July 1996, doctors in Australia could administer lethal doses of drugs to the terminally ill. The Dutch government has documented more than 1,000 cases per year in which physicians actively caused or hastened death without patient consent.

Death by Obligation

The concept of managed death has progressed rapidly and universally, and now death has joined the ranks of politically-correct "ism's" as a civil right. Keep in mind, however, that human objects of managed death often have little to say about their alleged rights. Candidates include the pre- and new- born; the comatose, disabled, or terminally ill; and those severely depressed or mentally impaired. Others seek for them their so-called civil right to a "good death."

For example, in the early 1980s the Indiana Supreme Court allowed the parents and the doctor of "Baby Doe" to starve the infant, who was born with Downs Syndrome and birth defects to death. As Baby Doe suffered death by obligation, so did hundreds of thousands of "superfluous" men, women, and children in pre-World War II Germany. Between 1939 and 1946, over a quarter of a million citizens were routinely exterminated for being "devoid of value." About 5,000 children, some for their badly modeled ears, were killed in the Nazi euthanasia program.

Death Education

America's youth today are well-conditioned to the normalcy of death at another's hand. According to a 1995 American Medical Association study, our nation's youth will have witnessed by television some eight thousand acts of murder before they reach puberty. Make no mistake: Death education is not limited to television viewing.

Introduced in the 1970s, death education in America's public education system is an ill-camouflaged effort to promote the godless agenda of the *Humanist Manifesto II,* which reads: "[We recognize] an individual's right to die with dignity, euthanasia [mercy killing], and the right to suicide." Since humanist change agents do not believe in God, they make fun of any religious views as openly as they dare.

In 1997 the U.S. Supreme Court refused to declare as constitutional the "right to die," yet the death culture continues to be transmitted to students through the educational publications of Simon and Schuster, Random House, and more (See Textbook Conspiracy). Take, for example, Sid Simon's *Values Clarification* handbook of practical strategies for teachers and students. Simon's "Fallout-Shelter Problem" goes like this: Given personal information about ten people, children must select who should (and who should not) survive if in an imaginary fallout shelter there is space, air, food, and water for six people only. Students are not given the opportunity to consider creative means for sustaining life; they must instead eliminate the least worthy.

Biblical Perspective

In addressing issues of the so-called "death culture," the idea is not to moralize about complex family health care decisions. Certainly, it is in love that caring family members refuse, or agree to terminate, artificial life support which prolongs bodily functions that may not define life from God's perspective. The point is rather to demonstrate the impact of the death culture in what the Bible calls end-times.

Perhaps unwittingly, but not without consequence, many will turn from sound doctrine (2 Tim. 3:7), and deceptions will be rampant (2 Tim. 3:13). Under the United Nation's concept of sustainable development, the population must be reduced (See Radical Environmentalism). In what will be termed an act of mercy, some will confer the presumptuous sentence of death on others (John 16:2; Luke 21:16). Still others will seek escape by pronouncing and executing their own death sentence. Either way, scripture indicates that delivering up the body to death profits nothing (1 Cor. 13:3).

God's Assessment: Life is Precious

Greeks and Romans alike advocated suicidal death as noble for both the feeble and aged. In stark contrast, Jesus brought new appreciation for the dignity of human life. Today's death culture fails to comprehend humankind's position as crown of God's creation (Heb. 2:6-8), destined to partake of the Divine nature (2 Pet. 1:4). To the believer, God is the God of life (John 1:4 with Col. 2:9; 1:9); Christ's was a ministry of life (1 Thess. 5:10); and ours is an abundant life in Jesus (John 10:10).

God's Command: Choose Life

If sin had not come into the world, death would not have been an option (Gen. 3:24). Because of the fall, death is inevitable (Heb. 9:27). It is not, however, a godly choice when self-inflicted. On the contrary, God clearly mandates life as the only viable choice (Deut. 30:19; Rom. 6:6). Taking no pleasure in death, God's clear command is to choose life (Ezek. 18:32).

Society's Skewed Perception of Human Worth

In May 1994 Federal Judge Barbara J. Rothstein of Seattle paired the right to abort with the constitutional right to commit suicide with medical help. In any case of managed death, society's definition of personhood, as defined by quality of life, becomes the salient issue. Accordingly, the death lobby has redefined what it means to be "a person." Psychologist Dr. Steven Pinker doubts the full personhood of neonates (infants) for their lacking "morally significant traits." Joseph Fletcher's fifteen indicators of personhood likewise exclude the pre- and new-born, as well as the seriously developmentally disabled.

When variables such as handicap, state of health, skin color, religion, age, or lack of perceived "personhood" determine a person's value, then society sets itself up as supreme judge. As was the case in pre-World War II Germany, the powerful determine who is worthy to live. By arguing benefit to the whole of society, they justify systematic extermination of those who fail to make the grade. For example, in *Confessions of an Eco-Warrior,* Dave Foreman categorically repudiates "Humanpox." This error of "self-god" is the essence of the New Age Movement. The Enemy's ultimate plan is systematically to rid the global community of God and His annoying people (Rev. 13:5-8), while at the same time sparing those chosen to usher in and thereafter sustain the New World Order.

God's Perception of Human Worth

Even in a comatose state, a person is of infinite worth. Just prior to her death, a Christian friend shared the oft-quoted Bible verse about God's giving placid sleep unto His beloved (Ps. 127:2). An equally valid translation reads, "God gives unto His beloved, even as they sleep." This suggests the remarkable possibility that even while the body is sleeping, or comatose, one's spirit can commune with God.

That the life of one who can pray, praise, petition, and serve is of limitless value does not categorically degrade the life of one who will not or cannot. The sum of the matter is that man's thoughts are not God's (Isa. 55:8-9). From the womb to the grave, it is God, not man, Who rightly determines the merit of any life. As the Psalmist proclaims, man's seasons of life are in God's hands (Ps. 31:15).

God's Just Judgment

The Bible makes it abundantly clear that the forthcoming one world order will glorify none other than Lucifer—the ultimate murderer from the beginning (John 8:44). In the book of Revelation (9:11), Satan is given the title Abaddon, meaning "destroyer;" he is author of today's death culture. His chief executive officer, Antichrist, will offer the empty promise of peace, which instead will yield utter destruction (Rev. 17:13-17; 1 Thess. 5:3).

Unrepentant perpetrators of Satan's lies (Rev. 9:21) will knowingly opt to serve Antichrist. Toward the close of the last days, these will desire and seek death; however, it will not be granted as escape from the sure wrath of God (Rev. 9:6). Having rebelled knowingly against God (Rev. 22:15; 21:8), murderers will themselves taste of the "second death" reserved for those cast into the Lake of Fire. Believers can be assured that God's judicious reasoning surpasses man's in both timeliness and justice (Job 4:17).

Deconstructionism/Post-structuralism

Fifth century B.C. Sophists (meaning "wise men") were Greek philosophers and itinerant teachers, who received fees for their lectures. As atheists and early humanists, they were less interested in the pursuit of truth than in political use of rhetoric. Protagorus was the leading Sophist who taught that "man is the measure of all things." Plato and Aristotle both thought Sophists to be dishonest for applying bogus reasoning. Plato called their argument-counterargument ploy of deconstructionism "antilogic," and sophistry came to mean false reasoning.

Deconstructionism is modern relativism applied to language; it is a sort of cerebral political correctness that questions traditional values and renders unrealizable any meaningful communication. Today's version is a French import with Algerian-born literary theorist, Jacques Derrida, as its key proponent. Scholar Stanley Fish of Duke University is the best known proponent in America today. Known also as post-structuralism, high theory, or postmodernism, it maintains that words have no meaning apart from relative interpretation; therefore, they can mean anything we want them to mean. Individuals create languate to win arguments, not to affirm truth. Right and wrong do not exist, only good or bad debate.

This being the case, it stands to reason that absolute values cannot possibly exist. Arguments are always directed against the absolute rather than in defense of one's own relative interpretation. The antilogic of modern deconstructionism is the philosophical basis for Secular Humanism, Multiculturalism (Diversity), Genderism/Radical Feminism, Afrocentrism, and Radical Environmentalism. While denying the existence of right and wrong, today's politically correct sophists contradict themselves with their affirmation that belief in God is wrong, but belief in no God (or self-god) is right. Sexism and racism are wrong, but intolerance for fundamental Christians is right. Discrimination is wrong, but reverse discrimination is right.

Biblical Perspective

Rotherham's *Emphasized Bible* speaks of end-time false teachers (2 Pet. 2:1) who defame the way of truth (verse 2). Forsaking a straight path of moral absolutism, they have gone astray (verse 15). While themselves slaves of corruption, they promise freedom with great swelling words of vanity (verses 18-19). They are like fountains without water (verse 17), yet many follow their wanton ways (verses 2-3). Given this Biblical scenario, deconstructionism is well-disposed to the enemy's plot to supplant the Judeo-Christian with the New Earth (or Global Civic) Ethic. The latter ignores the fundamental values upon which America purportedly is founded while promoting instead a form of global socialism, as scriptures foretell and as defined earlier in *Humanist Manifestos* and more recently in the report of the Commission on Global Governance, *Our Global Neighborhood*.

Depository Trust Company (DTC)

Headquartered in New York City, the Depository Trust Company is simply a private bank for securities. A brokerage clearing firm and transfer center, the DTC handles book entry transactions for banks and brokers, all of which secure their membership with it. Its Director of Training, Mr. Jim McNeff, identifies the DTC as the largest limited trust company, and likely the most powerful financial institution in the world. The DTC holds assets of over nine trillion dollars. As a private depository bank for institutional and brokerage firms exclusively, the DTC is virtually unknown to the general public.

Marriage of Convenience

The DTC is owned privately by the same stockholders as the Federal Reserve Corporation. Through the Treasury Department and the Federal Reserve System ("the Fed"), the Rockefellers and their global allies have effectively wedded America's fiscal and monetary policies with their own (See Global Economics).

Due to Federal Trade Commission and Security and Exchange Commission regulations, no bank or broker can place stock into its own firm's name; a fictitious name is used instead. Under federal mandate, the broker or bank must send each transaction to the DTC for ledger posting. As a bank, the DTC cannot hold the certificate in its name either, so the DTC transfers the certificate to its own holding company (CD and Company, or CeDe and Company). The Fed, therefore, holds assets in trust in an unknown entity's name.

Because the Fed mandates that the Depository Trust Company handle all transactions for institutional and brokerage firms, the DTC virtually controls all paper asset transactions. Keep in mind that institutionally managed funds, such as pensions consist of paper asset investments, such as stocks and bonds. Such certificates are held in the name of the DTC's private holding company. Experts agree that the Fed will pin the new dollar to gold prices, so that stocks and bonds purchased with old dollars will be significantly diminished in value, in which case only Federal Reserve stockholders will win.

Stock and bond certificates reside in the same New York City vault used to hold the Fed's gold taken from the hands of private citizens in 1933. Under either Executive Order or Presidential Directive, the President can enforce any new emergency under the War Powers Act, at which time citizens must then surrender all gold bullion and trade "old dollars" for "new" under threat of imprisonment. Furthermore, according to the 1917 Trading with the Enemy Act, the Fed could refuse to surrender back stock and bond certificates in the event of national emergency. Since the Fed already holds citizen's stocks and bonds in its fictitious name, it will likely cash them in for the government's failure to repay overdue loans.

Manipulated Depression

McNeff admits that Fed and DTC's owners deliberately manipulated what amounted to disaster for many Americans on what has come to be known as Black Monday. Given the success of this controlled test, many experts expect imminent repeat of the similarly orchestrated Great Depression.

Mandated Cashless Society toward Mark of the Beast

Twenty-two February 1996 marked DTC's switch to cashless transactions; now checks and drafts are no longer permissible. Fed Wire funds are electronic ledger transfers between the Fed member banks. Only Fed Funds are accepted for stock or bond transactions.

A type of Fed Fund ATM card is likely to be needed for citizens to transact any business at all. Some believe that this trend brings clarity to what Scriptures call the Mark of the Beast. Although we have yet to sustain this mark, we daily experience its precursors.

Biblical Perspective

See Federal Reserved System.

Dewey, John (1859-1952)

Born in Vermont in 1859, John Dewey was an avowed atheist and the first president of the American Humanist Society. A noted author, educator, and philosopher, renowned for his Dewey Decimal System, he was instrumental in introducing the nontheistic religion of humanism into America's public education system.

Dewey, the Author

Dewey authored *School and Society* (1989) and *My Pedagogic Creed* (1897); furthermore, he wrote and subsequently signed the *Humanist Manifesto 1* (1933). Co-signer C. F. Potter claimed every American public school as a disciple of humanism. Toward realizing this outcome, Dewey's so-called Progressive Education spread phenomenally throughout the thirties and forties.

Dewey, the Educator

Known as "patron saint" of public education, Dewey molded educational thought and methodologies more than anyone of the twentieth century. Dewey saw education as life adjustment, the school system as vehicle for Values Education, and its teachers as agents of social change (See Change Agents). In Dewey's leftist Hegelian system, there is no God, no soul, no permanent moral absolutes, and no eternity; therefore, there are no consequences or judgment for sin. Not surprisingly, by the time of Dewey's death in 1952, the Protestant character of early public schools had disappeared.

Professor of philosophy at New York's Columbia University, Dewey also headed its Teachers' College, which served as model for teacher education departments at colleges and universities across America. Dewey's influence on the educational faculty at Harvard was similarly strong. In the 1950s the Reece Committee investigated Rockefeller, Ford, and Carnegie Foundations' control over teacher training schools. Interestingly, Dewey's association with the Rockefeller family went back a long way. In fact, he taught four of the family's five brothers.

Dewey's indelible mark remains even today in the Outcome-Based Education (OBE) movement. Both Progressive and Outcome-Based Education subordinate individualistic traits to collectivist interests toward a New World Order. In forming the Intercollegiate Socialist Society (1905), from which SDS eventually came, Dewey aimed to place socialists into America's classrooms, pulpits, and labor unions.

Dewey, the Philosopher

Dewey's inspiration was psychologist and philosopher William James, whose pragmatism interpreted truth in terms of practicality. Believing that all knowledge is derived from experience, Dewey encouraged students to follow their own lines of scrutiny. Dewey made "inquiry" the essence of logic; hence, the so-called "discovery learning" (learning by doing) craze of the 1970s.

Dewey, the Revolutionary

Dewey called for a world community with redistribution of wealth and an end to the Christian belief system. Notable disciples of Dewey were Professor George S. Counts, Harold Ruggs, and Scott Nearing. Counts' seventeen volume reference for teachers is known as the blueprint for socializing America. Ruggs and Nearing shared with Counts the revolutionary notion of using public education to shape "a new public mind" toward world citizenship.

A Marxist/Fabian Socialist, Dewey helped organize the Marxist educational system in Russia. The Fabian Society was a gathering of intellectuals, not least of which was co-Masonic hierarch and Theosophist Dr. Annie Wood Besant. The society's accomplishments mirror the one world efforts of Weishaupt's internationalist Order of the Illuminati.

Biblical Perspective

Undermining God's Word and the Judeo-Christian ethic is essential to realizing the promised Antichrist utopia of the New World Order, under which illumined humankind hopes to reign supreme apart from divine intrusion. Despite beliefs of schooled humanists to the contrary, the Lord is a God of knowledge (1 Sam. 2:3). Of Him, through Him, and to Him are all things; and to Him alone is all glory due (Rom. 11:36). This being the case, He cannot rightfully be excluded from any true education, "progressive" or otherwise, nor can His Word be disregarded as somehow lacking relevance. Those who speak without due deference to it lack light (Isa. 8:20), regardless of the scholarly accolades lavished upon them.

Although godless, global efforts assuredly will come to naught, Paul warns us in Colossians 2:8 against being corrupted through philosophy (as with James' pragmatism) and vain deceit (of atheistic moral relativism) after the tradition of men (secular humanism) and rudiments of the world view (Marxist/Fabian socialism). In these end-times, we are admonished to beware lest any man—be it Dewey, Counts, Ruggs, or Nearing—divert us from Christ.

E

Ecumenical Movement/
World Council of Churches

World Council of Churches and Catholicism

The Greek term for "ecumenical" means "of the whole world." Ecumenicism is global unity of the entire religious community. Known as the first ecumenical council of the church, the Council of Nicaea (A.D. 325) issued its famous creed, sanctioned by the Emperor Constantine. Under Constantine, his aides, and the papacy, a type of ecumenical unity was successfully achieved, albeit at the price of religious syncretism, promising no rightful salvation.

Formed in Holland (1948), the World Council of Churches continues to push privately for unification with the Church of Rome, whose ecumenical goals are revealed by its ongoing dialogue with representatives of four major non-Christian religions. Under Catholic (meaning universal) leadership, the Louvain Declaration of 1974 appealed to religious communities of the world to propagandize the decidedly New Age perspective of "planetary citizenship" (See Revived Roman Empire).

World Council of Churches and Political Correctness

The WCC seeks to reunify various branches of today's diverse religious community into what Christian author Dave Hunt calls a "religiously pluralistic international community" not unlike that achieved under Constantine. Today, however, its common denominator and major test of orthodoxy is the eco-theology of radical environmentalism. Guilt for human abuse of the environment, especially by Christians, provides motivation for the global call to stewardship. Eco-justice demands our asking Earth, not God, for forgiveness.

Today's eco-menical movement has provided cover stories for all major religious publications from the Unitarian Universalist magazine, _Word_, to _Christianity Today_. The movement's primary proponent, nonetheless, is Upper Manhattan's Cathedral of St. John the Divine, the "Green Cathedral," which calls for global convergence of world religions by the year 2000.

Franklin D. Roosevelt was one of the Cathedral's chief fund raisers, and Al Gore serves frequently as lay minister. Among its associates are mystic Maurice Strong, the top environmental activist, and the New Age movement's shining star, David Spangler, who performs the Eucharist there. An esoteric order connected to the Knights Templar, the Gaia Institute resides within the Cathedral. It applies Earth-worship's concept of interdependence to ecological cleanup for the federal Environmental Protection Agency.

Surrounded by Shinto and Native American shrines, Cathedral congregants demonstrate their trendy pan-religious bent by performing Tai Chi rituals and Earth Masses. Forces of Nature dancers leap up and down its aisles while the Howl-eluia Chorus of some 200 politically correct Episcopalians display dubitable oneness with Earth by literally howling at the moon (See Pantheism). It was at St. John's that the ill-famed Mayflower Madam wed.

World Council of Churches and Freemasonry

The primary spirit guide of co-Masonic hierarch Alice Bailey, Djwhal Khul, betrayed the key roles of public education, the ecumenical Christian church, and Freemasonry in aptly preparing Earth for its one world religion in the coming New Age. Not surprisingly, the World Council of Churches is strongly influenced by the largest secret society in the world, Freemasonry; for Masonic authority Carl H. Claudy boasts of the society's tolerance for all religions. No matter their personal beliefs, all men in the brotherhood who swear to protect the brotherhood, right or wrong, are seen as "spiritual sons of God." Upon the altar of the thirty-third degree initiation ceremony are four "holy books"— namely, the Bible, the Koran, the Book of Law, and the Hindu Scriptures. According to many Masonic authors, "any god will do" (See Ancient Mystery Religions).

World Council of Churches and New World Order

The Washington State Interfaith Council purposes to set aside religious differences on behalf of the New World Order. Similar councils are springing up around the world as never before. There are more than seventy in the U.S. alone, and the number is growing. Toward achieving shared one world goals, the World Council of Churches collaborates with the World Constitution and Parliamentary Association, the forefront association poised to realize the global agenda on political, economic, and religious levels. Called "Positive Christianity," this push for global unity proclaims a sort of mish-mash "good news" that most can affirm. Korean Messiah Sun Myung Moon leads today's broad ecumenical movement.

Biblical Perspective

Unity among peoples of the world is clearly a Biblical principle (John 17:21-23). It must not be overlooked that God Himself has a glorious plan for theocratic globalism, which will be realized in the forthcoming Millennium. Clearly, God does not contravene unity itself—only unity opposed to redemption through Jesus Christ. You see, Jesus is the door to salvation (John 10:9). Apart from Him, no man, woman, boy, or girl is saved from sin and alienation from God (Acts 4:12; John 14:6).

This narrow perspective is not rooted in human pettiness, as some presume, for God's ways are far above the ways of man (Isa. 55:9). It is based instead on God's rightful concern for His Name above all names and for the well-being of those who presently bear it, or will bear it in the near future and throughout eternity (Phil. 2:9-11). Be assured, God excludes no person or group (Acts 10:34)—even sinners (Rom. 5:8)—from His boundless love (John 3:16). In Christ, no one is esteemed above another, despite gender or social class (1 Cor. 12:13); however, Amos 3:3 poses the fitting question, "How can two walk together except they be agreed?" The obvious answer is, "They can't."

Light cannot possibly fellowship with darkness and still remain light any more than milk can maintain its flavor or cream color when Hershey's chocolate is stirred into it. For this reason, the clear command of scriptures is to withdraw from those who walk "out of the ranks" of the straight and narrow, and do not join with them (2 Thess. 3:6;14). This includes idolaters (1 Cor. 5:11) and Earth-worshippers (Rom. 1:25). Make no mistake; interfaith ecumenism, as embraced by the World Council of Churches, stands opposed to the inspired Word of God and must not be embraced (See Authenticity of Scriptures).

Nonetheless, many rush to the broad, fashionable way, which

unfortunately leads to destruction, themselves having been deceived by false prophets who appear as sheep, but inside are devouring wolves (Matt. 7:13, 15). Their "one mind" signifies subjection to Antichrist (Rev. 17:13) and his beguiling brand of end-time global unity. Tragically, not only will these miss out on the blessing of worldwide unity under rule of the very Prince of Peace Himself, but they will also experience certain wrath of God for participating in blasphemy and for compelling others to do so (Rev. 14:9-11).

Out of love alone, the Father has sent the Son, not to condemn, but to save the world (1 John 4:1-14). Godly response is "love unfeigned" for one's brother (1 John 4: 20-21; 2 Cor. 6:6), but always with a single eye (Titus 2:13) so as to eschew the "spirit of error" characterizing this present age (1 John 4: 6).

End/Latter Times; Last/Latter Days

Biblical Perspective

Last-day theology is a major scriptural theme throughout the Poetic Books (Song of Solomon), Major Prophets (Isaiah, Jeremiah, Ezekiel, Daniel), Minor Prophets (Joel, Habakkuk, Zechariah, Zephaniah), Pauline Epistles (1, 2 Cor.; 1, 2 Thess.; 1, 2 Tim.), General Epistles (Jude), and the Book of Revelation. Matthew 24, Mark 13, and Luke 21 are known as the Great Eschatological Discourse, prophesying all-encompassing future events, especially in reference to Israel.

Having begun with the ascension of Christ, the end (or latter) times will see formation of a ruthless, destined-to-be-doomed global system of government and economics. Modeled after the European Economic Community, the New World Order will redistribute wealth and implement a cashless system for buying and selling (See Global Economics/Banking; Revived Roman Empire). Under Lucifer's headship, Antichrist and his False Prophet will fill key positions politically and ecclesiastically. Their pantheistic one world religion, smacking of ancient mysteries, will inaugurate a new, deceptively enlightened age marked by global interdependence (See New Age Movement).

The last-day church, known for brotherly love, will enjoy a remarkable outpouring of the Holy Spirit and will access a wide-open door to worldwide evangelism (See Holy Spirit Imparted). Resolved to refuse the Mark of the Beast, this Bride of Christ will suffer persecution for her unmixed faith, but ultimately will escape floods of self-god and eco-menical deception by means of the Rapture (See Ecumenical Movement/World Council of Churches; Radical Environmentalism). In contrast, politically correct world citizens remain on earth to suffer the Great Tribulation, followed by plagues of a magnitude the world has never known. Instead of Antichrist's empty promise of world peace, these will experience an astonishing nuclear holocaust (See Armageddon), which will be gloriously interrupted by the Second Coming of Christ with His previously raptured Bride (See Day of the Lord).

According to the Lord Jesus, the generation that witnesses restoration of the Jews to their homeland will not pass away until all these prophecies are fulfilled (Matt. 24:33-34). Israel was declared reborn as a nation in 1948, and the Jews recaptured Jerusalem in 1967. As a Biblical generation falls somewhere between forty to one hundred years, ours is this targeted generation. While routines remain mundane, a global flood of lawlessness crests in anticipation of imminent, unhindered release upon the whole inhabited earth (Matt. 24:38).

Signs of the End

That knowledge will be increased in these last days applies in a general sense to the information age of cyberspace technology (2 Tim. 3:7). More specifically, however, it refers to revelation regarding prophecies of monumental future events (Dan. 12: 4,9-13). To consecrated believers, end-time signs are as birth pangs announcing introduction of new life—increased intensity signals that God's Kingdom is indeed at hand.

These pangs are not to be confused with doomsday premonitions of "the end of the world." Even so, the latter days will be shaken by economic and political upheavals, a series of armed conflicts, breakdown of the earth's ecosystem, undermining of the Judeo-Christian ethic, religious deception, and persecution. Nonetheless, these shakings are balanced by fulfillment of the Plan of God for spiritual Israel and the wrap-up of the Seventy Weeks for national Israel.

Economic and Political Upheavals, and Armed Conflicts

The latter days are scarred by unprecedented rumors of wars and global outbreaks thereof, the focus of many being racial (*ethnos* against *ethnos*, Matt. 24:6-7). Combat leading up to Armageddon will center on the last-day regathering of dispersed Jews to Palestine in opportunistic hopes of settling once and for all the ongoing ancient feud between Ishmael (See Islamic Fundamentalism) and Isaac (See Israel).

Breakdown of the Earth's Ecosystem

Natural wonders will shake the earth in fear-inspiring ways (Joel 2:30-31). Increasingly, there will be earthquakes in diverse places (Matt. 24:7), not to mention severe famines (Matt. 24:7) and pestilence (Luke 21:11).

Breakdown of the Judeo-Christian Ethic

The end-time global village shuns Christ-like virtues of self-sacrificial love, faith, longsuffering, goodness, meekness, gentleness, and temperance (Gal. 5:22-23). In their stead, the New Earth Ethic gives way to sensuality. As a result, prideful self-love follows the incessant pursuit of self-esteem with discovery of so-called heightened human potential (2 Tim. 3:2); and unfeigned love is effectively cooled (Matt. 24:12).

Unwilling from their youth to obey rightful authority, self-actualized global citizens engage in love of pleasure, profane covetousness, and abounding lawlessness (2 Tim. 3:2, 4; Matt. 24:12). As fierce opponents of absolute values and Biblical fundamentalism, they lightly discard personal integrity, while yet boasting (2 Tim. 3:3-4). Their addictions are fed by lack of natural affection and lust (2 Tim. 3:3, 6).

Global Religious Deception

As scriptures prophesy, false prophets and deceivers claiming to have attained "christhood" are rampant (Matt. 24:5, 11). The seduction of powerful signs and lying wonders (virtual reality and holography, for example) bring strong delusion (2 Thess. 2:9, 11). Though access to limitless information defines these times, lack of the knowledge of truth sadly prevails (2 Tim. 3:7). Great apostasy seduces former believers with prosperity and complacency, which in turn dilutes the church with a gutless form of counterfeit godliness (2 Thess. 2:3; Rev. 3:14-17; 2 Tim. 3:5). Those reprobate concerning the faith join with the global community in facilitating worsening evil in the name of good (2 Tim. 3:8, 13).

Persecution of the Church (Mt. 24:9)

Homage will be paid the ever-faithful, end-time Philadelphia Church of brotherly love (Rev. 3:9); but this church, whose job it is to restrain the ongoing global effort (2 Thess. 2:7), does not escape retaliatory persecution. According to the Greek in Luke 21:28, end-time believers are to "unbow," which term assumes an outside source of restraint.

Preparation of the Bride

While lukewarm complacency grips a large segment of the church community, a remnant yet pursues purity. These believers are as a bride diligently preparing for marital union (Rev. 21:2). The heavenly Bridegroom does not fail to furnish her thoroughly that she might maintain a victorious testimony throughout these perilous last days (2 Tim. 3:1, 17). Believing that the vision will not tarry, the unmixed faithful cling to it and tirelessly promote it (Hab. 2:2).

This Bride sits patiently at the feet of her heavenly Bridegroom who, in turn, restores her to wholeness (Joel 2:25-26). Revived gifts of the Spirit accompany unparalleled anointing upon all yielded recipients (Joel 2:28-29). Spiritually equipped and empowered, believers boldly evangelize (Rev. 3:7-8; Matt. 28:19-20; Hab. 2:14). Precarious last days precede the Prince of Peace's thousand-year reign on earth, featuring global revelation of the matchless Name of Jesus (Rev. 3:8). Then, and only then, comes complete restoration, peace, and harmony in what unfolds as God's rightful world order (See Millennium).

Enlightened One

See Adept/ Initiated Adept.

Esoteric Philosophy

The Greek root of "esoteric" is *esoterikos,* meaning "private or confidential." Esoteric philosophy is not intended for, or understood by, the general public. Only an elite "inner circle" are so enlightened.

All ancient civilizations are known for mysteries. At their core is Pantheism, which proclaims all life to be god or part of god. Even today, Ancient mystery religions tarry in esoteric crafts of Freemasonry and Witchcraft/Wicca, not to mention the New Age movement. As with ancient mysteries, inner-circle Adepts undergo degrees of initiation toward achieving supreme enlightenment. Secret doctrine is revealed only at the highest, inner level (See Luciferic Initiation).

Biblical Perspective

The Christian's source of truth is not esoteric hieroglyphics; it is rather the "more sure Word" (2 Pet. 1:19; See Authenticity of Scriptures), but mystery is by no means foreign to Biblical Christianity. Christian marriage and the Rapture of Christ's Bride are two such mysteries (Eph. 5:32; 1 Cor. 15:51ff). God by nature is mysterious (Rom. 11:33), as are clouded prophecies— Daniel's Seventy Weeks (Dan. 9:24-27), for example. Enigmatic truths of Christ's veiled parables are concealed from the "wise and prudent" of this world, but revealed nonetheless even to "babes" in Christ (Matt. 11:25).

Hundreds of years before Christ, Jeremiah warned of a mighty, ancient nation of obscured language that would come from afar to destroy Israel. Although Babylon was the one world nation to which Jeremiah primarily referred, there is likewise a secondary, end-time application. "Mystery, Babylon the Great, mother of harlots and abominations of the earth" (Rev. 17:5), also with obscured tongue, once again intends to overturn Israel, both national and spiritual (Jer. 5:7,13,15-18). Instead, God will see to the destruction of this latter-day global eco-menical religion, which wrongly "swears by those who are no gods" (Jer. 5:7; Rev. 17:16-17, KJV; See Ecumenical Movement and Radical Environmentalism).

Eurocentrism

Eurocentrism defines the European-American world, noted for its Judeo-Christian ethic and free enterprise. Both oppose global efforts toward realizing the interdependent, socialistic New

World Order with its New Earth Ethic, which ignores fundamental values upon which America allegedly is founded (See
Global Economics/Banking; Radical Environmentalism).

To deconstruct Western civilization, specifically European-
American culture, politically correct educators attack as
Eurocentric indoctrination the canon of great books (e.g., Homer,
Plato, Aristotle, Virgil, Chaucer, Shakespeare, Dante, Milton,
Wordsworth, Twain, etc.). In 1991 the New York State Board of
Regents task force on minorities consulted with Leonard Jefferies,
chair of the Department of Black Studies at New York's City
University. The purpose was to eliminate Eurocentrism from the
state's curriculum. As a result, many students today are not fa-
miliar with Western culture or its great works.

Students are led to believe that Eurocentrism denotes white
male supremacy; furthermore, "white" presupposes genderism and
racism. While Afrocentrism and Asiacentrism take center seat,
Euro-American culture is reduced to that of victims and victim-
izers. Of course, white men are the supreme villains, despite the
fact that thousands of them died to eliminate slavery. Furthermore, a white male Republican President and Congress issued
the Emancipation Proclamation and passed the Thirteenth
Amendment to the Constitution, which abolished slavery.

These facts are conveniently skirted as middle schoolers,
relatively uninformed about the history of their own country,
learn instead of global cultures, their gods, and their greatness
(See Public Education). Promoting understanding of, and appreciation for, other cultures is not necessarily the issue (See Outcome-Based Education). Rather, the problem is undermining,
and otherwise distorting, Euro-American culture in lopsided
veneration of multiculturalism and diversity, keeping in mind
that so-called Eurocentric, Bible-believing Christians alone are
excluded from the ranks of the "celebrated diversity."

Biblical Perspective

See Political Correctness Movement.

Evolution

The theory of biological evolution contends that a single cell
is responsible for all matter—animal, vegetable, and mineral—
through a slow process of random change initiated without mas-

ter design over some 4.5 billion years. Evolution from simple to increasingly complex forms is effected by means of mutation and natural selection (survival of the fittest).

Derived from inferential conclusions, this godless belief can be traced to the first century B.C. It gained wide acceptance much later through the work of biologist Charles Darwin, who in 1859 introduced *The Origin of the Species.* Dr. Werner Von Braun (a key figure behind the space program) and Dr. Howard A. Kelly (a famed surgeon and medical professor) join Albert Einstein as three of many notable scientists who reject the theory of evolution. Even Darwinian supporter Thomas Huxley saw it as no more than a "tentative hypothesis." Nonetheless, evolution is taught as fact, not theory, throughout the American public education system and in secular universities worldwide.

Even so, the theory lacks sound scientific backing. Evolutionists have failed to find even one true fossil, or skeletal remain of a transitional life forms; moreover, both simple and complex fossilized organisms coexist in every strata of rock. Despite Darwinian claims, scientists know of no mutational change that has effectively produced increasingly complex heredity in chromosomes or DNA. To the evolutionist's shame, the Heidelberg apeman and Nebraska-, Piltdown-, Peking-, Neanderthal-, New Guinea-, and Cro-Magnon Men were all determined to be frauds.

Dating methods are controlled by factors of temperature, pressure, humidity, and light, none of which are constant; still, evolutionists presumptuously assume a uniform decay rate. Commonly employed carbon decomposition and radio-metric dating methods fail to prove life's slow evolution over millions of years. In fact, no documentation supports the notion that man has been in this world for more than the ten thousand years argued for in the Biblical view. The possibility of amino acids coming together to form life is not only slim, but would likely require far more time than 4.5 billion years; and statistical odds for life's creating itself through chance mutations (one in ten-to-the-billionth power) prove the theory's folly.

Biblical Perspective

It takes about one million mutational steps for a single "higher animal" to evolve. This being the case, and in view of the fact that, by nature, mutations are negative, evolution is virtually impracticable. Gregor Mendel's work on modern genetics further supports the Biblical contention that, despite extremely rare mutations, life begets "after its kind" (Gen. 1). That is to say, monkeys beget monkeys, not more complex humankind. This observable, repeatable fact of nature presents a strong case for Biblical Creation (Gen. 1:1-2:25).

There is but one chance in ten to the ninetieth power that all three hundred Messianic prophecies would be fulfilled; but, remarkably, they were, each and every one. Clearly, it takes more faith to believe in the God of random chance than in the God of Biblical Creation (John 1:3; 1 Cor. 8:6; Eph. 3:9; Col. 2:16), yet evolutionists openly mock Christian faith as groundless superstition.

Evidence of a Master Designer is seen in all of Creation, from the DNA molecule to the construction of galaxies. For example, the most primitive one-cell life form exceeds in complexity even the most advanced computer. Indeed, the human body houses fifty-five trillion cooperating cells with countless complex energy exchanges. Each feature of every cell is biochemically dependent on others. Without question, humankind is "fearfully and wonderfully made" (Ps. 139:14). Nature's delicate balance unmistakably supports teleology (design) rather than evolution (random chance). Ironically, while they champion random chance, brilliant scientists have attempted through years of research and planning to create life, demonstrating albeit unwittingly the need for an intelligent Creator.

Charles Darwin's philosophy of historic optimism is his true claim to fame. Both historic optimism and biological evolution oppose the proven Second Law of Thermodynamics, not to mention the Bible (2 Tim. 3:13), in their claim that life forms, especially humans, are by chance progressively bettering themselves. Both are crucial to the topic of globalism in that meticulously groomed Gaia-honoring world citizens deprecate creationists as enemies of the New World Order—namely, the Judeo-Christian doctrine and believers in it.

While biological Darwinism undermines authenticity of Scriptures, social Darwinism feeds into the New Age fallacy of multiple reincarnations toward ultimate flowering of human potential in the soon-coming Age of Aquarius. Both serve the purposes of the "prince of the power of the air," whose Antichrist spirit is ever at work in the global community (Eph. 2:2).

F

Federal Reserve System ("The Fed")

It's Establishment

Maternal grandfather of today's Rockefeller brothers, Senator Nelson Aldrich submitted the original proposal, the Aldrich Bill, to establish a central bank operated by private interest. However, Article 1, Section 8 of the Constitution prohibits private interests from issuing money or regulating its value; therefore, Congress rightly voted it down. In 1913 the bill came back slightly modified as the Owen-Glass Act. Many authorities believe that dogged efforts of illumined Freemasonry established the system to ensure European Illuminists a permanent role in American finances.

The Fed is not a government institution, as many presume, nor does it receive funding from the U.S. Congress. It is a privately-held corporation owned by stockholders. When the act was passed, Charles A. Lindbergh, Sr. was a member of the Banking and Currency Committee in the House. Lindbergh firmly opposed the act for its controlling features, such as scientific creation of panics, and for intruding upon essentially all American interests in business and at home.

It's Key Figures

Texan Colonel Edward Mandell House is the Fed's "unseen guardian angel." Arthur D. Howden Smith profiled House in the 17 July 1926 issue of *The Saturday Evening Post*, as one who thought the Constitution to be "outdated." Principal architect of the Council on Foreign Relations, House shared Karl Marx's dream of a socialist New World Order.

Appointed by the President with Senate approval, a board of governors in Washington, DC heads the system. These presidential appointees support financial interests of Global Economics/Banking. Through the Treasury Department and the Fed, the Rockefellers and their internationalist allies have effectively wedded the nation's fiscal and monetary policies with their own. Rockefeller holdings are primarily via the Chase Manhattan Bank (See Revived Roman Empire; Kings without Kingdoms).

It's Structure

The Fed consists of twelve federal reserve banks, their twenty-five branches, and other facilities throughout the country. For all practical purposes, the Federal Reserve Bank of New York is the Federal Reserve. Fewer than a dozen international banking establishments hold controlling interest, and only four of them are based in the United States. The remainder of the Fed's interests are European, most influential of which are the Rothchilds. In some way or other, all American interests are connected to this powerful London family.

It's Function

Probably the largest generator of debt in the world, the Federal Reserve regulates the country's credit and monetary policy as the independently-operated U.S. central banking system and note-issuing authority. Federal Reserve notes that we carry in our pockets are not "money" (i.e., "gold and silver coin"). Rather, they are "evidence of debt" (See USC Title 12 152; *Black's Law Dictionary*).

It's Power

One of the most powerful figures in government today, Fed Chairman Alan Greenspan is accountable to no one, not even the President. The Fed is essentially self-governing and unrivaled in it's role of forming and implementing monetary policy. In its over eighty years of existence, this government-granted private credit monopoly never once has been audited; yet overall economic activities, including inflation and interest rates, are governed single-handedly by the Fed's decision to enlarge or constrict the supply of money to our economy. For example, in anticipation of the Y2K Crisis, the Fed increased currency in banks by up to $50 billion.

The discount rate is what the Fed charges member banks who borrow money. By raising or lowering this rate, the Fed in effect regulates credit. It can apply additional control by requiring member banks to keep on hand larger or smaller amounts of their deposits as reserves.

Biblical Perspective

The Bible predicts a central authority which will control citizens' power to buy and sell under the one world government it forges (Rev. 13:16). Toward economic, political, and religious management of the New World Order, the technology of the Mark of the Beast will be installed by Antichrist and enforced by the False Prophet (Rev. 13:4-18; 14:9-11).

Keeping in mind that love of money (not money itself) is a root (more literal to the Greek than "the root") of all kinds of evil (1 Tim. 6:10), Scriptures caution us to be wary when money enables unified global power, which by nature opposes God, His people, and His plan. Along with the Depository Trust Company, the Federal Reserve System wields such power, and is, therefore, a deserving focus for the vigilant student of Bible prophecy.

Freemasonry; Masonic Order/Lodges

The *Encyclopedia Britannica* calls Freemasonry the largest secret society in the world. With an estimated six million members in 164 countries, "Speculative" Masonry today is tied to more than one hundred fraternal organizations. Men of affluence and status join what best-selling author Texe Marrs calls "the secret brotherhood," which includes the Bilderberger Group, Yale's Skull and Bones Society, and the Knights of Malta—not least of which are clandestine Black Lodges. These "brothers," he adds, have been called the Wise Men, the Hierarchy, the World Mind, or simply the Order.

Born officially in 1717, modern Masonry shares beliefs and practices of internationally linked organizations with a common code and a central theme of universality. By the 1800s its dominant power had shifted from Europe, specifically France, to the United States. The Shriners are purely American.

The Mother Supreme Council of the World is its governing body, to which absolute allegiance is sworn at the thirty-third degree ceremony. Grand Lodges recognize as leading authorities Henry Wilson Coil, Joseph Fort Newton, Albert G. Mackey, and Albert Pike. Boasting fifty or sixty thousand books with over two and one-half million papers in its archives, its 175,000-volume library is replete with Masonic Secret Doctrine.

Freemasonry and the Illuminati

Freemasonry's "mother lodge," the Blue Lodge, confers its three foundational degrees. When, in 1785, the Illuminati was exposed, outlawed, and forced underground, the order's founder, Adam Weishaupt, ordered infiltration into the lodges of Blue Masonry. Thereafter, on 19 July 1789, the president of Harvard University warned the graduating class of expanding Illuminati infiltration into American politics and religion. Sixth U.S. President and organizer of New England lodges John Quincy Adams issued similar warning. Many believe that Illuminists have since concealed subversive internationalist activities behind the front of Masonic philanthropy and humanitarianism.

Freemasonry and the Occult

Freemasonry is thought to have evolved from the Ancient Order of Druids, whose Celtic doctrine remarkably parallels that of the New Age movement. It's esoteric secrets are rooted in Gnosticism and Pantheism. In summarizing the "Master of the Royal Secret Thirty-second Degree," Masonic authority Henry C. Clausen expounded the wisdom of ancient mysteries.

Freemasonry's Council chooses who, through degrees of initiation, joins the mystical "inner circle." Scottish and York Rites are offered to those who wish to "go higher." The York Rite confers the thirty-two degrees of the Scottish Rite, plus the Knights Templar degree.

Spirit guides that inspired Theosophist Madam Blavatsky praised Masonry, and Arthur E. Waite included sections on the occult sciences in his Combined Edition of the *New Encyclopedia of Freemasonry*. Candidates swear bloody oaths to "ever conceal and never reveal" the lodge's secrets. On record in the New York City archives, Avery Allen verified the homicide of a so-called traitor, William Morgan. As a result of this 1826 murder by English Illuminist Richard Howard, about half of all Masons in the North District of the U.S. succeeded.

Freemasonry and the New Age Movement

Both New Age mystics and illumined Masons use buzz words affirming the enigmatic belief that man is inwardly divine. "Divine higher truth in all" allows "esoteric enlightenment." While at the same time forging a New World Order, "the initiated" attain to "higher consciousness" of the "supreme being" through the "religion of Nature." At the thirty-first degree, the Masonic candidate expresses hope for a better incarnation in the next life. His bidding is to advance in the New Age cycle of reincarnation.

Freemasonry and Unitarian Universalism/Mormonism/ New Earth Ethic

Metaphysically monistic (reality is reducible to one substance), Masonic deism is closely linked to histories of Unitarian Universalism and Mormonism. Its morality lacks values specificity; indeed, its sycretistic relativism makes place for the New Earth (Global Civic) Ethic (See Values Education).

Freemasonry and True Christianity

Called by heathen names, the Masonic god Jao-Bul-On is polytheistic. Jao is Greek for the god of Gnostics or Jehovah; Bul is for Ba'al; On is for Osiris, an ancient Egyptian god. Consistent throughout Freemasonry's unscriptural doctrine is the belief that man reaches immortality in the Celestial Lodge above by his own good works.

Freemasonry has effectively undermined Christianity in Masonic ritual by systematically erasing the name of Jesus from otherwise verbatim scriptures. Masons forbid prayer to or through Jesus, for He is said to be merely "a good man." Similarly, the Bible is regarded as no more than a symbol. Despite these flagrant departures from sound Biblical Christology, there are born-again Christians in the ranks of Freemasonry, who having failed to research voluminous Masonic literature, inaccurately presume Freemasonry to be no more than a charitable organization with a firm moral base.

Freemasonry and Humanism, Secular and Mystical

Freemasonry purposes to unite the world in teaching the brotherhood of man. Toward this end, Masons may embrace religion or secular humanism. Mystical humanists engage in spiritism.

Freemasonry and Women/Children

Invited men over twenty-one may seek initiation; however, co-masonry, or adoptive masonry, allows women. Women's groups include the Order of the Eastern Star, and there are also orders for boys (Order of DeMolay) and girls (Job's Daughters and Rainbow Girls). Nevertheless, Freemasonry remains male dominated. No meeting can be held without at least three male officers present. Unknown to many, the foundation of Masonic symbolism is phallic worship, and some claim the famed Masonic "G" really represents the "generative principle."

Freemasonry and Israel

Jewish Masonry was founded in 1843 through the Independent Order of B'Nai B'rith, whose chief aim, through internationalism, was to establish German Jews in all world affairs. Its branch was *L'Alliance Israelite Univerelle* (founded in 1860), distinguished by esoteric philosophy and cabal rule.

Freemasonry and Islamic Fundamentalism

In the early eighth century, Muslims overran the Moroccan city of Fez and slaughtered some fifty thousand Christians. As they dipped their caps into the blood of martyrs, murderers cried, "There is no god but Allah, and Mohammed is his prophet." In time, these blood-stained caps were called Fezzes. Today Shriners wear red Fezzes and, while kneeling before the Koran, take Masonic oaths in the name of the moon god, Allah. Nobles of the Mystic Shrine, the Ancient Arabic Order, is accessible to thirty-second degree Masons and Knights Templars.

Freemasonry Dominance and Danger

Freemasonry has been condemned by the papacy and in some countries suppressed by the state. A former Mason and Chief Justice of the U.S. Supreme Court, John Marshall, joined the ranks of Finney, Moody, and Torrey in denouncing Freemasonry as dangerously evil. Daniel Webster, Ulysses S. Grant, James Madison, and Millard Fillmore, the latter two having been Masons, agreed; nonetheless, with the possible exception of John F. Kennedy, every U.S. President since World War II has belonged to Freemasonry, the Council on Foreign Relations, or the Trilateral Commission.

In addition to fifteen U.S. Presidents, Freemasonry claims forty-one federal judges. Half the members of the Senate Judiciary Committee are Masons, as are eighteen senators and seventy-six members of the House of Representatives. Two former presidents of the U.S., an internationally prominent evangelist, and even a Scandinavian King were present at the thirty-third degree initiation ceremony of ex-Mason Jim Shaw. King Assad of Syria and the late King Hussein of Jordan are known to be Masons.

Biblical Perspective

(See Ancient Mystery Religions.)

G

Gay Rights

Since the 1970s, the homosexual movement has gained astonishing political power, so much so that the ACLU has committed an entire branch to lesbian and gay rights. The Human Rights Campaign is a leading international homosexual advocacy group, as well as America's largest gay lobby. Additional supportive groups include Amnesty International, Act Up, Outrage, and Rainbow Coalition. These are joined by Queer Nation (the most violent of the gay rights' groups) and NAMBLA (North America Man/ Boy Love Association). The *Lambda Report* is a magazine dedicated to monitoring the gay rights movement.

Gay Rights: "Mainstream" Classification

Homosexuality is presumed to be normal and healthy. The *Diagnostic and Statistical Manual of Psychiatric Disorders* (DSM) suggests treatment only when sexual orientation disturbs the homosexual. In developing their anti-discrimination theme, some offhandedly label all adversaries "homophobes."

Many gays demand special legal consideration alongside ethnic minorities and other historically disadvantaged groups. While portraying themselves as victims, radical gays work at making the public comfortable with their presence. So pervasive is mainstream classification for gays that even Orlando's family friendly Disney World tacitly endorses an annual "Gay Day," and the National Education Association seeks to recognize October as "Lesbian and Gay History Month."

Opponents object to mainstream classification for gays. After all, a 1982 study by the U.S. Centers for Disease Control revealed that the typical gay male has in his lifetime over five hundred sexual partners, often strangers. Furthermore, the now-famous Gay Manifesto insists on adult sex with children (Demand #55,1993 *March on Washington*).

Gay Rights: Historical Landmarks and Legal Efforts

The movement's voice was first heard in 1969 when a routine raid on a gay bar in Greenwich Village set off the infamous Stonewall Riot. Subsequent successful legal maneuvers include the 1972 Gay Rights Ordinance, which disallows discrimination in the workplace. Although it was defeated, the Employee Non-Discrimination Act would have forced employers to hire gays, transvestites, and even pedophiles. With strong support from President Clinton, homosexuals are working hard for another vote on ENDA. Significantly on 28 May 1998 President Clinton issued an executive order implementing sexually oriented quotas in federal hiring and promotions.

In 1973 the modern movement took root in the political arena of San Francisco. Today a group of eight New York lawyers seek to stretch American definitions of family and sexuality. Tireless efforts have effected momentous societal change. For example, in 1996 gays were granted the right to marry, but the order was stayed awaiting review by Hawaii's Supreme Court.

Voters finally approved constitutional amendments in Hawaii and Alaska, banning homosexual marriage; furthermore, Defense of Marriage laws were passed in twenty-six states (1997).

President Clinton's "don't ask; don't tell" policy allows gays to remain "free from harassment" in the armed forces. The 1997 Anti-Hypocrisy Act seeks to decriminalize consensual sex, adultery and sodomy in the nation's military.

Gay Rights to Special Privilege

The gay rights movement is not about equality under the law but rather about special privilege, spelling fewer rights for others. The growing class of "ex-gays" proves that gays possess no unchangeable characteristics. As its groups grace the ranks of the top one percent of political action committees (PAC's) nationwide, gays are far from politically powerless; moreover, with household incomes 41 percent above the national average, gays are easily the most affluent of any minority. Even so, radical homosexuals receive federal funding for such events as the San Francisco Gay and Lesbian Film Festival. Held in federal office buildings, the "Gay Jubilee" was partially paid for with tax dollars. Gay partnership benefits are awarded employees of NYNEX, Time Warner, Microsoft, Sprint, and more. Nonetheless, to the chagrin of civil rights activists such as Alveda King, radical gays continue to equate their crusade for special rights with the movement led by her uncle, Dr. Martin Luther King, Jr.

Gay Rights and Education

The movement's top industry is education, with publishing and social services following. NEA-commissioned educators, along with BANGLE (Bay Area Network of Gay and Lesbian Educators), are developing pro-gay training courses similar to Connecticut's "Pink Triangle" program. In the San Francisco United School District, a pro-homosexual curriculum for first-graders and kindergartners is called "My Family." It is promoted by the district's support services for gay, lesbian, and bisexual youth.

Through condom distribution and alternative lifestyle classes, the movement has thoroughly penetrated public education. For example, in February of 1997 students at Whitman Middle School in Seattle, Washington, were shown a play actively promoting the gay lifestyle. The alternative of monogamous heterosexuality, typified by the traditional family, was not allowed equal time, nor were parents previously notified of the assembly.

Pro-homosexual Project 10-type counseling programs are offered in jr.- and sr.- high schools. "Ten" stands for the falsification that ten percent of teens are gay when, in actuality, the figure is closer to one percent. Advocated heavily on college campuses across America, homosexuality is disguised as "diversity" (See Multiculturalism). Tax dollars fund "queer studies" in major universities as Stanford, Brown, and Duke. It is now possible to get a college degree in gay and lesbian studies, and politically correct students live in "gay friendly" residences.

Gay Rights and Religion

According to *Time* magazine (9 July 1990), Reformed Judaism was the first major U.S. religion to adopt a national policy sanctioning homosexuality. Today many churches welcome to their pulpits out-of-the-closet men and women of the cloth, and the General Theological Seminary of the Episcopal Church has revised its housing policy to allow committed same sex couples.

Gay Rights, Gay Diseases

Socrates described homosexuality as a "superior form of love," but a study by the Family Research Institute revealed dramatically reduced life spans for gays. Whereas heterosexual males and females can expect to live seventy-four and seventy-nine years, respectively, gays potentially may not reach the age of fifty.

Despite their expansive mainstream media campaign, gays purposefully avoid discussion of their unhealthy intimate behaviors. Gay Bowel Syndrome, parasitic colon disease, and fecal contamination are but a few health concerns faced by gay men, who are occasionally compelled to undergo reconstructive surgery.

Gay Rights and the United Nations

Former secretary-general of the United Nations Boutros Boutros-Ghali applauded childless homosexual unions for contributing to global population control efforts in tenor with the UN's banner of sustainable development. With American support, the UN has recognized NAMBLA as a legitimate organization. NAMBLA is an acronym for the North American Man-Boy Love Association, or "Boy Lovers." Their slogan is "Sex before eight, or else it's too late." Alyson Publications, such as *Gay Sex*, contain how-to instructions for pedophiles from NAMBLA. Incredibly, "Boy Lovers" and associates in Washington are working hard for "total elimination of all restrictions regarding child sex."

Biblical Perspective

In a gay newspaper, *The Advocate*, Steve Warren made the disconcerting admission that gays have on their side "the spirit of the age." According to the Bible, this spirit is decidedly Antichrist, and it has everything to do with the burgeoning New World Order, which champions population control and "tolerance" of all except for fundamental Christians.

Satan posed to Eve the provocative question, "Hath God said?" (Gen. 3:1). He further beguiled her by shedding favorable light on forbidden fruit. This was presented as reason enough to partake, despite God's command to the contrary (Gen. 3: 5-6). Eve fell for it, as do scores today with regard to gay issues (Lev. 18:22; Rom. 1:24-27; 1 Cor. 6:9-10).

Politically correct, end-time world citizens readily uphold the gay lifestyle characterized by what the Bible denounces as a lack of "natural affection" (2 Tim. 3:3; Rom. 1:25-28). Clearly, "the wicked freely strut about when what is vile is honored among men," Ps. 12:8 (NIV).

Questioning God's decrees is not new, but has been Lucifer's tactic from the beginning; his systematic sabotage of Biblical truth gives way to the coming New Age of selective tolerance (See Values Education; Authenticity of Scriptures). As Nero wrongly accused Christians of hating the human race, some radical gays align with the Tempter (Matt. 4:5; 1 Thess. 3:5) by berating straight counterparts as "hate-mongers," "breeders," and "homophobes" (2 Tim. 3:1-7).

Genderism/Radical Feminism

(See Political Correctness Movement.)

Many celebrate the fact that for decades the Women's Movement has effectively campaigned for social, political, and economic equality with men. Since early efforts by suffragists, this work has been highly visible and, most would agree, sometimes necessary.

The movement as we know it today gained global impetus after World War II. From the late 1960s its radical, militant wing has warred feverishly against sexism. Ironically, it can be said that feminist efforts have actually freed men, not women. It is not uncommon, in the wake of the movement, for single working women to support their families while former mates enjoy the financial and personal advantages of a self-reliant, career focused life.

In 1964 the U.S. Equal Employment Opportunity Commission was formed to end discrimination in hiring. So effective was this agency's work that women can now be found even in wartime combat units. A few stalwart men, such as General Krulak, a commandant of the Marine Corps, resist pressure to feminize the corps.

The National Organization for Women (NOW) was founded in 1966 in New York to further the movement's causes, which for some include pro-choice casual abortion, gay rights, and sexual liberty outside the confines of legal marriage. Extremists embrace the notion of female superiority. Some are responsible for making ludicrous demands: For example, the recall of Mattel's "Teen Talk" Barbi for her sexist phrase, "Math class is tough."

The feminist agenda clearly complements one world efforts. Signed by Jimmy Carter (1980), but not yet ratified, the United Nations Convention on the Elimination of Discrimination Against Women (CEDAW) mirrors the movement. Vague by design, this treaty supersedes our Constitution. Opponents allege further that it mandates global gender education to redefine the family and usurp parental authority in the name of human rights, all for advancement of the New World Order.

In 1995 the largest international gathering of women took place in Beijing. At this United Nations Fourth World Conference on Women, over forty thousand women met with intent to unify and transform the world by the Year 2001. There, the traditional family was pictured as a hotbed of domestic violence. Among the focuses were woman's right to abortion (See Death Culture), inclusion of homo-, bi-, and trans-sexuals in defining "gender" (See Gay Rights), and sex education (more accurately, indoctrination). In the fall of 1997 three new UN meetings were called to accelerate the Beijing agenda.

The religious community has not escaped the sway of politically correct genderism. Some presumptuously refer to God as "she," thus breaking a sacred biblical type.

The Clare Booth Luce Policy Institute serves as the top conservative organization opposing radical feminism in America's politics, businesses, and schools.

Biblical Perspective

Despite empty claims to superiority by males or females, single or married, God is no respecter of persons (Acts 10:34). All in Christ are one (Col. 3:11; Gal. 3:28). This spiritual oneness does not preclude individual differences, some of which are visible in gender-specific ways (i.e., women are generally smaller and less muscular than men, 1 Pet. 3:7). Despite all-inclusive definitions offered by radical feminists, gender specificity must not digress from the God-given model (Rom. 1: 25-27). For example, godly men are not to succumb to sexual misuse of their bodies, or to exemplify that which is "soft" or "delicate" ("effeminate" in 1 Cor. 6:9).

Many misguided feminists unfairly attack traditional Christianity for its supposed put-down of women. On the contrary, the Hebrew word for "virtuous" paired with the ideal godly woman of Proverbs 31 can mean "a force" or "power" (verse 10). She is literally "a woman of ability." Her talents are limitless (verses 13-24); and she is known, not for weakness, but rather for her strength (verse 25). A fearless woman, this wife rightly seeks the good of her husband (verses 10-12, 21, 25), all the while honoring his God-given authority (Gen. 3: 16). This leadership privilege is not to be abused, for husbands are enjoined to love, honor, and give to their wives after Christ's example (1 Pet. 3:7).

In no way is the traditional family, if properly submitted to Christ, a hotbed of domestic violence as some liberal feminists imply. Under her husband's leadership, the Virtuous Woman contributes to the worth (Prov. 31:16) and manages well the diverse affairs of her household (Prov. 31:27). Her well-nurtured children grow up to call her blessed (Prov. 31:28). The apostle Paul spoke the mind of Christ (1 Cor. 2:16), not politically correct human wisdom (verse 13), when he expressed his desire that younger women marry, bear children, guide the house, and give no occasion for reproach (1 Tim. 5:14).

Bear in mind that God's Word never intimates that it takes a village to raise a child. The strong traditional family serves this purpose well, but is nonetheless under attack by the radical feminist agenda. Perhaps it is no coincidence that the false one world religious system of these last days is depicted in Revelation Chapter 17, not as a comely Shulamite Bride (Song of Solomon), nor as the Virtuous Woman (Prov. 31), but rather as a "great whore" (verses 1, 15) whose rebellion is "as the sin of witchcraft" (1 Sam. 15:23). Although Paul had a clear picture of these perilous last days (2 Thess. 2; 2 Tim. 3), he did not concern himself with the guiding principle of sustainable development: "If you don't produce, you don't consume" (See Radical Environmentalism). For women to be among the producers, not depleters (as child-bearing, dependent housewives are considered), may classify them as good global citizens of the New World Order; however, they merit no favored distinction in God's economy.

Genetic Engineering

Originating in nineteenth century England, selective breeding, or eugenics (Greek, "well-born"), was abused in the 1930s by Nazis. To improve the hereditary qualities of the human population, the movement is ongoing. Its goal is to enhance human intelligence and, thus, inspire behaviors characterized by some as politically correct.

A specific goal of the nontheistic religion of humanism is a new race for the New World Order. The motto of this new race is "One World; One Species." Whereas the New Age mystic looks for a new species resulting from a planetary quantum leap to "christhood" (See Luciferic Initiation), the godless humanist hopes to control his own evolution by means of social and even genetic engineering. This is not as preposterous as it sounds. By biochemical techniques, genetic engineering deliberately manipulates hereditary material. This is frequently achieved by introducing new DNA, usually via virus or plasmid (small, mobile piece of DNA found in bacteria). Through this process, functionally-specific plants, animals, or bacteria can be bred.

To the horror of bioethicists, Dr. Robert Stillman at the American Fertility Society in Montreal (1993) started with seventeen microscopic embryos and multiplied them to forty-eight. One scientist noted, "This is Frankensteinian science at its best." "Frankensteins" in the scientific community are actually figuring out how to build living things. In Japan, Masuo Aizawa is growing colonies of nerve cells in an attempt to fabricate a living brain.

Genetic engineering has changed the pathway of biology more than any sole scientific development of the twentieth century. Genes are presently in use to target murderers and rapists. Virtually weekly, scientists discover a gene for yet another disease. Biologists believe the impact on humanity will be greater than that of nuclear power or even the computer.

Biblical Perspective

In reference to the "time of the end," Daniel prophesied that "knowledge shall be increased" (12:4). This speaks primarily of knowing God's purposes, as revealed by His prophets. Nevertheless, it can also refer to technological advance. For example,

Nanotechnology makes possible the engraving of twenty-eight volumes of the *Encyclopedia Britannica* on what is comparable to the head of a pin. Even more remarkably, it potentially allows a tiny robot to pass through the human bloodstream to inspect or remove diseased tissue from body organs.

According to the Rotherham translation, such knowledge can also imply calamities or wickedness. In the book of Revelation (9:11), Satan is given the title Abaddon, meaning "destroyer." Genetic engineering in the hands of Satan's emissaries could produce unspeakable, irreparable results, solved only by death at the hand of the experimenter (See Death Culture).

Illumined internationalists may seek to manipulate genetic and managed death options to supplant the Christian world order with a new one for the coming New Age of Group Consciousness (See Age of Aquarius). Highly-evolved, politically correct world citizens, who have discarded as obsolete the Judeo-Christian ethic, are essential in the godless New World Order. In the hands of such ones, genetic engineering can specify who among us survives, and in what condition, to usher in, sustain, and further the cause of so-called global enlightenment

Global Economics/Banking

(See Depository Trust Company; Federal Reserve System; Mark of the Beast.)

With birth of multinational corporations, deregulation, the World Bank, the G8 (partners of eight of the richest Western nations), the GATT (General Agreement on Tariffs and Trade), and the International Monetary Fund, there is no doubt that we have entered the global economics age. One need only witness how a crash in the New York Stock Exchange is felt instantly in Tokyo, London, and Bonn to discern how economically interconnected the world has become. According to the *Washington Post*, the EURO is "the dream of monetary union become reality." As of 1 January 1999, the EURO clearly denotes a turning point in global finance. Its implementation preceding political unification is nothing short of revolutionary.

Some believe global economics to be a result of the progressive process of our democratic free-market system; others believe in conspiratorial efforts. In *Tragedy and Hope*, Harvard trained

Professor Carroll Quigley of Georgetown University accessed confidential records of moneyed internationalists who, for decades, have given form to sundry governmental policies. Although Quigley dismisses the notion of conspiracy, he admits that this power-elite network of Round Table Groups is known to have cooperated with totalitarian regimes.

Curiously, the word "conspiracy" is derived from a Latin verb literally meaning "to breathe together." In planning for something criminal or evil, conspirators whisper with their faces close (as if breathing together) to come to one mind, not unlike the Round Table Groups. To be sure, many socialist progressives believe in an invisible government, if not a conspiracy, shown to exist years earlier by the Money Trust investigation spoken of by Charles Lindbergh, Sr. (See Federal Reserve System).

Foundation-omics à la Rockefeller

The drive toward global economics is by no means new. For virtually decades, international banking has been the Rockefeller's single most important business. Rockefeller family banks include the First National City and Chase Manhattan Banks. The latter is the undisputed heavy-weight champion of international banking, employing a full-time envoy to the United Nations.

By stockholding, making loans to industry giants, and scientific giving to foundations under Rockefeller dictate, the clan monopolizes vast segments of the economy. Herein is the Rockefeller advantage: Through foundations, control replaces ownership, and "not for profit" means "not for taxation."

Rockefellers have interlocking control over the other most powerful foundations, the Carnegie Group and the giant Ford Foundation. The five Carnegie foundations are but appendages of the Rockefeller octopus. Nonetheless, titans of finance are dwarfed by the collective system of global economics.

American computer companies and New York-based international banks have made possible the automation and centralization of global banking. Along with the Rockefeller's Chase Manhattan Bank, other families (and the banking institutions they own) virtually control the money supply of the world. These include the Rothschild Banks of London and Berlin; Lehman Brothers Bank, Kuhn Loeb Bank, and Goldman, Sachs Bank of New York; Lazard Brothers Banks of Paris; Israel Moses Seif Banks of Italy; and Warburg Banks of Hamburg and Amsterdam.

WCPA-nomics à la Philip Isely (Its Secretary-General from 1966)

Founded in Denver in 1959, the World Constitution and Parliament Association (WCPA) plans a total of five sessions leading up to the New One World Order. While guaranteeing jobs for all, especially in the environmental arena (See Radical Environmentalism), its plan proposes a single monetary system and currency (likely electronic; See Mark of the Beast). It further authorizes an Earth Financial Credit Corporation to oversee development of global trade and commerce on a regional basis.

In 1977 twenty-five countries adopted the Constitution for the Federation of the Earth at the second session of the World Constituent Assembly (now called The World Constitutional Convention), revealing plans for global control of all trade, banking, and finance. It calls for establishment and operation of a Planetary Accounting Office, Planetary Banking System, and Planetary Monetary and Credit System.

The World Future Society has become the world forum called for in the Club of Rome's 1972 book, *The Limits to Growth.* The WFS is where the political, spiritual, and economic aspects of one world government can all merge.

Globalization-omics à la Maurice Strong

According to a 1992 World Goodwill newsletter, uneven distribution of the world's resources coupled with colonialist domination must be overcome. The internationalist approach is to consider raw materials the common property of the whole world. Global resources include minerals, waters/ seas, forests, commodities, foodstuffs, and even people. Since the mid-seventies, countless unions, banks, forums, organizations, commissions, and corporations have joined presidents and prime ministers of a number of countries in shared effort to centralize world wealth. Collaborative commerce defined by strategic global alliances is destined to create the new hierarchy of concentrated economic power. In 1974 the United Nations General Assembly outlined a plan to redistribute wealth in a report entitled "New International Economic Order."

Globalization is transferring wealth under the principle of sustainable development. Sustainable development is part of the Declaration of the United Nations Conference on the Human

Environment chaired in 1972 by Maurice Strong, top environmental activist and noted New Age occultist.

Sustainable development underscores the Marxist/ Leninist maxim of "earning one's keep on planet Earth." Simply put, good global citizens add to Earth's resources; bad ones—i.e., the elderly, infants, infirmed, and at-home moms—deplete them (See Death Culture; Values Education). Because underdeveloped nations are not bound by the treaties that developed nations are forced under, the outcome is redistribution of the world's wealth. Communization concentrates global wealth into the hands of few. Although the concept is found nowhere in the U.S. Constitution, its eco-socialism, featuring mandated population control (See Planned Parenthood), is completely described in Chapter Two, Article 18 of the USSR Constitution (1977).

Dominant global banks with one world currency and stock exchange will be achieved by means of deregulation (tearing down financial laws of the land), technology (information super-highway of the G-8), and trade (cut-throating American business with purchase of less expensive foreign products). The idea is to devalue the dollar domestically, and increase it internationally, thereby transferring American wealth ("globalization") and eliminating borders of national sovereignty ("harmonization").

Eco-nomics à la Al Gore

The 1990 Moscow Global Forum of one thousand participants from eighty-three countries called for a planetary perspective involving "a new spiritual and ethical basis for human activities on earth." You see, radical environmentalism negates the Cartesian Theory, which distinguishes human life from earth, whose resources are intended by God to be used, albeit with good stewardship.

In starting the National Religious Partnership for the Environment, Al Gore endorsed eco-justice, which assigns to humans the blame for environmental impoverishment. Radical environmentalists, such as Gore, embrace British scientist James Lovelock's Gaia Hypothesis, which sees Gaia-Earth as a living, interconnected ecosystem, deserving human apologies. Gore's Global Marshall Plan calls for a New Global Economics.

The core document from which the global environmental agenda comes is the voluminous, Rio-presented Agenda 21 (1992), the UN blueprint for global eco-socialism. The Earth Summit, of which Agenda 21 was a primary product, mandates transfer of first world wealth to third world nations.

Consumerism is the targeted enemy of sustainability. While easing transition of all nation-states' economies to the UN concept of sustainable development, Agenda 21 proposed specific changes in human activities. It required reduced energy use in developed countries and balance of resources throughout entire eco-systems.

The UN is discussing world taxation as a means of funding environmental and population control policies. In *The Future of Federalism* (1962), Nelson Rockefeller called for "some free-world supranational political being with the power to tax." As he thinks of it, international taxation applies not to the mega-powerful rich, but rather to the masses; his is a mass-tax, not a class-tax.

NAFTA-nomics à la President Bill Clinton

The trend toward global economics is being pushed by President Clinton through the North American Free Trade Agreement (NAFTA, 1989), now dwarfed by the latest version of GATT and also most far-reaching trade agreement ever to be written, the "Final Act of the Uruguay Round" (1994). The latter locks nations into rules and regulations that exceed the authority of their own constitutions. NAFTA's merger among the U.S., Canada, and Mexico has created an even larger free-trading block of nations than the European Community. The goal of NAFTA is "equity" and "social justice" achieved by transferring wealth to underdeveloped nations.

Trilateralist and former Council on Foreign Relations President Wilson Ford admitted that by removing low wage jobs, NAFTA hurts Americans. Even so, he encouraged the release of some of our sovereignty. Trilateralist and Council on Foreign Relations member Henry Kissinger rightly described NAFTA as a first step toward the New World Order. Case in point: A provision in NAFTA created the Commission on Economic Cooperation, which consists of elitist international scientists functioning as a global Environmental Protection Agency.

Debt-usury-nomics à la World Bank and IDA

Officially called the International Bank for Reconstruction and Development, the World Bank was established in 1945 as an agency of the United Nations to provide loans at prevailing market rates, generally to developed countries. Its offshoot, the International Development Association (IDA), was set up in 1960, thus providing interest-free, long-term loans to finance economies of developing nations. To retard merely the interest on a debt, debtor countries pay ever increasing percentages of their national output. Today America is the largest debtor nation in the world.

For obvious reasons, debt-usury economy is destined to fail. Any real reform is delayed by disagreement over who should bear costs of debt relief. Analysts predict economic crisis exceeding that of 1929, when the United States was a creditor nation. One needs only to look to Japan's recent worst financial crisis of the postwar era to realize that the debt volcano is getting ready to blow.

In 1995 a congressional Declaration of Interdependence declared that the U.S. economy should be regulated by international authorities. Toward this end, the world scene is clearly being set. Much economic clout has shifted to the growing economies of Asia and Western Europe. As the most populous country, China will soon be the largest economy. Five former Soviet republics and Afghanistan have now joined the Economic Cooperation Organization (ECO) of Iran, Pakistan, and Turkey, creating what some call a formidable economic bloc; moreover, it is thought that six Arab families ruling on feudal thrones control forty-four percent of the world's oil reserves. Given today's economic pie of $3.6 trillion in global trade, the U.S. controls less than fifteen percent.

Electro-nomics à la E-cash

Privacy and use of cash disallow monitoring and control needed in the New Economic World Order; therefore, the World Trade Organization plans to bring about a global cashless electronic economy (See Mark of the Beast). Super computer hackers in the CIA have already developed powerful software that can monitor bank accounts worldwide.

Reporting for *The European* (15-21 August 1996), Elizabeth Philips claimed that virtual money, or e-cash, is destined to become the world currency of the future. Escalating crime and major financial collapse will encourage its materialization. In the name of combating crime, hitherto unthinkable laws are at present being proposed and even passed worldwide.

Cyberspace-nomics à la Y2K

Some warn that the much-publicized Millennium Bug threatens a world wide economic depression of such monumental proportion that Machiavillian measures will be warranted. The biggest problem associated with the Y2K Crisis is embedded chips, billions of which are in service globally. These serve as "unseen guardians of our lives" for they keep nuclear cores, intensive care units, military hardware, satellites, oil, gas, water, and electricity. Non-reprogrammable, they first must be located in order to be replaced; however, chips often are buried under the ocean floor.

Moreover, corrective changes introduce new bugs at an average error rate of one in ten. As a result of these and additional Y2K complications, at least one mission-critical failure may halt operations for agriculture, food processing, health care, education, and government services; moreover, air traffic control glitches might make it unsafe to fly over some nations. While many authorities believe the outcome will be catastrophic—inspiring civil unrest, political exploitation, and even governmental restructuring—others yawn in the face of its threat.

Biblical Perspective

Although he served as a government official, Daniel nonetheless had the gift of a prophet (Matt. 24:15). The apocalyptic book of Daniel outlines the inevitable course of world history. So accurate were Daniel's prophecies about Antiochus Epiphanes, a prefigure of Antichrist-to-come, that Christian opponent Porphyry wrongly insisted that Daniel's description must have been written after the fact.

The same argument cannot be applied today. Daniel could not have known about today's UN concept of sustainable development, yet he accurately foresaw end-time environmental and political efforts of eco-socialists. Daniel predicted with uncanny accuracy that Antichrist will "divide the land for gain;" that is, he will see to redistribution of the world's wealth (Dan. 8:25; 11:39). No doubt Antichrist aptly fits the description of the powerful "free-world supra-national political being" to which Nelson Rockefeller referred in *The Future of Federalism* (1962). Be assured, the Bible predicts a central end-time authority to control its citizens' power to buy and sell in the one world government it will forge (Rev. 13:16-17).

Gnosticism

From the Greek word, *gnosis,* or "knowledge," Gnosticism taught that man's slumbering spirit needs awakening in order to be liberated by knowledge. An esoteric cult of divine enlightenment, Gnosticism sprang from Kabbalism, which was at first an oral occult tradition. Branches of the cult were the earliest notable secret societies of the post-resurrection era. Although not recognized by Biblical authorities, its texts are widely known today as the New Testament Apocrypha.

Early church fathers Irenaeus, Hippolytus, Epiphanius, and Tertullian likewise refuted Gnosticism. Indeed, it blended heresies of Hinduism and Buddhism with Greek philosophy and ancient mystery religions of the Mediterranean. Gnostics also taught that man consists of spirit, soul, and body, the latter two being evil. The created order was said to be inferior, as is its "evil creator," the God of the Old Testament. Because enlightened ones perceived themselves as somehow superior, divisions between the so-called "spiritual" and their "fleshly" counterparts arose even in the early church.

Passed on through twelfth-century Knights Templars, the Gnostic belief system continues today in Freemasonry. Having devoted more than forty pages to Gnosticism in his Masonic classic *Morals and Dogma,* Albert Pike elucidated the misguided notion that enlightened ones will one day rule the world.

Biblical Perspective

Gnosticism taught that man is separated from God, not by sin, as the Bible teaches (Rom. 1:18), but by a number of cosmic spheres (usually seven) that surround the earth. These spheres are ruled by spiritual powers (archons) who allegedly guard them. Penetrating such spheres is accomplished by knowledge, revealed only to the initiated. Salvation is achieved, not by the atoning work of Jesus (Rom. 10:9-11), but by spiritual awakening and release from earthly captivity into divine light.

In these perilous last days, there remain those whose endless pursuit of false knowledge fails to yield truth (John 14:6; 2 Tim. 3:1, 7). Despite Gnostic heresy, God's creation is good; humankind (spirit, soul, and body), very good; and the Creator Himself, infinitely good (Gen. 1: 10, 12, 18, 21, 25, 31; Ps. 25:8). God's wisdom excludes idle speculations and fables to the contrary (Col. 2:8-23; 1 Tim. 1:4; 2 Tim. 2:16-19; Titus 1:10-16). The Bible is clear that wayward one world efforts, advanced by undercurrents of misshapen spirituality, are destined to take the fatal plunge (Rev. 19:20-21). Still, today's would-be Gnostics pride themselves for their presumed superiority (2 Tim. 3:2, 4).

Great Invocation

What the Lord's Prayer is to Christianity, the Great Invocation is to the New Age movement. Supposedly, it was given to Theosophist Alice Bailey through her spirit guide, Djwhal Khul. Leading star of mysticism David Spangler brashly claims to be the Great Invocation critical to calling forth the world "savior." One of the most widely publicized activities of Lucis [formerly Lucifer] Trust, the Great Invocation is simply an overture to the Hierarchy of Initiates, who through the process of evolution, presumably have mastered esoteric philosophy, themselves having achieved Luciferic Initiation.

Simply put, the Great Invocation is a prayer to usher in globalism by letting "light, love, and power restore the Plan on earth" (See Satan's Counterfeit Plan), and by letting these three and death "fulfill the purpose of the coming one" (See Antichrist). By definition, globalism is a worldwide design to undermine the sovereignty of nation-states and establish a spiritually deceptive New World Order with redistribution of the world's wealth and, therefore, its power.

For some forty years, World Invocation Day has been observed. The idea is mass distribution of the Great Invocation through the mainstream media.

Biblical Perspective

On Mount Carmel the great prophet, Elijah, challenged many diviners of Baal (meaning "lord" or "possessor"). From morning until noon, so-called seers cried, "O, Baal, hear us," but to no avail (1 Kings 18:24, 26). New Age prayers to the Hierarchy of Initiates are similarly in vain because they ask amiss (James 4:2). Salvation, glory, honor, and power belong unto the Lord, our God, and to Him alone (Rev. 19:1). In these last days, representatives of all peoples, nations, multitudes, and tongues, even unwary Christians, will fall prey to Satan's deceptive counterfeit (Rev. 17:1, 15; 2 Thess. 2:11; Matt. 24:24). Nonetheless, the Millennial Kingdom of Christ will ultimately prevail over any one world scheme promising pseudo-light, love, and power apart from Jesus Christ (John 1:4; 1 John 4:8; Matt. 28:18).

Great Tribulation; Time of Jacob's Trouble

Biblical Perspective

(See Day of the Lord; Seventy Weeks of Daniel.)

General Tribulation

Tribulation means affliction, trial, distress, or suffering; the Latin word for tribulation means "threshing-sledge." To experience this threshing-sledge is to have tested one's endurance, patience, or faith. Scriptures often refer to tribulation in this general sense (Ps. 13:4; Matt. 13:21; John 16:33). Every human suffers tribulation, albeit to varying degrees, throughout the course of life (Rom. 12:12; James 1:27). The psalmist assures us, however, that weeping endures but for a night. The joy of relief assuredly comes in the morning (Ps. 30: 5). That is to say, God in His own time mercifully provides a way out of every possible temptation, known commonly by all to some degree (1 Cor. 10:13).

In certain cases, tribulation serves as chastisement for sin (Rom. 2:9). Indignation refers to God's displeasure with Israel, national and spiritual, for their rebellion and apostasy (2 Thess. 2:3, 11). Lest one be inclined to point the finger, keep in mind that Jesus Christ "knew no sin," yet He, too, endured great tribulation. For the sake of righteousness, the disciples shared in His sufferings (Rom. 5: 3; Acts 14: 22) that they might be cleansed, refined, and thus suited for their heavenly habitat. So splendid is eternal glory prepared for Christ and His Body that these passing sufferings are unworthy of comparison (Rom. 8:18). Having survived blindness, murderous plots, being left for dead, shipwreck, imprisonment, an incurable bodily ailment, and more, Paul called these but light, short-lived afflictions when put in perspective (2 Cor. 4:17). On the other hand, as primary tools of the purging process, through which God nonetheless works for good (Rom. 8:28), Satan and his emissaries will endure instead the ultimate fate of what amounts to eternal tribulation in the Lake of Fire (Rev. 20:10).

Specific Tribulation

In Matthew 24:21, 29 and Mark 13:19, 24, we read of a distinctively unique Great Tribulation preceding Christ's Second Coming. Daniel prophesied of end-time fury to be unleashed against national Israel at the hands of Antichrist and his ungodly one world coalition (Dan. 11:36; 2 Thess. 2:10-12; Rev. 12:13-17; See New World Order). Further reference to this period is found in Revelation 7:14, which alludes to "Great Tribulation" (lit. RV, "the Tribulation, the Great One"), specifically "the time of Jacob's Trouble" (Jer. 30:7). The "abomination that desolates" signals its onset (Matt. 24:15; Mark 13:14 with Dan. 11:31; 12:11). Prefigured in A.D. 70 when Jerusalem was destroyed, this abomination primarily refers to the Antichrist and his forthcoming declaration of New Age godhood while in the very Holy of Holies itself (2 Thess. 2:4).

Not just national Israel, but all nations will be subject to this "hour of the Trial" (Rev. 3:10). There is, however, one exception: A specific company of faithful end-time believers from all nations, who have not denied the name of Jesus. These will be taken from earth at the Rapture "from out of" (Greek, *ek*) this, "the hour of the Trial" (Rev. 3: 8, 10), that they might be "put in a hold [for the purpose of preservation and protection]." In other words, a specific group of God's people, the dead in Christ included (1 Thess. 4:16-17), will enter protective chambers to escape the punishment of earth's inhabitants for their iniquity (Isa. 26:20-21).

Day of the Lord; Jacob's Trouble; Great Tribulation

Given these facts, keep in mind that the Day of the Lord, the time of Jacob's Trouble, and the Great Tribulation have several things in common. The latter two involve the same time period, and the Day of the Lord covers, or at least includes, the same time period. All three connote trouble and tribulation (Zeph. 1:14-17; Jer. 30:7; Dan. 12:1, respectively), as associated with birth pangs (Isa. 13:6-9 and 1 Thess. 5:2-3; Jer. 30:6-7, respectively). For all three, this trouble is great (Zeph. 1:14; Jer. 30:7; Matt. 24:21 and Rev. 7:14, respectively) and even unparalleled (Joel 2:1-2; Jer. 30:7; Dan. 12:1 and Matt. 24:21, respectively).

Each is called "that day" (Isa. 2:12, 17, 19-21 and Zeph. 1:7, 9-10, 14-15; Jer. 30:7). With reference to the Great Tribulation, the Septuagint (Greek translation of the Hebrew Old Testament) translates "a time of trouble" (Dan. 12:1) as "that day of tribulation." After seven years of tribulation and plagues (three and one-half years of each), there will come great cosmic disturbances immediately preceding the Second Coming of Christ (Joel 3). Christ's return with His previously raptured Bride serves as grand climax of the judgment phase of the great and terrible Day of the Lord described by Joel (2:31) and Malachi (3:2-5).

Many previous "days of the Lord" were but secondary applications pointing in type to this primary future and singularly great Day of the Lord, referred to by Isaiah, Joel, Zechariah, Malachi, Paul, and Peter. Unlike past days of the Lord, this great day, to occur even beyond the writing of Paul's epistle (1 Thess. 5:1-11), will stand out from previous such days because it involves divine judgment of all nations.

H

Hierarchy

Hierarchy of Initiates/Spiritual Hierarchy of the Earth/ Planetary Hierarchy; Uburmenschen (German)

See Adept/Initiated Adept.

Holy Spirit Imparted (Former and Latter Rains)

Biblical Perspective

Approximately eight hundred years before Christ, Joel prophesied of a future time when God will pour out His Spirit upon all believers, and it will be manifested in prophecy, dreams, and visions (Joel 2:28-29). On the Day of Pentecost, one hundred-twenty tarrying Christians were filled with the Holy Spirit, as indicated by their speaking with other tongues (Acts 2:2-4). Peter related this celebrated occurrence to Joel's account (Acts 2:16).

As with all Biblical prophecies, primary and secondary applications with greater and lesser degrees of fulfillment hold true (See Authenticity of Scriptures). In this case, for example, Pentecost fulfilled Joel's prophecy, as Peter boldly proclaimed, but not wholly. In order for wonders of the magnitude described by Joel to be seen, more of God's Spirit must yet fall (Joel 2:27-32). While referring to former and latter rains which would produce plenty and restoration, Joel did not exercise his skills at meteorology; rather, he pointed to Holy Spirit deluge, the greatest measure of which is forthcoming (Joel 2:21, 23-26).

The Hebrew root for the former rain identifies it as an earlier teaching rain. Moderate in measure, Spirit anointed teaching prepares hearts for the end-time harvest of souls (John 4:35). At the appointed time, this former rain will accompany a violent spring shower, which combination will allow bountiful reaping of the then-readied crop of souls (Joel 2:23-27). Despite the devastation associated with its violence, this spring rain will yield fantastic blessing to the Kingdom just prior to the Rapture of Christ's Bride (Joel 2:24-32).

Speaking in Tongues

Pentecostal baptism in the Holy Spirit will persist until Christ's body is perfect [i.e., mature] and with complete knowledge (1 Cor. 12:8-12). Although experienced in part during this Gospel Age, full maturity and knowledge have yet to define the church of Jesus Christ; consequently, tongues have yet to cease.

The Greek word for speaking in tongues is *glossolalia*. A believer who speaks in tongues yields his most unruly member (James 3:3-8) to the Holy Spirit, who, in turn, provides a prayer language—heavenly (of angels) or earthly (known of men), 1 Corinthians 13:1. The *Amplified Bible* calls tongues "different, foreign languages," not formally studied by those who speak them (Acts 2:4). The term, "charismatic," is from the *charismata* or "gifts" of the Holy Spirit (1 Cor. 12: 4) and is sometimes used of Christians who are Pentecostal in experience, but not necessarily of the Pentecostal denomination.

Jesus knew how to pray as He ought, and had no need for one to intercede on His behalf; moreover, the Holy Spirit was not yet given until Jesus was glorified, following His natural death (Rom. 8:26; John 7:39). For these reasons, Jesus Christ probably did not speak in tongues. Even as Christians, we do not know how to pray as we ought. When Jesus imparts the Holy Spirit Baptism (Matt. 3:11; Luke 3:16; John 1:33), the Spirit intercedes through believers for personal groanings too deep to be uttered (Rom. 8:26-27). The Holy Spirit gives utterance so that the prayers of recipients are perfect, hence certain to be answered (James 4:3).

Speaking in tongues can represent any of these several occurrences:

• the initial manifestation of the baptism in the Holy Spirit through a receiving Christian (Acts 2:4; 10:46; 19:6);

• the ongoing personal prayer life of a charismatic Christian (1 Cor. 14:2, 4, 5, 18; Jude 20);

• a corporate gift of the Spirit, operating in conjunction with interpretation, to edify the church (1 Cor. 12:4, 6, 10, 30). [Not all who speak in tongues operate the gift of the Spirit in the corporate body (1 Cor. 12:10, 30)]; and

• worship in heavenly song, individually or corporately (1 Cor. 14:15).

By earnestly coveting the "best gifts" (1 Cor. 12:31), Paul did not casually dismiss tongues, but rather he emphasized their appropriate manner of delivery (*in love*, 1 Cor. 13) and impact (*edification*, 1 Cor. 14:4; and *thanksgiving*, verse 17) as they are operated corporately. When referring to "best gifts," Paul's focus is more group than individual edification. That Paul also desired group edification does not retract his wish that all would speak in tongues for self-edification (1 Cor. 14: 5).

Historical Occurrences of Tongues

Speaking in tongues is part of the Great Commission (Mark 16:17-18). Believers are followed by signs, one of which is speaking in tongues. Healing, deliverance, and miracles likewise constitute this heavenly package. History proves that speaking in tongues was not limited to a single day at Pentecost (Acts 2:1-13); indeed, tongues occurred in the church at Corinth (1 Cor. 12, 14) more than thirty years after Pentecost; also, in the home of Cornelius (Acts 10:44-11:17) and at Ephesus (Acts 19:6). Post-apostolic Christians Justin Martyr (died 165), Irenaeus (died 202), and Tertullian (died 220) acknowledged tongues, which were likewise exercised throughout the Middle Ages by Francis of Assisi (1182-1226), among others. During the Reformation, Luther and the Huguenots were among those who spoke in tongues.

Throughout the nineteenth century, Great Britain experienced the phenomenon of tongues under the ministry of Edward Irving in Scotland and London. In the 1700s and 1800s, Charles G. Finney, Dwight L. Moody, and Charles H. Spurgeon spoke in tongues, and British Bible expositor F. B. Meyers wrote about frequent exposure to speaking in tongues in Estonia. The Azusa Street Revival in California was springboard to the twentieth century worldwide Pentecostal Revival. Tongues-speaking Christians now number into the tens of millions, among whom are respected ministers of traditional and evangelical churches.

Counterfeits Expected

Whenever God gives something good, Satan introduces his counterfeit version. Yielded Christians speak in tongues (Isa. 28:11), but so do some of differing world religions (e.g., Islam), cults (e.g., Children of God), and the occult (e.g., New Age). Still, the true believer can trust that if (s)he asks even an earthly father for bread, he most generally will not impart a stone. If (s)he asks for a fish, he will not give a serpent; and if (s)he asks for an egg, he will not respond with a scorpion. How much more will the Heavenly Father give the Holy (not unholy) Spirit to one who asks aright (Luke 11:9-13)?

According to Acts Chapter One (verse 14), the Holy Spirit Baptism, evidenced by tongues, fell on believers demonstrating *homos* ("same") and *thumos* ("mind"), Greek for "one accord." This unique unity is counterfeited in the single-mindedness of Antichrist's end-time coalition. Both cases of spiritual unity were God-incited (Acts 1-2; Rev. 17:13, 17). Despite these facts, tongues cannot be "of the Devil," or God would not have promised them (Acts 1:4), inspired prophets of old would not have anticipated their outpouring (Isa. 28:11; Joel 2), and post-Pentecostal apostles would not have engaged in tongues-speaking (1 Cor. 14).

Glossolalia and Globalism

The Holy Spirit imparted with evidence of speaking in tongues is crucial to the subject of end-time globalism. It is through this gift that God shows us of things to come and guides us in truth (John 16:13). Given the advancing great deception of Antichrist, Christians need to be armed fully to avoid delusion (2 Thess. 2:11; Matt. 24:24). Finally, according to Acts 2:11, tongues speak of the "magnificent, splendid, grand" works of God (Greek root, *megaleios*). Therefore, today's believers have an advantage, as did those at Pentecost, and Paul later, to pray in the spirit (tongues) and with understanding (native tongue) that God might be suitably acknowledged for His magnificence, grandeur, and splendor (1 Cor. 14:15), especially in the face of escalating wickedness (2 Tim. 3: 13).

Humanism/Secular Humanism

Not to be mistaken with humanitarianism, secular humanism is that doctrine, attitude, or way of life centered on relativistic human values that exalts the dignity and worth of man based on self-determination through reason (See Values Education). Simply, it dethrones God and, in turn, exalts man as the measure of all things.

By 1650 a strong influx of humanism spilled over from Europe into America, resulting in the moral darkness of the early 1700s. This was combated by the Great Awakening (1740-1750); nonetheless, humanism is alive and well, even today. Brands range from scientific/rationalistic to mystical/ religious (as Unitarianism) and from secular/enlightened to democratic/Marxist. For many, today's brand of choice is mystical humanism, emphasizing self-god. In all cases, the scriptures of humanism are the *Humanist Manifestos I* (1933) and *II* (1973), promising the dawn of a New Age, beginning with humans, not God. Its true revolution gives birth to the New World Order, based on transnational federal government.

John Dewey, father of America's supposedly "progressive" public education system, advocated and signed the 1933 manifesto. Among forty-two professors who signed the 1973 version was the father of operant conditioning, B. F. Skinner, who forged the base for many instructional practices (See Outcome-Based Education).

As a result of two U.S. Supreme Court cases (1961, 1964), humanism is a "nontheistic religion" Its four goals follow:

• Science-based one world religion, whose god is man or the state, as described in *A Common Faith* by John Dewey.

• New economic system to redistribute the world's wealth by exchanging the free enterprise system for some alternative form (See Global Ecomonics/Banking).

• New World Order—anti-Christian; anti-American "world community" with its Declaration of Interdependence and arbitrary law for the good of society at the given moment.

• New race, its motto being, "One world; one species." Whereas the New Age mystic looks for a new species resulting from a planetary quantum leap to "christhood," the godless humanist hopes to control his own evolution by means of social or genetic engineering.

Humanists are good tacticians. They target the youth by means of teacher training programs (See Teachers' College, Columbia University) and textbook and children's literature industries (See Textbook Conspiracy).

Historically, educators like Dr. Horace Mann, John Dewey, and his disciples were instrumental in promulgating humanism's agenda. Likewise, the international Aspen Institute for Humanistic Studies, a private, non-profit organization, attracts leading officials of the Trilateral Commission, the Rockefeller Foundation, and the White House to attend advanced seminars in global ideology. Most materials developed there find their way into public school textbooks (See Textbook Conspiracy).

Humanism is at the root of the public school's teaching evolution, political correctness, and moral relativism (See Abortion; Death Culture; Safe Sex). Many of today's teachers and professors proudly see themselves as change agents. While assuming a facade of neutrality, they advance humanistic moral skepticism.

Biblical Perspective

Decades of godless humanism, promulgated through public education, has given rise to an inner void prompting recent generations to yearn for some sort of spiritual fulfillment. Increasingly open to mysticism, seekers fall prey to New Age counterfeits with their empty promises of self-esteem (See Solipsism), the spark of deity within (See Adept/Initiated Adept), global harmony and accountability (See Pantheism/"All is Energy"; Radical Environmentalism), and peace for the New World Order of an anticipated New Age.

Blatantly excluded from the celebrated diversity (See Political Correctness Movement), sanctified Christians choose not to emulate unbelieving humanists (Jer. 10:2) or to embrace their gods of worldly wisdom and self-importance (Deut. 12:30), for God will never transfer His glory to another (Isa. 42:8)—be it Lucifer, Antichrist, or "illumined," eco-indoctrinated world citizens. Godly believers exalt not in humanity, but rather in the Lord alone (1 Cor. 3:21; 1 Cor. 1:31). Despite the flood of deception round about them, these are strengthened in prayer to flee the things that shall come to pass and to stand before the Son of Man (Luke 21:36; See Rapture).

I

Ideal

(See Adept/Initiated Adept)

Illuminati, Order of

Bavarian Roots: Adam Weishaupt

At the bequest of the House of Rothschild, the secret society of the Order of the Illuminati was founded in Bavaria on 1 May 1776 by Adam Weishaupt (known to fellow Illuminists as Spartacus) and was later revived under the name German Union. Born a Jew, Weishaupt became a Jesuit-trained professor of canon law. He was indoctrinated in Egyptian occultism and inspired by radical philosophies, such as Jacobism. In fact, the Jacobin Society named Weishaupt its "Grand Patriot." Having been instructed by occultist Kölmer (from what today is Denmark), his entire lodge and he were initiated into the secret teachings of Lucifer.

Illuminists, or "enlightened ones," profess to have a special intellectual or spiritual acumen. The Illuminati featured pyramid style chain of command with Rex Weishaupt at its pinnacle. Led step-by-step into the "higher mysteries," initiates progress through ranks of "Minervals" to "Illuminatus Minor," then "Major," respectively. From lower-rung neophytes to the inner-circle Rex, candidates were convinced that the order would one day rule the world. The society's avowed goal was, and remains, *novus ordo seclorum,* or new secular [Godless] order (See New World Order; Ancient Mystery Religions.).

The plan was to gain a foothold in key policy-making circles of European governments. An alliance between illumined Freemasonry and the Rothschild banking network provided needed funds. It was Baron Adolph Von Knigge (Philo) who reorganized the Order of the Illuminati along Masonic lines, but he finally defected (See Freemasonry).

The order operated under the principle that "the end justifies the means." The idea was to create a world government by abolishing all ordered government, private property, inheritance, patriotism, religion, marriage, and family. For example, Weishaupt developed a philosophy that virtually parrots today's feminist agenda (See Genderism/Radical Feminism). In 1786 Bavarian authorities seized Illuminist documents that included a tea recipe to procure abortion for Weishaupt's "new, liberated woman" (See Death Culture).

The French Revolution

It was not until the summer of 1782 that the order's influence migrated from Bavaria to France, where French writer and philosopher Voltaire directed the club's media campaign. When in March of 1785 the Bavarian government heard four leading Illuminists testify of Satanic involvement, the Bavarian government banned both the Illuminati and the Freemasons.

Through the Jacobin Society and Napoleon Bonaparte, who later seized power as dictator in 1799, Illuminists incited the terror-by-design French Revolution, thought to be progenitor of all contemporary totalitarian regimes.

The French Revolution forcefully created a new secular order, but the 300,000 peasants who should have profited instead were killed. In *Fire in the Minds of Men* (1980), James H. Billington, now head of the Library of Congress, traced and documented revolutionary activity lifted from the Bavarian Illuminati.

American Roots: Albert Pike and Jacob Schiff

Deists Thomas Jefferson and Alexander Hamilton both studied Weishaupt. The former infiltrated Weishaupt's order into the newly organized Scottish Rite of New England. In the late 1800s Albert Pike was selected to head Illuminist activities in the United States. Admirer of the Kabbalah, the oral occult tradition from which gnosticism emerged, Pike established a Satanic cult called the New and Reformed Palladian Rite. The Mazzini-Pike Plan called for three world wars; the final one, Armageddon, was to be sparked, as scriptures foretell, by controversy between Israel and the Islamic world (See Islamic Fundamentalism).

After World War II, Jacob Schiff emerged in New York as key Illuminist. The German-born son of a rabbi, Schiff was recognized by Rothschild as a financial wizard; therefore, Schiff's mission was to gain control of the U.S. money system (See Global Economics/Banking; Depository Trust Company). The leading architect of the Federal Reserve System was Schiff's chief executive and courier, Colonel Edward Mandell House. That same year (1913) the progressive graduated income tax was first imposed. Schiff targeted men who, for a price, would support internationalist causes. What's more, he was instrumental in spearheading minority group strife and in undermining religion, particularly Christianity, in America (See Political Correctness Movement).

Illuminati Alive, Well, and Undercover

The *Communist Manifesto* was said to be a rehash of Weishaupt's writings. His society operated a unique system of mutual espionage not unlike the Gestapo, with each member spying on the other. It adopted the Babylonian symbol of the All-Seeing Eye, indicating "Big Brother's watching." This chilling occult symbol is found on the backs of one dollar bills.

Since 1776 at least three U.S. Presidents (George Washington, for one) have warned the public of Illuminist activities. On 4 July 1794 the president of Yale College, Timothy Dwight, issued a memorable warning against the occult doctrine and global plan of Illuminists. Although the Order of the Illuminati ceased to exist officially after its exposure in the 1780s, Illuminist efforts nonetheless continue through the Grand Orient Lodge of France. Moreover, the order was revived in Berlin by Leopold Engel (1906), and its ideology persists in America today through the Council on Foreign Relations.

Biblical Perspective

In assessing the worth of any belief system, one principle prevails—that is, let God be regarded as true, and every opposing man, woman, group, or demon spirit, a liar (Rom. 3:4). Christians are admonished to touch no unclean thing lest they be enticed to depart from the true faith (2 Thess. 2:3, 11). It is wise to "learn not the way of the heathen" (Jer. 10:2), nor to "inquire after their gods" (Deut. 12:30), as do wayward one world occultists in pursuit of godless global government.

The Christian exalts no man or group of men (1 Cor. 3:21), but the Lord alone (1 Cor. 1:31). His source of truth is not esoteric illumination, but rather the "more sure Word" (2 Pet. 1:19). Only inerrant scriptures are God-breathed and, as such, altogether profitable to impart wisdom unto salvation through faith in Jesus Christ (See Authenticity of Scriptures).

Insiders/Eastern Liberal Establishment

The Eastern Liberal Establishment is an euphemism for a deliberately anonymous prestigious membership, whose collective viewpoint is called globalism. In its place, the term "one world" was used formerly, but today is deemed less fashionable. The "90s" term, globalism, was coined to signify the Establishment's world-wide, but age-old, design—reflecting the "Great Work" of Freemasonry and "the Plan" of New Agers—to abolish nation-states for bio-regionally defined representative transnational federal government in what has come to be known as the New World Order.

Over the years, America's defense has been dominated by Insiders, who in managing our military-industrial complex have been responsible for what have proved to be calamitous foreign policies. German-born U.S. diplomat Henry Kissinger is among the most prominent of Insiders, whose numbers include both Democrats (e.g., President Clinton) and Republicans (e.g., Newt Gingrich).

The Council on Foreign Relations, the Establishment's brain, consists of a couple thousand of the nation's Insiders in fields of high finance, academics, politics, commerce, the foundations, and the mainstream media. Insiders, who meet under the auspices of the Council on Foreign Relations and its spin-off groups (Trilateral Commission and Bilderbergers), most likely plan to use the United Nations and the European Community as models for other regional groupings of nations (See Illuminati, Order of).

America's executive department is dominated by Establishment Insiders. Former President George Bush is perhaps the most prominent one ever to have attained the position of President. He is distinguished as the first top-ranking Insider to use the term "New World Order" openly and in public. State and Treasury Departments are especially hard hit by Insider sway. Still, the Establishment's principal instrument of control is the private credit monopoly of "the Fed," or Federal Reserve System. Among many private groups forming the Eastern Liberal Establishment are the Royal Institute of International Affairs, Dartmouth Conference, the Atlantic Institute, and the Aspen Institute for Humanistic Studies.

While warning of its power and control over our financial system and certainly a large segment of industry, Senator Jesse Helms has pinpointed the vast wealth and influential social connections of the predominantly Rockefeller-controlled Eastern Liberal Establishment. According to former government liaison Gary Kah, "Nelson gets the ink; David wields the power" (See Global Economics/Banking).

Biblical Perspective

The concept of globalism is not foreign to the serious student of Bible prophecy. Daniel's vision (Chapter 7) defined a global power system to follow those of Egypt, Assyria, Babylon, Medo-Persia, Greece, and Rome (verses 4-6; Rev. 17:10) and to precede the Second Coming of Christ (verses 13-14). Daniel further described the Satan-incarnate Antichrist as diverse from predecessors and given to speaking very great things (verses 24-25). Antichrist's genius promises not only to resolve the global eco-crisis, but also to settle the age-old Middle East conflict (See Israel; Islamic Fundamentalism.). Without doubt, a green banner will fly atop the anticipated New World Order (See Radical Environmentalism).

This world dictator will wield dynamite-like power (*dunamis* in the Greek) in signs and "wonders of falsehood" (2 Thess. 2:9) while he shamelessly blasphemes God (Rev. 13:1, 5; 2 Thess. 2:4). Because peace is so coveted in these unsettling latter days (Rev. 17:17), allied powers, who likewise are reprobate concerning the faith (2 Tim. 3:8), will be induced to share "one mind" with Antichrist and his False Prophet (Rev. 17:13).

The expected New Age of harmony will prove to be but a brief season of pseudo-peace. Before long, the Antichrist regime will "tread down" and virtually "devour" the whole earth (Dan. 7:23). Despite one's camp of choice, secular humanism or mystical New Age, politically correct globalists will have labored in vain building the broad walls of spiritual Babylon, revisited in end times (Jer. 51:58). When the Revived Roman Empire called

"Babylon, the Great," falls—and fall it must—collaborators will lament greatly for their futile toils (Rev. 18).

Isely, Philip

Organizer of Action for World Federation (1946-1950), Philip Isely first surfaced in the 1940s as a leader in the one world movement. From 1954-1958 he organized the North American Council for the Peoples World Convention, which culminated in Lakewood, Colorado (1959) with the formation of the World Constitution and Parliament Association. The WCPA served as organizing agent for the Provisional World Parliament and preparatory committee for the 1990 World Constituent Assembly, its motto being "one earth" (See Radical Environmentalism). In 1958-1959 Isely headed the Committee for the World Constitutional Convention and, in time, became its secretary-general. From 1966 Isely served as the WCPA's secretary-general. Business woman and nutritionist Margaret Isely serves as Treasurer alongside her husband, Philip, on the WCPA Executive Cabinet.

As the WCPA's key figure, Isely was instrumental as writer and integrative engineer in the association's assembling of a Provisional World Parliament. The WCPA's plan includes a ten-region world government, as delineated in the Club of Rome's handbook (See Council on Foreign Relations). A total of five sessions were originally planned in order to establish the New World Order. Since 1982, a number of sessions have already been held.

Spiritual leaders behind the WCPA are yogis and swamis from the Far East. Not surprisingly, the Preamble of the Constitution for the Federation of Earth reads like a New Age occult manual [See Pantheism "All is Energy"].

Biblical Perspective

See Insiders/Eastern Liberal Establishment.

Islamic Fundamentalism

As Christianity has differing denominations, with wide range of character among adherents, so it is with Islam. With this in mind, it can be said that extreme Islamic perspective is decidedly

fatalistic. While a resident of Kuwait, I observed that some devout Muslims seem to think as follows: "If I live, I live; if I die,
I die. Whether or not I conduct my affairs carefully, according to
laws of physics, and in harmony with universally accepted mores,
my plight in life rests solely in the hands of Fate. So be it." Given
this thinking, every event—big or small, spiritual or mundane,
sober or foolhardy—is punctuated with *Insh'Allah,* "God willing."

Islam properly pervades every aspect of daily life. In fact, the
word "secularism" does not exist in classical Arabic. The Muslim
Brotherhood is a movement founded in Egypt (1928) by members of the Sunni branch of Islam. Active in Jordan, Sudan, and
Syria, it aims to establish a universal theocratic state headed by
a "supreme guide." To the Muslim, Allah is great, but not necessarily personal. He is nonetheless invariably on the Muslim's
side.

Evangelicals represent less than one percent of the entire
population of the Islamic Near to Middle East. During one of
my six visits to Iran in the early 1970s, I was greeted by a huge
sign draping the front of a mosque. It read, "Christians are not
welcome here. They will be losers in the afterlife." Notwithstanding, according to Islamic belief, every human is born Muslim, and, if necessary, must be forced into submission. A form of
cultural imperialism, Islamic Fundamentalism elevates to the status of divine mandate the spirituality and culture of seventh-
century Arabia. Its global charge is summarized in the creed of
Iraq's Baath party: "One Arab nation with an eternal mission."
Michael J. Horowitz of the Hudson Institute has documented
murder of Christian believers in Iran and Ethiopia and widespread enslavement of Christian children in militantly Islamic
Sudan, following the principle of *dhimmitude.* That is, Christians
and Jews may be permitted to live, but only under Islamic domination.

Jihad

The Muslim's singular hope for eternity is that the good
accomplished in his life outweighs the bad. Alternative and in-
stant access to Heaven—replete with seventy-two awaiting vir-
gins—is achieved by death in *jihad,* or holy war. Integral to the
Prophet Mohammed's teaching is that Islam is a religion of the
sword. It is said to be an angry religion, in search of a fight.

Jihad means "struggle," spurred on by belief that all of Israel is on Islamic sacred land, and this land must be retaken as a Palestinian-Arab state. This central Islamic belief was clearly demonstrated when I taught at the American School in Kuwait. There we received a shipment of inflatable plastic globes purposely rendered useless. Because "Occupied Palestine" was preferred nomenclature, every mention of "Israel" was cut out by officials, apparently with a knife.

Islamic Terrorism

Arab rage over U.S. support of "Israel" virtually guarantees continued worldwide Islamic terrorism. For decades, Russians have financed the PLO and other Middle-Eastern based terrorist groups. Communist China and North Korea also supply munitions and training.

HAMAS is the Arabic acronym for Islamic Resistance Movement, meaning "brave zealot." Unlike syncretistic religions (See Ecumenical Movement), Islam allows no compromise; therefore, its most ardent followers are fanatics, willing to engage in terrorism on Allah's behalf. HAMAS are sustained by several thousand members claiming thirty percent support among Palestinians in the Gaza Strip. With proponents in Iran, Sudan, Jordan, Syria, Lebanon, Saudi Arabia, and the United States, the HAMAS are based in Saudi Arabia, Tehran, the West Bank and Gaza Strip.

The Hezbollah (meaning "party of God") are also hyperfundamentalist religious warriors who embrace the war cry of the HAMAS' founding documents: "The war is open until Israel ceases to exist and until the last Jew in the world is eliminated" (See Death Culture). Documented in an August 1871 statement which is still catalogued in the British Museum, Illuminist Albert Pike predicted involvement of Political Zionists and leaders of the Muslim world in yet another World War (See Armageddon).

Nation of Islam

Khalid Abdul Mohammed is the spokesman for Louis Farrakhan, a Black Muslim given national recognition and dubious credibility as leader of the Nation of Islam. His seething sentiments against "blue-eyed devils" and "crackers," as well as "bloodsucking" Jews, are heard as far away as Great Britain, whose dominant religion is fast becoming Islam, and the United States, known by Muslims as "the Great Satan" (*Newsweek* [14 Feb. 1994] 48).

A small cult founded in Detroit in the 1930s, the Nation of Islam breaks from orthodox Islamic doctrine by insisting that Allah has visited mankind in the flesh through one Elijah Mohammed, whose son assumed leadership of the Black Muslim movement upon his father's death. Unbelievably, Blacks were said to belong to a tribe descending from outer space via UFO some sixty-six trillion years ago. A mad Black scientist supposedly produced the race of White "devils" (See Afrocentrism).

Farrakhan broke from the two million-member group to declare himself the new messiah. His own sect boasts some ten to fifteen thousand members. In a video tape series, *Farrakhan: Charismatic Beacon or Cult Leader,* he claims to represent Jesus; but in a March 1984 radio broadcast, he called Blavatsky-inspired Hitler "a very great man" with "a good name." In October 1996 Farrakhan hosted a World Day of Atonement rally at the United Nations Plaza in New York. This is not his first international foray in attempt to go global (*Newsweek* [21 Oct. 1996] 44.).

Takiya

The code of the desert allows seducing, marauding, tricking, and lying. Modeled by the Prophet Mohammed at Hudayblya, *Takiya* is the right within Islam to "fake peace" when one is proven to be weak. The idea is to wait for better timing in order to conquer the enemy. I recall a political cartoon from the Kuwaiti news in 1972. While kissing the nose of an apparent enemy, the Arab pictured was hiding from view a mallet poised behind his back for opportunistic use. This comically depicted a famous Arab saying, "When your enemy is strong, kiss his hand [or nose] and pray that it will be broken one day."

Dar al Islam

Given these perspectives, *Dar al Islam* (House of Islam) no doubt poses a great threat to the Judeo-Christian World Order, or *Dar al Hob* (House of Infidels). Of the world's 5.2 billion inhabitants, twenty percent embrace Islam. Muslims now control, to some extent, about fifty of the world's most important countries and hold most of the world's oil supply. Terrorism expert Neil Livingstone warns that if Saudi Arabia were to succumb to radical Islamic Fundamentalism, it would spark a global economic catastrophe that would impact stock markets worldwide (See Global Economics/Banking).

Experts in the intelligence community tell us that with the presumed failure of Soviet Communism, the most destabilizing conflict in the world is the one between Islam and the West. Make no mistake, Islam is the fastest growing religion in the world, destined by 2025 to reach two billion; and it is set upon imposing seventh-century Arabian religion on all cultures worldwide. Iran's global ambitions have grown steadily since the Iranian Revolution in 1979 and the Ayatollah Khomeini's rise to power.

The leader of the New Islamic World Order, Iran, seeks to exert her military authority in the region and, at the same time, her spiritual authority over the entire Muslim world. Former Iranian President Akbar (meaning "the greatest") Hashemi Rafsanjani explained Islamic Fundamentalism's "Grand Design" as follows. In uniting all Islamic nations under the leadership of a coalition led by Iran and Syria, the West, first, must be driven from out of the Middle East, thus "liberating" Palestine. Next, the Judeo-Christian World Order must be supplanted with an Islamic one. Under her new president, Mohammed Khatami, Iran has reaffirmed its support for terrorist groups, Hezbollah, and Islamic *jihad.*

Islam has become the fasting growing religion in Europe. A total of seventy of the world's one hundred eighty-four countries are considered part of the "House of Islam." The role of Islamic Fundamentalism in these end times is pivotal and must not be dismissed lightly. Spread by force and upheld by *jihad,* Islam is a powerful tool in the hand of the Enemy toward shaking Earth's inhabitants to cry out for a dictatorial union under Antichrist.

Islamic Mysticism

Founded by Turk Sultan Veled, the Mevlevi Order for hundreds of years has practiced the Sema Ritual, through which an altered state of consciousness is achieved. Whirling dervishes revolve around themselves, while balancing on one foot and propelling themselves with the other. Under leadership of the spiritual master, stages of the ritual represent knowledge, awareness, and finally union with divine truth (See Adept; New Age Movement: Omega Point; Pantheism).

Biblical Perspective

Progenitor of the Hebrew race in the bloodline of Christ, Isaac is the "heir of promise" (Gal. 4:30), a type of Christ in countless ways. Half-brother Ishmael's seed was likewise to be made "a great nation" (Gen. 17:20). Indeed, all Arabs following the prophet Mohammed's example claim descent from Ishmael. With his Egyptian wife, Ishmael bore twelve sons and a daughter, who became princes and progenitors of many tribes (Gen. 25:17). However, Scripture calls Ishmael "a wild ass of a man." Even today, his hand is against every man, and every man's hand is against him (Gen. 16:12). An amplified translation of Romans 6:4 refers to carnality as "the lower, Ishmael nature."

To the Iraqi, Nebuchadnezzar is seen a national hero because he conquered the Jews and captured Jerusalem. The infamous Baghdad Butcher, Saddam Hussein, sees himself as a sort of Nebuchadnezzar reborn. According to a Hebrew and Chaldee dictionary, "Arab" comes from a primary root word meaning "to lie in wait" or "to engage and meddle with" [Louis Bahjat Hamada. *Understanding the Arab World* (Nashville: Thomas Nelson Publishers) 41]. It is no wonder Jeremiah calls Babylon (also in Iraq) the "hammer of the whole earth [to be cut asunder]" (50:23).

That Israel is on Islamic sacred land and must be retaken as a Palestinian-Arab state is simply not true. God promised to Abraham's seed the land from the River Nile to the Tigris/Euphrates Rivers (Gen. 15:18). Because of Israel's rightful inheritance, all nations will be united against Jerusalem (Zech. 14:1-2). God's promise nonetheless will be realized in full during the Millennium with the reuniting of Northern Israel and Southern Judah (Ezek. 37, 39). Especially then, and in measure before, Israel will blossom as a rose even in the face of rigorous opposition to her and her supporters (Isa. 35).

Israel: National and Spiritual
Biblical Perspective
Israel: Nation, Spiritual Type, Land

Israel means "to prevail with God" or "prince with God." It is used in Scriptures to designate the son of Isaac (Jacob) or his descendants, the twelve tribes of the Hebrews. Also, it refers specifically to the nation's ten northern tribes, as opposed to Judah in the south. Daniel 9:24-27 contains a complete history of Israel from Daniel's time to that of the Messiah, thus confirming God's continuing plan for her (See Seventy Weeks of Daniel).

Next, the term Israel refers to "spiritual Israel" in reference to New Covenant, Spirit-filled believers, "born from above" (John 3:3), some of whom are destined to receive their full inheritance at the Rapture (See Holy Spirit Imparted; 1 Pet. 2:4-5, 9). The Two Witnesses/Olive Trees/Lamps of the Great Tribulation are thought by many to represent the Messianic Jewish and Gentile remnant of believers left behind, who nonetheless resist Antichrist and preach, with signs following, for 1260 days (3½ years) until they suffer martyrdom (Rev. 11:7-8; Rev. 6:9, 11, 14).

Scriptures likewise use the term Israel in reference to the apostate church. She is pictured as the separated "natural branch" in need of grafting into her own olive tree (Rom. 11:24-25). Finally, Israel is a territory of just 7,993 square miles. This, the promised land, will ultimately extend from the Nile to the Euphrates Rivers. Seen in Scripture as "the center of the earth" (Ezek. 5:5; 38:12), its full appropriation most likely will be realized in the Millennium.

Ancient Vendetta

Israel is the subject of a four-thousand-year-old blood feud between Ishmael and Isaac, the second of three Hebrew patriarchs who were progenitors of the Jewish race (Gen. 17:19). Springing from this vendetta, the "City of Peace," Jerusalem, remains today the center of passion to Jews, Muslims, and Christians alike. She is said to hold the key to the end-times (See Islamic Fundamentalism; Armageddon).

Ironically, all who come to living faith in Christ, no matter their heritage—Jewish, Muslim, nominal Christian, or other— are called and chosen to compose the New Jerusalem Bride in whom God tabernacles here and now and throughout eternity (Rev. 21:2-3). "Whosoever will" may come (John 7:37). Notwithstanding, the essence of age-old controversy is this: Islam wrongly claims Ishmael as first-born "seed of promise." The word, Arab, means "to set an ambush," which plainly is against the chosen of God, Israel (national and spiritual). Both vie tirelessly for the position of the elect and for the land of promise.

Israel and Eschatology

In 1897 the First Zionist Congress convened in Switzerland to discuss the vision of creating a homeland in Palestine for then-scattered Jews. Many started moving to Jerusalem, then under Turkish control, and Hebrew became the state language. By the 1920s, collective farms, or colonies, were founded. Arab dissension continued to mount, but Hebrew resolve remained firm.

Scriptures affirm that the generation that sees Israel reestablished as a nation will not pass away until the entire Eschatological Discourse is fulfilled (Matt. 24:32-34). Some use 1948, the end of British mandate and recognized beginning of the *Diaspora's* return, as the countdown starting date. Others use 1967 when Jews took sovereign control of Jerusalem and held on to her for the first time in 2,500 years. Either way, the general time frame for the end-time is clearly in view.

Israel's Promised Prosperity

Ezekiel (38:8) describes national Israel as "living securely" after returning from many nations. In these end-times, Israel is foreordained to "blossom as a rose" (Isa. 35: 1). She is destined to lend, not borrow; to reign, not be reigned over (Deut. 15:6). Already Jerusalem is seen as a Golden City. Virtually every newspaper carries her story daily. Perhaps "Snap" (new, inexpensive electricity developed with desert air and sea water); untapped priceless mineral deposits in the Dead Sea; and/or a budding tourism industry, given the rebuilding of the Temple, will facilitate this destined prosperity.

Remarkably, Israel is said to "live securely" despite the fact that her Jewish population is roughly the size of the population of Iowa, and her more than 140 million enemies cover a surrounding land mass exceeding that of the entire U.S. Moreover, today's militia groups and some anti-New World Order sects are identified, among others, with anti-Semitism. To guarantee Israel's security, some experts believe that, in time, she will sign a covenant with Antichrist to protect her from the Revived Roman Empire; others disagree with this interpretation of Daniel 9:27.

Israel's Ultimate Armageddon

At any rate, her Final Battle is part of the war of the Great Day of God Almighty, World War III, or Armageddon (Rev.

16:14-16; Zech. 12:2-3). It will take place after a short-lived period of pseudo-peace (Ezek. 38:8). Started by a dispute over Jerusalem, it is destined to be the greatest holocaust in history.

According to the prophets Ezekiel, Daniel, and John the Revelator, four spheres of political power will come against national Israel. These include: "King of the South" Arab Confederacy; Northern Confederacy, headed by Russia; "Kings of the East" Asian Confederacy; and the Revived Roman Empire of the United States of Europe.

"A cup of staggering" and "a burdensome stone" to surrounding nations (Zech. 12:2-3), Israel will be shaken by what some authorities say will be three all-out nuclear exchanges (Ezek. 39:9-12); but at the Second Coming of Christ, she shall be spared total annihilation.

J

Jacobism (The "Philosophies")

Voltaire, Rousseau, Diderot, and other members of the Paris Academy formed the intellectual base of Jacobism, founded at Versailles in 1789. The club later used a former Jacobin (Dominican) friary as its headquarters in Paris. George Washington denounced Jacobism as an extremist republican club of the French Revolution. Through the Jacobin Society and Napoleon Bonaparte, who subsequently seized power as Chief Consul in 1799, illumined Freemasonry allegedly incited the French Revolution (1789-1799).

Assisted by Danton's speeches, extremist Jacobins proclaimed the First French Republic. They overthrew the moderate Girondins and had the king guillotined (1792-1793). Through the infamous Committee of Public Safety, the Jacobins began the Reign of Terror, led by Robespierre, after whose execution in 1794, the club was abandoned. At that time, the term Jacobin passed into general use for any left-wing extremist.

The Jacobin Society named as its "Grand Patriot" occultist Adam Weishaupt, who forged the political power base for illumined Freemasonry. Their plan was to gain a foothold in key policy-making circles of European governments, and alliance between illumined Freemasonry and the Rothschild banking network provided needed funds (See Global Economics/Banking).

Weishaupt's Bavarian Illuminati and "enlightened" (or High) Freemasonry are based on principles of Jacobism. Although the Illuminati ceased to exist officially after its exposure in the 1780s, its efforts continue through the Grand Orient Lodge of France. The Illuminati's agenda, which continues in America today through the Council on Foreign Relations, corresponds to that of the New Age. Its blueprint contrives a New International World Order with a global government and religious congruity.

Biblical Perspective

See Illuminati, Order of.

Jung, Carl Gustav (1875-1961)

Founder of analytical psychology, Jung is admired by some for demonstrating moral conviction in standing against addictions, lack of ethical responsibility, and cross-cultural insensitivity. He apparently understood the value of adversity and daring aspiration. Known for his theory of the collective conscious, Jung perceived the unconscious to be the source of spiritual insight. He is known for differentiating between intro- and extro-version, and his books include *Modern Man in Search of a Soul* (1933). Jung's followers come from among the educated. Joseph Campbell is known as the champion of Jungian syncretism.

Having once collaborated with Sigmund Freud, Jung broke his association with the father of psychoanalysis (1912) over the significance of sexuality at the root of psychological problems. Despite this estimable disassociation, this Swiss psychiatrist and evolutionist is known to have rejected fundamental doctrines of Biblical Christianity (See Evolution).

Marilyn Ferguson authored a best-selling classic, *The Aquarian Conspiracy*, which endorses the New Age movement. She surveyed practices and beliefs of leading proponents. When asked to name those whose ideas most influenced New Age occultists, she mentioned Pierre Teilhard de Chardin and Carl Jung. No doubt the influence of Jung's esoteric grandfather and mother was considerable.

According to Jung's pantheistic view, God is within each person, and He, too, has a "dark side." Jung believed the Tibetan Djwhal Khul to be Theosophist Alice Bailey's "higher self." According to the Tibetan, as channeled through Bailey, Jews and true Christians are "forces of darkness." Jung referred to ascended masters as archetypal images, or "Ideal Forms," who by definition have achieved Luciferic Initiation. Jungian psychologist Hal Zina Bennett claimed never to have met a person, who within thirty minutes of coaching, could not contact an inner guide.

Clarissa Penkola Estes directs the C. G. Jung Psychoanalytic Institute in Denver. A shaman given to howling as a wolf, Estes is a member of Colorado's Authors for Gay and Lesbian Equal Rights. Corporations who employ this Jungian psychoanalyst submit to hypnosis and induced imagings of sexual encounters with the Earth goddess, Gaia (See Radical Environmentalism).

Jungian analyst and Episcopal priest Morton Kelsey was instrumental in bringing occult practices into the mainline church. These practices include automatic writing, channeling, transcendental meditation, mantras, and shamanism, or witchcraft (white magic).

Biblical Perspective

Trembling in view of his imminent fate at the hands of the Philistines, and realizing that the windows of heaven appeared closed to his prayers, Saul sought illegal comfort when he inquired of the witch at Endor. Not a familiar, but rather an unfamiliar spirit—that of Samuel—appeared, and this at the bidding of God. The woman was surprised, for she expected the usual appearance of her "familiar spirit." As Saul's spiritual errors earmarked his reign's eventual ruin (1 Sam. 28: 5-20), Jung's spiritual errors render tainted the whole of his intellectual pursuits.

A prominent mystic, Carl Jung is among last-day scholars whose primary quest is knowledge apart from Biblical Christianity. According to the Rotherham translation, such ones, though ever learning, are "never unto a personal knowledge of Truth able to come" (2 Tim. 3:7). Knowledge is known to "puff up"—that is, bellow, inflate, or blow up (1 Cor. 8:1). New Age claims to self-god certainly do that. Followers of self-divinity are "poor and foolish" for their failure to know the way of the Lord and the judgment of God (Jer. 5:4).

From such as Jung and New Age associates as Alice Bailey, Christians are to separate themselves. Jesus warned against deception (Matt. 24:4), for many in the days preceding Christ's coming will make false claims, as those of Carl Jung and his associates (verse 5).

K

Kabbalism, or Cabbalism

The *Kabbalah* ("tradition" in Hebrew) was unique in that it dealt specifically with Israel. The Hebrew word QBLH (*Cabalah*) is derived from the root QBL (*Qibel*), meaning "to receive." A medieval book of the occult, the *Kabbalah* presents a mystical, magical interpretation of the Bible. The *Kabbalah* is rightly compared to the Egyptian and Tibetan *Books of the Dead*. Akin to neo-Platonism, Kabbalism was at first an oral occult tradition from which Gnosticism emerged.

Cabalistic writing reached its zenith between the thirteenth and sixteenth centuries. Against strong opposition, its charismatic leaders spread Kabbalism throughout Eastern Europe during the eighteenth and nineteenth centuries. Throughout a period of more than fifteen hundred years, "Kabbalah" is but one of many terms used to designate its teaching. Others include "Masters of the Mystery," "Inner Wisdom," "The Understanding Ones," "The Science of Truth," "Masters of Knowledge," and more (See Adept/Initiated Adept).

Using numerical associations, as did Babylonians and Greeks, the *Kabbalah* explained the Old Testament from an occult perspective. The *Kabbalah* is divided into two parts, the symbolical and the real. The modern Kabbalist seeks to reformulate its doctrine to address society's needs today. For example, in her *Cabalah Primer*, Henrietta Bernstein brings "new thoughts for the New Age."

The Hebrew Connection

Founded in eighteenth-century Poland, the Hassid sect of Orthodox Judaism was based on study of Kabbalism; however, only a minority of Jews acceded to it. Current Judaic thought likewise rejects Cabalistic writings as medieval superstition, yet it lives on today in the Hassid sect, whose men wear conservatively maintained black suits and broad-brimmed hats of eighteenth-century European society. While denouncing the academic approach of Talmudic academies, Kabbalism stressed intense emotion in worship. A later, more intellectual approach emerged and is now based in New York City.

The Occult Connection

According to the world's leading authority on the *Kabbalah*, Gershom Scholem, the *Kabbalah* is related to today's practice of white magic, palm reading, and Satanism (See Witchcraft). The *Kabbalah* teaches that there are two great worlds: They are the higher world (macrocosm) and the lower world (microcosm). Kabbalist belief includes a form of reincarnation in which the soul of one man, because of imperfection, transmigrates into the next, then the next, until all 613 precepts of the law are finally kept; and he supposedly becomes God.

Its ancient esoteric philosophy was woven with threads of pantheism, the belief that all living things are god, or part of god. At Gorbachev's November 1997 State of the World Forum, the Dean of the International Research Center of the *Kabbalah*, Rabbi Philip Bergs, encouraged attendees to exercise the spark of the god-force within (See Pantheism).

Early nineteenth century occultist Eliphas Levi was among the first to combine fortune-telling, Tarot, and *Kabbalah* into one system. The *Kabbalah's* Hebrew and English aspects, along with Tarot, are said to enhance one another.

The Masonic Connection

Not only is it an important source for sorcerers, the *Kabbalah* is the definitive one for Freemasonry and its many internationally linked organizations. In *Morals and Dogma*, Freemason authority Albert Pike called the *Kabbalah* a "second, more excellent bible," a key to occult sciences and source for all mystical Masonic secrets and symbols.

Biblical Perspective

Although some respected Christians thrill at its eerie affirmation of the authenticity of Scriptures, others link the popular *Bible Code* by journalist Michael Drosnin with Jewish occult mysticism of Kabbalism. Rooted in ancient mystery religions, Kabbalism is founded on other than the sure bedrock of Jesus Christ (1 Cor. 3:11). No matter the intensity of emotion, worship is to no avail if it springs from doctrine after the tradition of men and not God (Mark 7:7). Paul warned the Colossians to beware lest any man (Pike included) impair their spiritual discernment after such tradition. This is the mainspring of the world, propagated through philosophy and vain deceit (Col. 2:8); it is no "second, more excellent bible." God's Word alone is Spirit-breathed (See Authenticity of Scriptures; 2 Tim. 3:16). In sum, particularly these perilous last days, believers are to shun fellowship with unfruitful works of darkness (Eph. 5:11), even when they are falsely called "light" (Isa. 5:20).

Knights Templar

During the Middle Ages, knighthood was a fraternal order. Entering it conferred royal favor, or reward for public services, upon its initiates. These medieval fraternities were sometimes secular, sometimes religious.

The Knights Templar and Knights of St. John were top-class religious knights united by sacred vows of poverty, chastity, and obedience. Founded by nine French knights in Jerusalem (1118), the Knights of the Temple of Solomon devoted themselves to recovery of Palestine from its Islamic stronghold. They actively participated in the twelfth and thirteenth century crusades. In so doing, their stated charge was to safeguard pilgrims on their way to the Holy Land.

The order grew quickly. In 1128 papal protection was bestowed. Recognized for their extraordinary bravery, the Knights Templar became extremely wealthy and powerful through gifts of land and money given in exchange for assurance of safe pilgrimage. Ultimately, the Knights Templar abandoned military function to become European bankers (See Revived Roman Empire: Kings without Kingdoms).

The order adopted heretical religious beliefs of Gnosticism and the barbarous Arabic military Order of the Assassins, founded in Persia (1090) by Hassan Saba as a conspiracy against Orthodox Islam (See Islamic Fundamentalism). Templar rites of initiation included, among other depravities, sodomy and spitting on the crucifix. While Knights Templar appeared to be a Christian order, their inner circle worshipped Satan and venerated the Baphomet, an idol of Luciferians (See Ancient Mystery Religions). As is the case with Freemasonry and other ancient mysteries, the Knights Templar had a public image contrary to its secret doctrine, which was reserved for the masters alone (See Adept/Initiated Adept).

In 1307 a former member of the order charged it with blasphemy and immorality. When France's Philip IV had these allegations examined, Knights confessed unnatural vice and heretical oaths against Jesus Christ. It was for atrocities as these that Grand Master Jacques De Molay was burned at the stake (1314). Incredibly, today's Masonic Order of De Molay is reserved for impressionable young men.

Following public outrage with Pope Clement V's being forced, despite great reluctance, to abolish the order (1312), it continued to operate covertly. Modern day perpetuity of Knights Templar is found in Masonic Lodges. Freemason authority and occultist Albert Pike elucidated the purpose of the Knights Templar in his classic Masonic volume, *Morals and Dogma*: "We shall be rulers over the Masters of the World." For such a purpose, wealth provides the means; forces of occultism, the power.

Biblical Perspective

The spirit of Antichrist opposes God while exalting itself. This end-time spirit will manifest as a Satan-incarnate global dictator, who will claim godhood (2 Thess. 2:4). The Antichrist spirit was present in Paul's day (verse 7) and thereafter in the blasphemous rites and ambitious secret mission of the Knights Templar. Yet the Word is clear: The Lord shall first reveal, and then paralyze and slay, that lawless one (verse 8). All the wealth of the world, all the demons in hell, will not thwart the certain end of the matter. Judgment will be swift and sure to all who forsake love of the truth in aiming to rule as so-called Masters of the World (verses 10, 12).

L

Lucifer (Satan)/Luciferic Initiation

Biblical Perspective

The true light of the world is Jesus Christ (John 1:9), and His followers walk as children of light (Eph. 5:8). To the mystic, however, Lucifer is "the Light." A beautiful, anointed cherub, Lucifer was indeed "the Shining One" (*helel*); but pride demanded more. Exalting himself above the stars (believers), Lucifer wanted humankind's position as crown of God's creation. Even more, he wanted to be as God (Ezek. 28:11-19; Isa. 14:12-20; 1 Tim. 3:6).

Whereas Lucifer is but one entity, his subordinate fallen spirits, called demons, are legion. A legion is the largest single unit (about six thousand) in the Roman army (Eph. 6:12; Mark 5:9). To this day, Lucifer and his demons are hostile to all that is good (Job 1:6, 12; 2:1; Zech. 3:1).

Meaning "light-bearer," "morning star," or "the shining one," the name Lucifer appears only once in the Bible (Isa. 14:12) in a literal description of the overthrow of a tyrant, the king of Babylon. The passage more accurately speaks of Lucifer, who rebelled against the throne of God and, consequently, was "brought down to Sheol, to the lowest depths of the Pit" (verse 15). Pride drove Lucifer to become chief of fallen angels who shared his ambition; however, ensuing rebellion was short-lived. Lucifer is seen in Scripture as one who fell as lightning from heaven (Luke 10:18). Thus cast from the Mountain of God (Ezek. 28:16), Lucifer forfeited his once high and holy position. Following this rebellion, Lucifer became known as Satan.

Satan means "adversary," or "opposer." He is the Devil, *diabolos,* "one who riddles through [with false accusation]" (Rev. 12:9). He does not want to be second from the Sun, but first, thus usurping humankind's destiny as the Bride of Christ (John 17:21; See Plan of God). Dust (referring to man, Ps. 103:14) is this serpent's meat (Isa. 65:25). For these reasons, the Devil stands before God day and night accusing believers of wrongdoing (Rev. 12:10). In thus opposing humankind, the Devil is able to go only as far as God allows (Job 1:12; 2:6; Luke 22:31). If he cannot manifest himself through men who resist him (James 4:7), Satan chooses even swine over non-matter (Luke 8:33).

Scripture uses a number of titles for Lucifer, including Accuser of the Brethren (Rev. 12:10); Adversary (1 Pet. 5:8); Beelzebub (Matt. 12:24); Belial (2 Cor. 6:15); Deceiver of the Whole World (Rev. 12:9); Great Dragon (Rev. 12:9); Evil (Wicked) One (Matt. 13:19, 38); Father of Lies (John 8:44); God of this World (2 Cor. 4:4); Murderer (John 8:44); Old Serpent (Rev. 12:9); Prince of this World (John 12:31; 14:30); Prince of the Powers of the Air (Eph. 2:2); and Tempter (Matt. 4:3; 1 Thess. 3:5).

The Goat Motif

In Leviticus 17:7, demons are referred to as hairy, rough he-goats (*sair* for "devils," with reference to false gods or demonic spirits). The late Anton LaVey's *Satanic Bible* identifies Greek mythology's Pan—a man playing a shepherd's panpipe, but with horns and hoofed legs of a goat—as but one of many infernal names of Satan. (See Ancient Mystery Religions.)

Lucifer's Mission

Scriptures liken Lucifer to a number of ruthless tyrants, such as Nimrod, Nebuchadnezzar, Belshazzar, the Prince of Tyre, Antiochus Epiphanes, and Antichrist, whom Satan one day will control and inhabit. As Christ Jesus was Immanuel, "God with us," Antichrist will be Lucifer incarnate. In Christ dwells the fullness of the God-essence (Col. 2:9); signs and wonders follow Him (Acts 2:22). In Antichrist will dwell the fullness of Lucifer (2 Thess. 2:4); counterfeit signs and wonders will follow him (Matt. 24:24).

An apropos title of Lucifer is Abaddon ("Destroyer," Rev. 9:11), also a secret, sacred word of the Masonic Scottish Rite (See Freemasonry). Satan's sin is that of *ponoros*, or "active evil." Not content to face perdition alone, he wants to destroy with him as many as he can. Toward this end, he would deceive, if possible, the very elect of God (Matt. 24:24). As Satan tempted Eve with the promise, "Ye shall become as gods," he likewise tempts humankind throughout the ages. As with all ancient mystery religions and Lucifer's fall, as well, promise of "becoming god" is the bait.

Using supernatural intelligence and power, Satan effectually deceives by blinding the minds of unbelievers (2 Cor. 4:4). It was he who sifted Peter as wheat (Luke 22:31-32) and who buffeted Paul with a thorn in the flesh (2 Cor. 12:7). As a roaring lion, he stalks his prey (1 Pet. 5:8). Demons may attempt to associate with the righteous (Acts 16:16-18). Therefore, Christians are to test or try the spirits to determine if they are unfallen messengers from God or fallen demons (1 John 4:1). For demons to wreak havoc with a Christian, one's volition is necessarily involved. Christians must therefore remain sober, vigilant, and willing to please God in all things (1 Pet. 5:8), remembering that at no time can the Devil put a barrier between them and the love of God (Rom. 8:38).

Luciferic Initiation
(Counterfeit Baptism in the Holy Spirit, Acts 1:8)

According to occultists, Lucifer is the grandest of ideals, an angel proud enough to believe himself to be God and brave enough to buy his independence from God. His plan is to tear down the individual by teaching evolutionary origins and existential despair philosophies, and then, to come in with the pantheistic lie that "I am a part of God; I AM God."

The New Ager claims to attain this false sense of christ-, cosmos-, or group-consciousness, having affirmed oneness with the universe and, hence, with God (See Pantheism).

A mass planetary quantum leap via Luciferic Initiation, achieved by pledging loyalty to Lucifer as "god" (actually, demon possession referred to as "transformation"), promises to usher in the anticipated New Age of Aquarius. The earth then will become a sacred planet under a New International World Order under its New Age "christ," actually Antichrist.

Lucifer's Fate

The Bride of Christ will join her heavenly Bridegroom in the task of judging fallen angels (1 Cor. 6:3), but even now Satan and his cohorts are defeated and reserved unto judgment (2 Pet. 2:4). Until that judgment is consummated, believers take assurance that their Enemy cannot go beyond God's permissive will;

furthermore, God will not allow His own to suffer temptation more than they are able to bear. God faithfully provides a way of escape (1 Cor. 10:13).

The good news for believers is that Satan was defeated by Christ at Calvary (Col. 1:16; 2:10, 15). If they but resist him, he must flee (James 4:7). God is infinitely greater than this wicked one in the world (1 John 4:4). Consecrated, Spirit-filled Christians have power over Satan and all demons (Luke 9:1). They can tread on these diabolical hosts (Luke 10:17-20), and in Jesus' Name, cast them far away (Mark 16:17), for even demons believe and tremble (James 2:19). Better yet, during the Millennium, Satan will be bound and thus prevented from harassing humankind (Rev. 19:20; 20:2). Ultimately, Satan's fate is to be eternally doomed in the Lake of Fire (Matt. 25:41; Rev. 20:1-3, 7-10).

Lucis (formerly Lucifer) Trust

Lucis Trust is a non-governmental organization (NGO) and parent organization to the Theosophical Society, representing a form of ancient Gnosticism, an esoteric cult of divine knowledge. Boasting over six thousand members, today's Lucis Trust joins many foundations that support New Age causes, one of which is globalism. Connected with the highest levels of illumined Freemasonry, Lucis Trust was established in 1922 by occultists Alice and Foster Bailey. Foster was a thirty-third degree Mason; both Alice and her mentor, Madam Blavatsky, were co-Masonic hierarchs.

A number of Luciferic organizations were established in the 1920s and 1930s by the Theosophical network of Bailey and Lucis Trust—for example, the Arcane Schools of New York, London, Geneva, and Buenos Aires, which provide special training in high-level networking of the New Age movement. World Goodwill and Triangles are two other organizations whose idea it is to promote the New International World Order. World Goodwill, for example, is composed of the "New Group of World Servers." In 1961 it joined with World Union, involved heavily in world government efforts.

Given that the New Age crowd perceives the UN as a chosen instrument of God, Lucis Trust was appropriately headquartered, until recently, at United Nations Plaza in New York. Lucis Trust's weekly broadcasts are beamed worldwide from Costa Rica's United Nations University for Peace. An UN non-governmental organization (NGO), Lucis Trust has been a key player at recent UN summits. Occult tenets of the cabalistic and powerful Lucis Trust continue to influence key members of the United Nations and the Council on Foreign Relations. Robert McNamara, Henry Kissinger, and David Rockefeller are among notable financial and political leaders who have belonged to Lucis Trust.

Biblical Perspective

The Bible warns of a coming world government (Dan. 4:19-27; 7:2-8; Rev. 12:3; 13:1, 5; 17:9-12), whose Antichrist leader promises a pseudo-peace at odds with God's plan. The New International World Order with its global government and religion, as promoted by Lucis Trust and companions, will not fail to come. Be assured, however, that no lasting peace will accompany it, for then shall wickedness be revealed. With the very breath of His mouth, the Lord will slay Antichrist, and his "sacred secret" of iniquity. At His *parousia,* or "presence," believers will escape his grasp (See Rapture); and thereafter at the Second Coming, Jesus Christ will paralyze, and thus render ineffective, Lucifer's deception (2 Thess. 2:7-8).

M

Mainstream Media

The Council on Foreign Relations purposes to establish a New International World Order. Its 1987 report identified as members 262 journalists, correspondents, and communications experts. On 30 October 1993 *Washington Post* ombudsman Richard Harwood did a piece about the role of the CFR's media members. According to Harwood, these do not merely analyze and interpret, but rather "help make" foreign policy (compatible, of course, with CFR global goals).

The Chicago CFR sponsored a series of surveys (1978-1990). Among opinion leaders involved were government officials and mass media news directors, editors, and columnists. Goals at the top of their list (weaponry, arms control, and environment) were all globalist (See Radical Environmentalism). Leaders showed to be clearly more internationalist than the public they work hard to influence; however, the Gulf War proved to be a turning point for the American public in support of Bush's publicly declared New World Order.

Television

Retired anchor for CBS News, Walter Cronkite, is known among globalists as "the poster boy" for the World Federalists Association. Mr. Cronkite is not alone in being soundly linked with Gorbachev's New Paradigm. Each of three major television networks is almost completely dominated by members of the Council of Foreign Relations, and its spin-off, the Trilateral Commission. Presidents of the entertainment divisions of these three major networks helped support the Environmental Media Association (EMA) in advancing global themes of radical environmentalism in TV series. Television networks are also influenced by the Rockefeller's family bank, the Chase Manhattan (See Global Economics/Banking). Five percent ownership of the stock of a widely held corporation is usually enough to assure minority control. The Rockefellers far exceed this minimum in major networks and, thus, bias the media in astonishing ways.

Newspapers

The State Department, Pentagon, and White House claim the right to manage all news; therefore, "we the people" hear what they want us to hear. Major newspapers have CFR interlocks. The Rockefeller-controlled Council on Foreign Relations has made significant strides toward gaining control of the wire services, which supply much of our news. Privately-owned newspapers are becoming rare, with less than fifty families virtually controlling America's newspapers. Because major networks all run the same stories, our European counterparts find Americans curiously ignorant of world affairs.

Magazines

At the University of Iowa (1970), I studied propaganda analysis. Primary texts were not Marx's *Das Kapital/Capital,* or other expected selections. They were instead *Time* and *Newsweek* magazines, and for good reason. Major magazines in the CFR link are *Life, Money, People, Fortune, US News and World Report, Time, Newsweek,* and more. At a gathering of the Bilderbergers in June of 1991, David Rockefeller commended *Time,* among others, for forty years of discretion with regard to global government plans. He further endorsed the supranational sovereignty of an intellectual elite and world bankers.

Book Publishers

Prominent publishers have been represented on the CFR. Among these are IBM Publishing and Printing, Xerox, Viking Press, Harper and Row, Random House, and Harper Brothers. Many specialize in publishing textbooks (See Textbook Conspiracy). Along with major networks, newspapers, and magazines, the Rockefeller establishment has a certain lock on book publishing.

Anti-Christian Strategies

A recent Freedom Forum poll revealed that 91 percent of Washington journalists admit to being "liberal" (*The Washington Times* [3 Sept. 1996] 1). Being liberal may not necessarily discredit writers to whom the label applies; nonetheless, the admission clearly compromises the media's acceptability as the primary, supposedly objective source of values-charged information.

Failure of the media to cover Christian issues makes it difficult to get public support for legitimate causes that are not deemed politically correct or otherwise advantageous to the global community. Writers are quick to coin derogatory terms for Christian concepts. For example, the monogamous heterosexual is called "homophobic," and pro-life proponents are called "anti-women" (See Gay Rights and Abortion). If a group is known to be pro-family, pro-God, and pro-Bible, it is identified as an extremist "tool of the Christian right."

Internet

Many believe that with the advent of the personal computer, the monopoly of the mainstream media is being crushed by the Internet, which could serve in the years to come as an underground medium for the benefit of Christians.

Biblical Perspective

Habakkuk's message to the righteous of his day applies all the more today. The prophet compared himself to a watchman called to write the vision so plainly that one can run while reading it. As vigilant watchmen, we too are to join Habakkuk in standing against the spirit of one who gathers unto himself all nations (Hab. 2:1-5; See New World Order; Antichrist). In so doing, we are to embrace the vision, not a counterfeit, lest we perish (Prov. 29:18). Even more importantly to the Kingdom of God, we are to publish that vision manifestly, despite the deluge of mainstream opposition. Our battle cry is this (Matt. 24:35): Heaven and earth will pass away, but God's Word? Never! (See Authenticity of Scriptures.)

Manchild Ministry

Biblical Perspective

Scripture defines the Body of Christ as having a Head (Jesus Christ) and a Body (believers). In several contexts (Isa. 66; John 16; Rev. 12), a unique part of this Body is called the "manchild." The doctrine of the manchild, as presented here, is not to be mistaken for teachings heavily influenced by William Branham—for example, those of John Robert Stevens and the Manifest Sons of God Movement. A Detroit attorney, author, and New Age authority, Constance Cumbey has explored literature of followers Bill Britton and David Ebaugh. In so doing, she has documented what she perceives as clear parallels between the New Age and Manifest Sons of God Movements.

Contrary to the Manifest Sons of God belief system, the Biblical doctrine does not suppose humankind can attain divinity, perfection, or "christhood," as esoterics mistakenly promise via New Age enlightenment. Though sometimes misinterpreted, the Biblical doctrine of the manchild and its ministry nonetheless hold valuable truth for every serious student of Scripture.

The Manchild Dispute

The identity of the manchild has been the subject of much controversy among eschatologists. Many believe that the manchild of Revelation 12 represents Christ, and the woman who gives birth, Israel; but this cannot be so. In Revelation 1:1, the angel took John in spirit to a future vantage point, allowing him to look "back to the future," so to speak. The angel showed John "things which must shortly take place" in John's future, clearly beyond the natural life of Christ on Earth (Rev. 1:3; 22:7, 10, 18-19). Furthermore, the manchild of Revelation 12 remains unborn until the period of the end, referring to the time of the Dragon with seven heads (world government).

The last and seventh head of the Dragon (Lucifer) is the Beast (Antichrist), who in causing the whole Earth to worship his image and to take his mark, will wage war against believers (See Mark of the Beast: 666; Rev. 13:15-18). Other verses prove this Beast to be in the end times, not the time of Jesus' earthly ministry, again showing that Jesus cannot possibly be the manchild of Revelation 12 (Rev. 14:9, 11; 15:2; 16:2, 10, 13; 17:3, 7, 8, 11-13, 16, 17; 19:20; 20:4, 10).

The Greek word for "signified" in the King James translation of Revelation 1:1 literally means "signs and symbols." Because the book of Revelation is by nature symbolic, we can assume that the manchild of Revelation 12 symbolizes something or someone other than Christ.

Given the context and established Biblical types, this woman best represents Christendom, the mother-church, whose offspring termed "manchild company" picture a victorious remnant thereof.

This less common position is held by many authoritative sources, not least of which is an Assemblies of God publication, the *Worrell New Testament with Study Notes.*

Identity of the Woman

The woman-church of Revelation 12:1-2 is clothed with the sun (Christ Himself), and the moon of the Old Covenant (having no light of its own, but reflecting that of the sun/Son) is under her feet. These pictures speak to the honor and dignity attached to this woman, who gives birth to the manchild, then flees to the wilderness of Great Tribulation (Rev. 12:5-6). There for three and one-half years, she is nourished and protected by God from the flood of destruction emitted by the seven-headed Dragon who pursues her (Rev. 12:6, 14-16).

The woman also wears a crown of twelve stars. The numeral "twelve" indicates completeness of God's kingdom, and the stars represent twelve tribes of Israel, each with 12,000 members, totaling 144,000 (Rev. 7:4-8; 14:4). As some of their Jewish brethren confirmed the covenant with Jesus during His three and one-half year ministry, the first half of the "seventieth week," these Messianic Jews will complete the prophecy during the last three and one-half years of plagues preceding the Second Coming of Christ (See Great Tribulation; Seventy Weeks of Daniel). Four hurtful blasts at the opening of the Seventh Seal will be held back until these "first fruits" are sealed to move unscathed among those upon whom the plague will fall (Rev. 7:2-3). The 144,000 will be redeemed from the earth, from among men, and out of Great Tribulation (Rev. 14:3) before Armageddon (Rev. 7:1-8; 14). Eventually they will rule and reign with Christ throughout the Millennium.

With "Christ the first fruits" (1 Cor. 15:23) at their head, end-time first fruits of mature sons and daughters of God (Rom. 8:29) include, but are not limited to, these 144,000 (Rev. 14:4). With His extended first fruits "in Christ," God will confirm His covenant for a week of years during the second half of the seven-year Great Tribulation to finish the transgression (Heb. 9:15; Isa. 53:5), make an end of sins (John 1:29), make reconciliation for iniquity (Heb. 2:14), bring in everlasting righteousness (Isa. 51:5,8; Joel 3:17), seal up the vision (Isa. 61:1-3), and anoint the most holy (Mark 1:9-11). To summarize end-time, full-term (that is, fully matured), Holy Spirit baptized manchild believers, inclusive of the 144,000, will finish the ministry of Christ on earth, and thus fulfill the Seventy Weeks of Daniel (Dan. 9:24). The Lord will use the offspring of the woman of Revelation 12 as chariots like a whirlwind to render His anger with fury (Isa. 66:15). Those nations gathered at the Lord's prompting (Armageddon) will behold His glory in judgment through the fruit of the mother-church's womb (Isa. 66:18).

Characteristics of the Manchild

The Greek term for manchild is used rarely. In Revelation 12, it comes from two Greek words, *arsen* and *huios*. The former speaks of a male in the sense of his being stronger for lifting purposes; the latter signifies the tender relationship of offspring to parents. The Greek phrase in the Revelation context speaks of a son's coming to full strength, or maturity, while in loving relationship with his Heavenly Father. Elsewhere in Scripture, those led by God's Spirit are said to be sons and daughters (*huios*) of God (Rom. 8:14).

Remember that the compliant Christian's life journey results in total fulfillment of the Plan of God to fabricate over time the "whosoever wills" among men into the very likeness, or inner character, of the Father. The model is Jesus Christ, first in position and in time (Phil. 2:9-11; Rom. 8:29). Many "sons" (male and female) follow the prototype, Jesus, into full-age maturity (Rom. 8:17; 29-30). These many sons include the latter-day manchild company.

• <u>With Regard to Gender</u> (strength-relationship motif)

In Matthew 19:4 Jesus used *arsen* with respect to God's making humankind male (*arsen*) and female. Having created male and female, God named them Adam (Gen. 5:2). We learn further from Galatians 3:28 that in the spiritual realm, there is neither male (*arsen*) or female, for all in Jesus Christ are one. The manchild company includes these "all in Jesus Christ," who in the end-times attain full-grown stature as equal heirs of God with Christ (Rom. 8:17). These possess the defining masculine quality of strength (*arsen*) as well as the characteristic feminine ease in nurturing tender familial relationships (*huios*).

Identified by her virtue, the woman of Proverbs 31:10 represents in type the Bride of Christ throughout the ages. The Hebrew word for "virtuous" suggests ability, force, and power. Christ's Bride is described as a dove (Song 2:14), yet she is defined by her force and power. Accordingly, Christ's fully ar-mored end-time Manchild Church is a consummate "warrior-bride"—that is, a lover, while at the same time a formidable foe against rulers of darkness (Eph. 6:11-18).

• With Regard to Nature and Calling

As Christ grew in wisdom, stature, and favor with God and man (Luke 2:52), so grow His followers (Eph. 4:11-13). "The servant is not greater than the Master" that (s)he should escape adversity (John 13:14-16). Christ and believers in Him are des-tined to suffer persecution (1 Pet. 4:13), to take up the cross and endure its shame (Matt. 16:24). Just as Christ was hated by the religious men of His day, so the manchild will be hated for His Name's sake (Isa. 66:5; Matt. 10:22; 24:8-9; Mark 13:13). Be-cause of the singularly impressive attribute of honoring God's Word above enshrined human traditions, even brethren will hate this manchild (Isa. 66:5).

Christ's ministry was short, only three and one-half years, but its impact was unparalleled. If all that Jesus accomplished in His short ministry were recorded, the world itself could not con-tain the books that should be written to proclaim them (John 21:25). It is not unreasonable to surmise that Christ's Body, too, will participate in similarly uncommon feats. Certainly, this has happened in measure; however, the works Christ did, and greater ones, will be accomplished by His Church (John 14:12). This is not because individuals will shine, as He did (Phil. 2:9-11), but rather in part because of sheer numbers of believers spanning the earth beyond Christ's limited reach of Palestine and its environs.

These "greater works" may refer to the power of love shed abroad from the hearts of manchild company believers, pictured in the Philadelphia Church Age. Even while in the womb of the visible mother-church, the invisible manchild is matured by this shared love (1 John 4:7-9). The "greatest commandment" Jesus gave His disciples includes loving one's neighbor as self, a dis-tinction of the Philadelphia Church (Mark 12:29-31), for surely a man cannot say he loves God whom he has not seen, yet hate his brother whom he has seen (1 John 2:3-6, 9-11; 4:20-21).

To be presented blameless, believers must be conformed to the image of Christ. This they do by taking on the form of servanthood, deferring one to the other (Phil. 2:1-5;12-15). Death to self (Gal. 2:20) and serving one another (Matt. 23:11) typify the less-chosen, narrow path (Matt. 7:14) of those who no longer live for self (Rev. 12:11). Dead to the "self life," they are crucified with Christ. It is He who lives within (Gal. 2:20), so that disciples can do all things through His infused strength (Phil. 4:13).

• With Regard to Multiple Birth

The manchild refers to a singular birth, as well as the birth of an entire nation. Consider Sarah, who miraculously bore a son in her old age. In this singular birth, she was destined to give such to plural "children" (Gen. 21:7). Isaiah wrote of a woman delivered of a manchild, which is described in the same context as a "nation of children," whose birth prompts great rejoicing (Isa. 66:7-8; 10). Both birthing women experienced miraculous deliveries, prompting questions of incredulity: "Who hath heard such a thing?" and "Who hath seen such things?" The manchild is unique in that it represents a "holy," or set apart, nation brought forth all at once, maturing as a corporate body of believers (1 Pet. 2:9; Isa. 66:8).

• With Regard to Supernatural Birth

Since the death and resurrection of Christ, the womb of the Church has remained virtually barren. Her efforts, though at times splendid, have failed to effect any permanent significance on earth with regard to its "bondage of corruption."

That is to say, the curse remains and, thus, puts somewhat of a cap on Scriptural promises that have not been fully realized (Isa. 26:17-18; Eph. 4:13; Rom. 8:20-23). The woman-church has yet to yield mature offspring whose spiritual stature reflects the fullness of Christ, provisionally and experientially. Toward this aim, the manchild fetus even now kicks rigorously against the walls of the womb, representing church tradition. Happily, these pangs will be cut short, for indeed the mother-church will produce the long-awaited manchild, even before her time of travail (Rom. 4:17-25; Isa. 66:7).

• With Regard to "Manifestation of the Sons of God"

In the eighth chapter of his epistle to the Romans, Paul anticipated the manchild's appearance. In fact, the whole of nature waits expectantly, longing earnestly for God's fully-matured offspring to be made known (verses 19 and 22). Their appointment as mature representatives of the Father exercising full delegated authority will yield rejoicing (verse 21), for then will the "bondage to decay and corruption"—i.e., the curse—be gloriously broken. The whole creation (of irrational creatures) has been moaning together in the pains of labor until now (verse 22, *Amplified*), but to date only wind has come forth. Cries of the whole of nature, represented in the woman-church's birth pangs, have wrought no universal or permanent deliverance in the earth; neither have the inhabitants of the world fallen (Isa. 26:17-18).

The manchild's phenomenal birth will bring forth the long expected victory. This birth will fulfill God's promise of the Church's bringing forth a universal body of believers that are truly "one," as indicated in Christ's prayer (John 17:11-12).

Through this manifestation of fully-developed sons and daughters of God (Rom. 8:19), the hand of the Lord shall be known toward His servants, and His indignation toward his enemies (Isa. 66:14). God will use the manchild ministry to overcome His enemies. As the Lord's chariot, a veritable whirlwind, this anointed company will render God's anger with fury (Isa. 66:15; Rev. 12:11) and, thereafter, rule or shepherdize all nations with Christ, the Head, throughout the Millennium (Rev. 12:5; Matt. 25:21, 23).

• With Regard to Spiritual Maturity

Identified with the Philadelphia Church of Revelation 3, the manchild will not deny Jesus' Name; it will experience "a little power" and a wide-open door for ministry (Rev. 3:8, *Amplified*). The manchild of Revelation 12 refers to a body of believers willing to be led by God's Spirit, for these are the *huios* of God (Rom. 8:14). *Huios*, you recall, speaks of full-age relationship.

John 16 also alludes to the birth of this notable manifestation of God's workmanship in picturing the woman-church, who having endured grief for a season, finally rejoices that the "manchild" has been born into the world (verse 21). This manchild enjoys full spiritual maturity (Isa. 66:10). It is no wonder that is the Devil's utmost desire is to devour the manchild at birth (Rev. 12:4).

• <u>With Regard to God's Word</u>

Manchild believers are known for loving the Word of Truth and desiring to obey it, no matter the consequences (John 17: 14-17; 7:16-17; 4:23). These value God's truth above traditions of men (Col. 2:8; Mark 7:8-9). Recognizing the authenticity of Scriptures, they study them diligently (2 Tim. 3:16-17). The manchild trembles in awe at the Word of God (Isa. 66:2) and demonstrates an overcoming word of testimony (Rev. 12:11).

While thus growing in knowledge of Truth, manchild Christians draw closer to Jesus and to those of like mind (John 5:39-40). This manchild company represents the many membered embodiment of "the perfect ['mature,' 'complete'] man," Christ in His full stature (Eph. 4:13).

• <u>With Regard to the Rapture</u>

Many scholars believe that the manchild is prefigured throughout Scripture. For example, the "man who walked with God," Enoch, and the fearless reformer, Elijah, were translated without tasting death, foreshadowing the promised translation of those alive and ready when Christ comes. In Revelation 12:5, the manchild is "caught up" to God and to His throne. The Greek word for "caught up" is *harpazo,* meaning "to seize" (in various applications) or "catch away/ up; pluck, pull, take by force." In reference to the presence of Jesus Christ, the same Greek word, *harpazo,* is used for believers who are "alive and remain." They shall be "caught up" in the clouds together with the dead in Christ to meet the Lord in the air (1 Thess. 4:17; See Rapture).

Unlike the lukewarm Laodiceans, who are deceived by encroaching cares of life (Rev. 3:17), these are found to be "watching and praying" (Luke 21:34-36). Because manchild Christians have kept the word of Jesus' patience, they in turn are kept *ek* ("from out of") "the hour of the trial," which shall come upon all the world to try them that dwell upon the earth (Rev. 3:10; See Great Tribulation).

Identity of the Remnant

In a widely accepted interpretation of Revelation Chapters 2 and 3, the seven churches represent seven stages, or "ages," through which the Church goes.

Given this interpretation, Revelation 3:14 speaks of the lukewarm Laodicean church on the heels, as it were, of "brotherly love" and worldwide evangelism (i.e., Philadelphia Church Age). These lukewarm believers are the woman's "remnant" of Revelation 12:17, further identified as Two Witnesses (Messianic Jews and Gentiles) who prophesy for three and one-half years during the Great Tribulation. Unable to destroy the crowned woman, the seven-headed Dragon makes war instead with this remnant. Through the refining fire of Tribulation (Rev. 12:17), these Laodiceans repent of their lukewarmness (Rev. 3:18-19), but ultimately suffer martyrdom (Rev. 11:1-14). Although they will sit with Jesus on His throne, they are not mentioned as reigning with Him and the manchild company.

Summary

Many scholars believe the manchild company to be pictured throughout Scriptures. In Revelation 12, the manchild cannot rightly represent Christ. However, as was the case with Christ, the manchild's birth (beyond Christ's time) will be miraculous. Although a tangible part of its mother-church, the manchild company will be distinctive in character and portion. Newly born, it will demonstrate remarkable full-stature maturity.

With both male and female components, this company of end-time believers will demonstrate the male nature of a warrior and, at the same time, the female nature of a bride. Given that God is no respecter of persons, and "whosoever will may come," these believers are not elitist, nor is the manchild the New Age counterpart of the hierarchy. Christians, who circumvent Scriptures with private egotist interpretations, mimic this New Age error.

The manchild company is pictured in the Philadelphia church, set in contrast to the lukewarm Laodicean church of Revelation 3. The Laodiceans represent the remnant of the woman-church's seed, and they are present in the Tribulation as Messianic Jewish and Gentile witnesses with whom the seven-headed Dragon wages war. The manchild company will escape Great Tribulation and plagues, respectively, by means of the Rapture and supernatural protection of the 144,000 blood descendants of the patriarch Jacob (Rev. 7:4). Except for God's grace in marking and sealing the 144,000, judgment and ruin under sounding of the Fifth Trumpet would instantly break over the globe, but instead are delayed until the manchild completes the work of Christ on earth and, thus, fulfills the Seventy Weeks of Daniel prophecy.

With red-hot love for Jesus (Song 5:9-16), the manchild company will not deny His Name. With but a little strength, they will take full advantage of the wide-open door of ministry set before them; moreover, manchild Christians will effectively restrain the work of Antichrist. For this reason alone, the manchild ministry is vital to the study of globalism (See New World Order).

Mark of the Beast: 666 and Related Technology

Biblical Perspective

"Mark of the Beast" is one of the most broadly-known prophetic phrases in the Bible. Its context being end-times, this mark is connected with three key players—namely, the Dragon (Satan), who will give power to "the Beast" (Antichrist) and his False Prophet. According to the Biblical account, the False Prophet one day will cause all to receive a mark in their right hand, or on their forehead. Speaking as the Dragon, he will make an image of Antichrist, and then force its worship under penalty of death.

More literally, according to the Greek, the Mark of the Beast will be a "stamp" or "brand," as of a slave, to attest to ownership and subservience. To participate economically in Antichrist's New World Order, this branding must be received despite the recipient's stature or socioeconomic standing. Simply put: No mark; no buying or selling (Rev. 13:4-18). To acquire this mark will further signify a volitional global pledge of allegiance to the New World Order, coupled with willful worship of Antichrist (Rev. 14:9-11). In no way is it to be construed as some inadvertent act that a Holy Spirit led Christian would engage in.

Mark of the Beast: 666

The numeral 666 is said to be the number of the mark. It is also the number of Antichrist, Satan-incarnate world ruler. We see, then, that the mark itself is in effect both a number and a name. Significantly, the numeral six is the Biblical number of mankind. Each of the three sixes likely represents a key aspect of the New World Order—namely, economic, political, and religious control.

Mark of the Beast: The Electronic Purse

To govern all buying and selling, as he must, the soon-coming world dictator will need to eliminate cash altogether. Otherwise, commercial activities could take place outside the system. Already, the locals of Place Dumon in suburban Brussels are conducting their own experiment with electronic (virtual) cash, or the programmable and portable e-purse as a replacement for old-fashioned notes and coins. Proton is the world's largest purse scheme; Mondex is its British-based rival. In use worldwide are fourteen million cards with Proton's reloadable chip.

The notion of a cashless society in itself is a good one. In *The Road Ahead,* Microsoft chairman Bill Gates describes the convenience of tomorrow's wallet PC. With it, a father can digitally slip five bucks from his own to his son's wallet—no problem.

Not only is it convenient and efficient, but it is also an evident deterrent to crime. In such a system, black-market activities are severely curtailed, and the medium of exchange for drug dealers virtually vanishes. Every debit card purchase casts a "data shadow," permitting incredible surveillance; furthermore, debit cards permit transactions to be conducted electronically without need for future payments or high interest charges. As prepaid stored value or "smart" cards are more widely circulated in North America with debit card function, cash will soon be obsolete.

Smart cards cannot easily be counterfeited or duplicated. They contain a small microchip one-sixth the size of a postage stamp, usually in the top left corner. One type has memory only. It can store incredible amounts of information, the equivalent of sixteen thousand pages of single-spaced typed text. The other has a microprocessor allowing update of information. Even smarter smart cards allow payments by inserting cards into telephones of computers.

Mark of the Beast: Verification Technology

PINs (Personal Identification Numbers) are being supplanted by such biometric alternatives as hand geometry, retinal reading, signature dynamics, voice recognition, and fingerprint reading. Arguing that the government must track illegal immigrants, tax cheaters, and "deadbeat dads," Public Law 104-193 requires all Americans to submit to biometric national identification (finger-printing) before issuance of drivers licenses (effective in 2000). Simpler yet, to eliminate need for such expensive verification technology, plans are being made to implant the microchip from the smart card under the skin.

Thus, one smart card augmented to address health care, education, licensing, voter registration, car insurance, and the like can become part of its owner without possibility of theft, damage, or loss (See Certificate of Initial Mastery). This syringe-implanted transponder will use radio waves to identify its bearer permanently.

Equipment needed to track the whereabouts and transactions of every person on earth has already been developed. In May of 1995 Britain's government announced the possibility of planting such a chip in the royal heir, Prince Charles, and also the late Princess Diana. Hospitals are likewise hoping to plant chips into newborns, ostensibly so they cannot be "switched at birth." Even now, tiny microchips about the size of a grain of rice are being placed surgically under the skin of animals to track their whereabouts.

In 1991 the Gulf War introduced the high-tech Global Positioning System, which provided continual electronic confirmation of every soldier's location, thus enabling troops to find their way safely around sand dunes. Consider the implications under the Antichrist, who would be able to locate anyone, anywhere, any time.

Mark of the Beast: National Precedes International Identification

It may come as no surprise to hear that the current U.S. administration is putting exhaustive effort into a de facto national identification card, backed by the National Governors Association. In the summer of 1996 Congress passed the Kennedy-Kassebaum Health Insurance Bill. One provision in the new law requires that every citizen be assigned a "unique patient identifier" by the end of 1997. Toward its imminent utilization, President Clinton advocates use of smart cards tied to Social Security account numbers. This being the case, every child at birth would be numbered. Once in a national database, that child could be tracked for life.

Issued without congressional approval, Clinton's Executive Orders No. 13010 and 13011 create an expanded, very powerful unified information system not unlike its more sophisticated global counterpart called for by the United Nations. Microsoft chairman Bill Gates contends that the information revolution is too limited if restricted to the already industrialized world. Gates envisions a personal computer in every village [Peter Blomquist, "Computer Needed in Every Neighborhood of the Global Village," *The Seattle Post-Intelligencer*, Friday, January 3, 1997].

Mark of the Beast: the Electronic Information Age

Through the years, the nature of the Mark of the Beast has been hotly debated. Some believe the mark to be in the form of an invisible laser tattoo not unlike product labeling with invisible bar codes read by scanners. They claim further that the numeral 666 is invisibly borne on ninety-five percent of all products bearing this Universal Product Code (UPC).

To some futurists, the linking of human brains to computers, called "wetware," renders virtual telepathy just generations away. Not until this current "electronic information age," so dubbed by the U.S. Department of Justice, are suppositions like this drained of their inherent science-fictionalized absurdity. Make no mistake, although we have yet to experience the Mark of the Beast, we daily experience its many precursors.

Millennium
Biblical Perspective
Millennium Defined

In Latin, "millennium" means one thousand years. Although their time frames mesh, the Biblical Millennium is not to be confused with A.D. 2000 at the turn of the century. It refers rather to a particular, post end-times period when Christ and His co-regents will rule and reign on earth. Theirs will be a theocratic global world order not unlike the Garden of Eden prior to humankind's fall.

Antichrist's so-called New World Order is the antithesis to, and Lucifer's counterfeit for, the Biblical Millennium. Then, Christ's "rod of iron," indicating swift and decisive correction for all rebellion, will topple end-time lawlessness (2 Thess. 2:3). At long last, the prince of this world—i.e., the prince of the powers of the air (John 12:31; 14:30; Eph. 2:2)—will give way to the Prince of Peace, the mighty King of kings Himself, as He returns to earth with myriads to put conclusive end to Lucifer's malevolence (Jude 14; See Second Coming). Throughout this thousand-year reign, the whole creation will be delivered from the "bondage of corruption" into the glorious liberty of obedient children of God (Rom. 8:21-22).

Millennial Subjects

There are a number of Millennial subjects: Christ, His co-regents, the 144,000 of Revelation 7:4-8 (and 14:4), believers' offspring, Satan, unfallen angels, and rebels.

- Throughout the Millennial Reign, Jesus Christ will sit upon the ruling throne, culminating at the Great White Throne Judgment (Matt. 25:31-32).
- Now possessing incorrupt, immortal bodies (1 Cor. 15:51-54), those previously-raptured warrior-bride manchild saints who have partaken of the wedding feast (Rev. 19:7) will reign as co-regents with Christ (Rev. 20:5-6).
- Formerly sealed at the outpouring of God's wrath, the 144,000 servants of God, first fruits from all the tribes of the children of Israel, will also live and rule with Christ (Rev. 7:4-8; 14:4; Rev. 5:9-10; Matt. 19:28).
- We know that there will be offspring, for the sucking child shall play without harm on the hole of the asp; and the weaned child shall put his hand on the adder's den (Isa. 11:8-9).
- At the onset of the Millennium, an angel will come down from heaven to bind Satan (Rev. 20:1-3). Thus bound, Satan and his hordes will be cast down to the pit (Isa. 24:21-22; Jude 6).
- Toward the close of the Millennial reign, when Satan is loosed for a short season, he will be permitted to test the loyalty and devotion of humankind under this theocracy.

Rebels will be gathered together as the sand of the sea. Scripture refers to Gog and Magog, literally in Russia, when referring to this circumstance (Ezek. 38:2; Rev. 20:3-10). However, rebellion will not take its full course.

Millennial Location

The Millennium will take place on earth, which will be greatly altered by former cataclysmic events during the Great Tribulation and subsequent plagues at the seventh vial, seven being the number of spiritual completeness, or perfection (Rev. 19:11-21; 16:17ff; 11:15ff; 14:14ff; 20:1-7).

Millennial Time Frame

The Millennium starts with the overthrow of Antichrist and his confederates at the Second Coming of Christ with His previously raptured Bride. It ends with a "little season" of rebellion, the destruction of rebels by fire from Heaven, the casting of Satan into an eternal Hell of torment, and the Great White Throne Judgment (Rev. 20:7-11).

Millennial Purpose

The Millennium is made possible by the power, foreplanning, and execution of Almighty God, coupled with the yieldedness of Christ and His glorious Bride. This thousand years begins an altogether new dispensation on earth toward the restoration of all things (Joel 2:25).

Foiled—the ungodly New World Order with its promised evolution into a supposed golden age of pseudo-liberty and peace! Dethroned—Lucifer, Antichrist, and the False Prophet! God finally assumes His rightful place. No longer is the world subject to lies of the prince of the power of the air (Eph. 2:2). Instead, every knee bows to Jesus, confessing Him, and Him alone, to be Lord of the universe (Phil. 2:9-11)!

As a result, righteousness shall remain in the fruitful field—its effect being peace, quietness (confidence), and assurance for ever (Isa. 32:16-27). There will be regeneration and renewal (Matt. 19:28), great light and prosperity, and binding of the breach of God's people (Isa. 30:18-20). Moreover, there will be no more sickness (Isa. 33:24). Mankind will be blessed with uncompromised spiritual revelation, righteous leadership (Ps. 77), and subduing of the animal kingdom (Isa. 11:6-9). Not only will the child play safely on the hole of the asp, but he shall be as a prince under God's undisputed rule (Ps. 45:16).

Montessori Method

Dr. Maria Montessori was an Italian physician and educator (1870-1952) who developed a holistic philosophy and system of learning which involved the young child's use of educational equipment while stressing perceptual training. Itard, Sequin, and Montessori addressed the senses of mentally retarded and academically underachieving youngsters (Ball, 1971).

The Director-General of UNESCO recognized Montessori's "fundamental influence on all modern methods of education" (See United Nations). Montessori called her work "a social movement," peace being its vital issue. Her cosmic plan was to encourage realization of human potential (See Solipsism). Toward this end, she called for more constructive economic forces (See Global Economics/Banking). In *To Educate the Human Potential,* Montessori profiled citizen duties in a "civilized Common-Wealth of the World," steadily moving toward globalization (redistribution of wealth) and harmonization (eliminating barriers of national sovereignty). Other Montessori publications include *Education for a New World* and *Reconstruction in Education* (See Public Education).

Montessori's concepts are unmistakably New Age, for she saw embryonic man as emerging into liberation, or true birth, with conscious realization of humanity's holy cause, which, not surprisingly, sets its focus on the New World Order, its cornerstone the environmental crisis (See Radical Environmentalism). Carrying a huge "Honor Your Mother Earth" banner, Jarrow Montessori schools in Boulder, Colorado, paraded in a tribute to Earth Day.

Biblical Perspective

According to Biblical admonition, believers are to abstain from even the appearance of evil (1 Thess. 5:22). Here, the Greek word for "abstain" is in the middle voice, indicating "for self interest." The context is the forthcoming Day of the Lord (verse 2). As the end-times unfold, it is in the Christian's best interest to steer clear of those in spiritual darkness, for they proclaim global harmony in vain. Truly, there is no peace apart from the

Prince of Peace (verses 3-4). Therefore, children (literally "sons," verse 5) of light are to "put to the test," or "examine," all things, holding fast to good (verse 21).

Multiculturalism (Diversity)

(See Political Correctness Movement.)

Sometimes called diversity, multiculturalism emphasizes differences based on ethnicity, race, gender, disability, and sexual orientation. The word "diversity" simply means having a certain number of ethnic minorities, women, handicapped, and homosexuals represented in the workplace, school, or any group for that matter (See Afrocentricity, Genderism, and Gay Rights).

This politically correct notion at first appears noble; however, an explicitly liberal political agenda supersedes all other considerations. Furthermore, the movement's program deconstructs Western civilization, specifically European/American culture. Forgetting that "Christian" America has a culture that in itself is distinguished, multiculturalism redefines it essentially out of existence.

Those who oppose the movement are tagged racist, sexist, homophobic, and oppressive in their attempt to preserve what adherents see as impoverished, slave-driving colonialism and white, heterosexual male preeminence. Use of such epithets, selective revision of history, and labeling opposing arguments as "anecdotal evidence" are dishonest tactics often employed by those deemed politically correct.

Nonetheless, four-year public universities have, for the most part, introduced "multicultural changes"; over half have diversity requirements. College mascots are accused of trivializing American Indian culture, and the song "Dixie" has been outlawed as a "racist leftover of slavery." Enlightened society has joined the bandwagon. Most celebrate production of the Wheel-Chair Barbie doll, no doubt an admirable attempt at embracing the handicapped; however, that "animal companions" are no longer appropriately labeled pets is broadly regarded as extreme political correctness. Presumed advancements are credited to heightened multicultural awareness, which erroneously elevates the right not to be offended to the status of a constitutional amendment.

By dividing American society and culture against itself, diversity contributes to dissolution of national definition and sovereignty, and thereby advances the New World Order. Anything "traditional" is the movement's target—namely, traditional values, family, work ethic, the Constitution of the United States, and Judeo-Christian faith.

Biblical Perspective

Toward New Age globalism, national sovereignty must be abolished, cultures merged, and Judeo-Christian traditions undermined. Advocates of the so-called politically correct Sophist antilogic of diversity are as those professing to be wise, while in fact they are foolish (Rom. 1:22). Ironically, in opposing discrimination, they themselves discriminate on the basis of ethnicity, race, gender, handicap, and lifestyle.

God's system for human distinction is altogether different. Although chosen attitudes and behaviors do matter, and all are held accountable with consequence, in no way does God favor or disdain anyone, regardless of ethnicity, race, gender, disability, or even sexual orientation (Acts 10:34).

In Christ (note that distinction), there is no Greek or Jew, circumcised or uncircumcised, bond or free (Col. 3:11); nor is there male or female, for all are one despite cultural background, gender, physical prowess, or socio-economic status (Gal. 3: 28). In contrast to the one Body of Christ, there are those who have yet to hear or receive the Good News, along with those who knowingly disregard Biblical mandate. These form the only other recognized group in God's economy; yet these, too, are beloved of God (John 3:16; 1 Tim. 1:15).

The book of Revelation uses many pictures to separate the two camps. For example, the Manchild company, Two Witnesses, and 144,000 unite as one; all are joint-heirs of God with Christ (Rom. 8:17). The Body of Christ is clearly diverse, yet decidedly one (1 Cor. 12:4-14). Lucifer, Antichrist, the False Prophet, the Harlot Church, and their dupes form the opposing group. Destined to an eternity in the Lake of Fire, the latter fail to qualify for over thirty thousand scriptural promises reserved exclusively for those who love and obey Jesus.

That "heathen have something to offer" opposes God's warning to "learn not the way of the heathen" (Jer. 10:2) or to "enquire after their gods" (Deut. 12:30). "Man's ways are not God's ways," nor should they be given "equal time" or celebrity (Isa.

55:8). To be sons and daughters of the Almighty, who are "one in Christ," believers are to "touch not the unclean thing" (2 Cor. 6:17), as defined by God's Word alone—not culture, nor even Judeo-Christian tradition (Col. 2:8; See Authenticity of Scriptures).

N

National Assessment of Educational Progress (NAEP)

For over a decade, a strictly confidential testing program, the National Assessment of Educational Progress (NAEP), has been administered, usually in March, to selected students in the public education system. Federal law (P.L.100-297) authorizes its administration. State participation is voluntary, but one day all children may be compelled to participate. Called "The Nation's Report Card," the NAEP is a longitudinal study, meeting at least two criteria. First, individual identity is involved—this, in violation of the Federal Privacy Act (Sec. 552a of Title 5, U.S. Code). Next, participants are retested in four years.

The NAEP assesses instructional basics and other subjects included in National Education Goals associated with America or Goals 2000. The parent information letter from its *Manual for Assessment Administrators* reads, "The National Assessment is a continuing survey of the knowledge, skills, and *attitudes* [emphasis added] of young Americans and the subjects they are taught in school." If students fail to respond with desirable attitudes of the politically correct global citizen, implicated teachers and parents are likely to be pinpointed and perhaps even penalized.

For the time being, the "parent survey" has been abandoned; nonetheless, selected students fill out twenty "background questions" that have nothing to do with reading and mathematics. Entries include consumer-oriented queries addressing family income, material possessions, activities, and values.

The National Center for Education Statistics (NCES) oversees collection of NAEP data. Strict confidentiality does not guarantee anonymity. The federal government and twenty-nine research organizations, academic institutions, companies, and contractors have access to restricted use of NAEP databases that contain individually identifiable information. William Randall, chairman of its National Assessment Governing Board, assures parents that students' names and numbers do not leave the school.

However, once these end up in the National Data Bank, parents have no control over what happens next.

Biblical Perspective

(See Outcome-Based Education.)

For their efforts to reach full potential, the intellectual elite of the New World Order must undermine and eventually overturn the right to privacy while at the same time compelling conformity to a singular global ethic. Believers still have a God-given right to privacy, or the "quiet life" (1 Tim. 2:2-3), and to follow the example of Jesus, who declined to answer personal questions posed even by authorities, whose positions may have been imposing, but were not sanctioned by God (Matt. 26:62-63; 27:14 and Mark 15:3; Luke 23:9).

National Education Association (NEA)

The National Education Association was founded in 1857 as a professional association. In 1906 the U.S. Congress chartered it, and in 1978 the IRS declared it a union. Largely financed by Rockefeller and Carnegie Foundations, the NEA today is the nation's chief education lobby. It ranks among the ten largest political action committees according to the most recently filed Federal Election Commission reports. With some 2.2 million members, the NEA creates regulations and certifies teachers to carry out its admittedly radical agenda.

Partisan Politics

Unlike federal government unions, teachers unions are not subject to Hatch Act restrictions on political activity. In fact, former U.S. Education Secretary William Bennett identifies the NEA as "the absolute heart and center of the Democratic Party." Because of its labor union status, the NEA can legally organize members into an army of campaign volunteers.

The hefty annual budget of its Political Action Committee (NEAPAC) is used to tap legal, political, and economic powers of the U.S. Congress. Yet to be determined is the amount of taxpayer money used to pay teachers while engaging in union activities.

The NEA works hand in glove with Planned Parenthood and the Sex Information and Education Council of the U.S.

(SIECUS). Gay rights activists form an extremely powerful faction in the NEA, which promotes tolerance for homosexuality and commends gay contributions throughout history. At its annual conference in July 1995, the NEA passed a resolution recognizing October as Lesbian and Gay History Month. Due to public outrage, the resolution was amended.

Privilege

NEA dues are a fixed proportion of the average teacher's salary, and its relationship with insurance companies on behalf of its membership is likewise financially profitable. Taxpayers fund its National Board for Professional Teaching Standards, not to mention retirement benefits for union staff. Until recently the NEA shared rare privileges with organizations like the American Red Cross and the Boy Scouts of America, thus exempting it from income and property taxes on its $65 million headquarters in Washington DC. Congressman Robert Dornan introduced the bill to strip the NEA of its National Charter privileges.

The Press

Forbes magazine recognizes the NEA as America's "largest and richest brass-knuckled labor union"; moreover, the NEA saturates most of the nation with its fifty-two state-level and 13,000 local-level affiliates. Nonetheless, the NEA gets surprisingly little attention from Washington's colossal press corps (See Mainstream Media).

Power

John D. Rockefeller made his first move on education when in 1902 he formed a sort of U.S. Ministry of Education, the General Education Board (GEB). The family since has given billions to champion international causes. Under Jimmy Carter's administration in 1980, the NEA demanded and subsequently got the Federal Department of Education, whose budget exceeds $35 billion annually in support of over 240 authorized programs. A payoff for the political support of educators, the DOE moved control of education to the federal level, outside of the parents' grasp. The NEA and the AFT (American Federation of Teachers) are considering a merger, creating an even more powerful force in public education.

Philosophy

Former president of the NEA Catherine Barrett applauded the teacher's true calling as "change agent," conveying values more than dispensing information (See Values Education; Political Correctness Movement). Dr. John Goodland of the NEA wrote a report entitled "Schooling for the Future" in which he acclaimed Dewey's concept of behavioral change (resocialization) as education's desired outcome.

By 1934 the NEA had adopted and incorporated into the classroom Dewey's brand of humanism, socialism, and globalism, forever changing the face of America's public education system. Today's Goals 2000 plan pushes schools toward the Outcome-Based Education model. Under OBE, human resource development for the global community supplants traditional teaching. Education author Samuel Blumenfeld criticizes the NEA's goal of gaining "more power, more money for the educational establishment [without] the foggiest concern for children."

Purpose

The year of America's Bicentennial (1976), the NEA unveiled its plan of education for the New World Order under Goals 2000. The Summary Report of the NEA Bicentennial Program reveals its goals "to change the course of American education for the twenty-first century by embracing the ideals of global community and the equality and interdependence of all peoples and nations." The NEA Earth Day curriculum has targeted 45 million public school children with what Mikhail Gorbachev has coined "the cornerstone for the New World Order" (See Radical Enviromentalism). This one world concept is not new. In 1946 a former editor of the NEA *Journal,* Joy Elmer Morgan, called the school "the very heart" of world government.

Prognosis

According to *Forbes,* the thirty-year decline in American education is "directly linked" with rise of the NEA. Its escalating power has precisely matched the discouraging scenario of increased spending with worsening results.

Biblical Perspective

Scripturally, children are commanded to obey their parents (Eph. 6:1: Col. 3:20); yet we know that in these last days, disobedience to parents is rampant (2 Tim. 3:1-2). Organizations such as the NEA contribute to this by demeaning family values, and by transferring responsibility for a child's education from the family to the federal government, or global village.

The Biblical admonition is to train up a child "in the direction of his duty" (Rotherham)—that is, primarily toward God (Prov. 22:6). An effective tool in the hands of globalists, the NEA supplants heavenly citizenship with cosmic citizenship. Contrary to the Bible, the NEA promotes syncretism (1 Tim. 4:1), genderism/radical feminism (1 Tim. 5:14), sexual freedom and perversion (Col. 3:5; 1 Thess. 4:3-5; Rom. 1:26-32), and a godless New World Order (Rev. 13:1, 7).

National Education Standards and Improvement Council (NESIC)

A provision in Goals 2000, the National Education Standards and Improvement Council is a new federal bureaucracy. The equivalent of a national nineteen-member school board, the council is appointed solely by the President of the United States and is run by bureaucrats at the Department of Education.

The NESIC purposes to control teacher certification, dictate public school curriculum, and control the granting (or withholding) of federal moneys to local schools. Keep in mind that local schools accepting Chapter One funding grants through Goals 2000 are compelled to implement the national curriculum of Outcome-Based Education (OBE).

Given its three-fold function, the NESIC is extremely powerful. U.S. Senator Nancy Kassebaum has introduced a Senate Bill (323) to eliminate the council with its misplaced authority to convert voluntary guidelines into mandatory ones.

Biblical Perspective

Big-government transfer of local, parental authority and values to an all-powerful police-state controlled by the Department of Education rides the tide toward federalized world government and restricts our moral and constitutional right as believers to speak, teach, and live by Biblical values (Deut. 6:7).

National Endowment for the Arts

In 1965 former President Johnson signed the National Endowment for the Arts into existence. In recent years the NEA has become one of the most controversial agencies. As an NEA promoter and representative, actress Jane Alexander identifies this controversy as a simple matter of taste. Artists funded have a right, she claims, to freedom of expression, even if it is not to another's liking.

However, the American citizen whose tastes differ to the point of being offended must pay for this dubious privilege. You see, the U.S. government allots the NEA its $100 million-dollar budget to fund projects perceived by many as being anti-Christ, and even obscene—for example, Robert Maplethorpe's homoerotic photos and the video, *It's Elementary: Talking about Gay and Lesbian Issues in Schools.* In one of the video's closing scenes, grade-school children all wear the symbol of homosexuality, pink triangle lapel pins, as they assemble for "Gay and Lesbian Pride Day" (See Gay Rights). Advocates may dismiss the NEA's budget as paltry when compared with the national budget, but opponents argue that thirty-three percent of the NEA budget directly serves only six percent of the population.

Through its grant selection process, the NEA functions as a kind of art arbiter. Its federal endorsement of particular works is tantamount to applying a U.S. seal of approval to what many view as pornographic and even blasphemous. For example, grants have been used to air sex lives of homosexual Black men and lesbian peep shows of girls age twelve and younger. Other "works of art" depict oral sex, "cruising" through public lavatories, and sado-masochism. In cases like these, defamation is funded with government moneys.

Biblical Perspective

With frequent exposure and popular affirmation, people tend to become desensitized to visual stimuli that once were highly objectionable. By repeatedly presenting to the American people federally approved "art," many are swayed in their personal tastes to accept the unacceptable, and in time even to prefer it. Lot, for one, made worldly choices that altered his tastes and judgment (2 Pet. 2: 7-8; Gen. 13:10-11); notwithstanding, he was a religious man, vexed by the evil of Sodom. Paul speaks of the last days as being similarly "hard to bear" (2 Tim. 3:1, *Amplified*). No doubt people who do not know God will become increasingly profane (verse 2) and loose in morals (verse 3). In their love of pleasure above God (2 Tim. 3:4), allied anti-God factions will oppose Christ and His followers (Rev. 17:13-14). With toppling of the Judeo-Christian ethic and world order, a New World Order, a godless one, can and will emerge.

Naturalism

Modern thinking has its roots in late nineteenth-century naturalism. Naturalism is the belief that all of life is explicable only by means of scientific data; all phenomena, therefore, reflect natural causes devoid of supernatural intrusion. Natural law alone governs. Given that only matter is reality, there is no need for moral or spiritual dimensions. To the naturalist, religious verities are illusory. Throughout the course of his natural life, man can expect only existential despair; death is mere oblivion (See Death Culture).

Naturalistic thought emphasizes that the world is fundamentally amoral, and humans are without purposeful free will. Lives are governed exclusively by genetic and environmental factors. Therefore, criminal behavior is a product of genetic, social, and economic circumstances beyond one's control. Criminals themselves are perceived as victims lacking power to make cognizant decisions to resist wrongdoing (See ACLU).

Biblical Perspective

The Bible plainly opposes naturalistic thought by differentiating between the "natural man" and the "spiritual man." In the Rotherham translation, the former is called "a man of the soul" (1 Cor. 2:14), one who is insensitive to the spiritual dimension. He does not welcome the things of the Spirit of God, nor can he get to know them. To him, they are but foolishness. His reality is the natural sphere apart from any supernatural intervention.

To the Christian, spiritual intervention defines reality, for the Spirit searches all things (1 Cor. 2:10), revealing what is rightfully his or hers in Christ (verse 12). God's "yea and amen" promises (2 Cor. 1:20) ensure abundant living (not existential despair) in this natural world (John 10:10) and throughout eternity (Matt. 19:29).

Decades of godless humanism, rooted in naturalistic thought and promulgated through public education, have contrived a vacuum so vast that more recent generations of America's youth are increasingly curious about, and open to, the spiritual deception of New Age occultism. While lacking spiritual discernment, these youth yearn for spirituality, and they fall prey to every wind of doctrine by the sleight [literally, "deceitful craft"] of men (Eph. 4:14; See Ancient Mystery Religions).

As equal heirs with Christ, believers inherit God Himself (Rom. 8:17). Ironically, it is not God's reluctance, but rather man's free will (influenced no doubt by genetic and environmental factors) that exclude him from these "exceeding great and precious promises" (2 Pet. 1:4). The good news is that "whosoever will" may share in this unspeakable inheritance; sadly, many instead will buy into the New Age deception of a burgeoning New World Order.

New Age Movement

(See Ancient Mystery Religions.)

The widely funded New Age movement is a worldwide coalition propelled by an esoteric belief system and united by its global agenda promoting Earth worship, sustainability, collectivism, and illuminism. Author of *The Aquarian Conspiracy,* Marilyn Ferguson, defines the New Age Movement as an essentially leaderless network, but powerful nonetheless in "spontaneously uniting as conspirators for the sake of the Earth." Lucis Trust is the "brains" of the movement, and David Spangler is its "leading star," claiming to be the Great Invocation.

By definition, the movement is a mystical religion by direct experience. Each one is responsible for discerning the "truth within." To this end, the New Age mystic is vitally interested in public awareness of self-esteem and conflict resolution. New Age mystics are known to dabble with psychic powers, ESP, telepathy, clairvoyance, subliminal persuasion tactics, astral-projection (out-of-body experiences; space travel), and 3-D image making (sculpture). They are fascinated by UFOs, near-death studies, shamanism, and Tarot methods of fortune-telling. The notion that people can shrink themselves through visualization is not uncommon among New Age curriculum developers, and flotation tanks are part of the New Age's spiritual technology.

To the New Age mystic, humans are gods-in-the-making. "Christhood" is considered an attainable position, and Jesus is but one of the many masters on equal footing with others such as Buddha. New Agers are open to any non-monotheistic belief system, but they are blatantly rancorous toward Christianity. Whereas not all humanists believe in the mythology of the New Age movement, they do recognize the need for new myths in a New Age. Perhaps not surprisingly, the 1973 *Humanist Manifesto* uses New Age buzz words.

New Age: Seven-Branched Plan

Advocates refer to the movement as "The Plan." Seven branches of this Plan address major fields of world work, and the custodians are "ascended masters." These seven branches follow: political (See New World Order; Radical Environmentalism; United Nations), religious (See Ancient Mystery Religions; Ecumenical Movement), educational (See Outcome-based Education; Public Education: Christian to Secular to Mystical; Textbook Conspiracy), scientific (See Evolution; Genetic Engineering; Mark of the Beast: 666 and Related Technology), philosophical (See Pierre Teilhard de Chardin; Solipsism), psychological (See Carl Jung), and economic (See Global Economics/Banking).

New Age: Four Pillars

Four pillars that uphold the movement include Evolution, Astrology, Reincarnation, and Eastern forms of religion (See Buddha). Indian swamis and yogis entice large followings in the West. New Age occultists consider Eastern religious leaders to be foremost authorities. The most revered mentors are Tibetan monks, presided over by their master, the Dalai Lama.

New Age Movement: Historical Stages

The anticipated New Age with its hollow promise of Utopia has already undergone distinct categories of readiness:

• <u>Preparatory</u> (1875-1890) under Helena Petrova Blavatsky, co-Masonic hierarch known as "spiritual godmother" of the New Age movement;

• <u>Transitional</u> (1919-1949) under Alice Bailey (Female Freemason who authored over twenty books on how to be demon possessed);

• <u>Revelatory</u> (1975 ff.) through the mainstream media (newspapers, magazines, radio, television, movies); and

• <u>Experiential</u> [e.g., the glorified garden plot in Northern Scotland, the Findhorn Community (upheld today as an Aquarian Mecca and utopian model of sustainability)].

New Age of Aquarius

New Age theology teaches that every 2,160 years of cyclic time, a new age emerges with its new revelation. "Planetary light bearers" are presently moving out of the Age of Pisces (Age of the Individual) into the Age of Aquarius (Age of Group Consciousness). The latter will be a golden era of unprecedented opportunity, peace, and worldwide collaboration, bringing unlimited well-being and universal brotherhood. Every new age has a new Savior (Maitreya) to lead the world into discovery of the "higher self."

New Age, New Species

To the New Ager, global unity is perceived as imperative to proper flow of the god-force (See Pantheism: "All is Energy"). Toward this end, a modern and superior species fitted for higher level of existence is arising on planet Earth. When humanity takes its "quantum leap" to this higher destiny, it will receive mystical powers, and a New World Order will emerge. A significant segment of humanity will, in fact, take this quantum leap, thereby creating a new species, *homonoeticus*. However, a great number will not yet be ready to participate. New Agers believe that these will suddenly be removed to a nonphysical dimension, where their karma can catch up before they are allowed back to the physical plane. This likely will be a New Age explanation for the Rapture of the Church. UFO abduction is yet another.

New Age: Omega Point (Pierre Teilhard de Chardin)

One of the movement's fundamental unifying factors is attaining a climactic Omega Point. "Peak experiences," as Maslow calls them, are accomplished through a variety of centering techniques to quiet mind and body. The *Donning International En-cyclopedic Psychic Dictionary* defines the Fifth Dimension as "the Kingdom of the Mind, a type of cosmic consciousness one can enter through altered states." This is perhaps the most addictive, and no doubt the most hazardous, aspect of New Age occultism.

Techniques for attaining the Omega Point include visualiza-tion, transcendental meditation, the martial arts, some forms of stress management, and yoga (which means, "yoking with Brahma"). Interestingly, relaxation biofeedback tactics are known by some as "the yoga of the West." Some New Agers engage in Tantric Yoga, a sexual form of black magic (See Witchcraft/ Wicca).

Hypnotherapy, or auto-suggestion ("enchantment," Lev. 19:26), is perhaps the most effective method for aligning the subconscious with the conscious mind, leading to a state of re-laxation. During hypnosis, a person's critical abilities are reduced to create a sort of "trance logic." In this altered state, the patient is vulnerable to suggestion, hallucinations, and demonic inter-vention not unlike experiences common under stimulation of psychedelic drugs. The phrase "taking a trip" is euphemistic for achieving a New Age altered state of consciousness. Hard-core occultists consider consumption of mind-altering drugs, such as LSD and heroin, to be "the lazy man's way" of achieving this coveted state of consciousness. Smudge is a well-known nonregulated drug that produces hallucinations and altered states.

Some use hypnosis to travel back to "past lives" (called past-life regression); others have distinct visions about future events (called fortune-telling or divination). While in altered states, New Agers follow their spirit guides by engaging in "channeling," the ancient practice of necromancy, or "calling back the dead" (actu-ally, demons). They also produce demon-manipulated automatic writing inspired by ascended masters.

New Age Associations: Political and Economic

The founder of the New Age Planetary Initiative is clearly tied in with the United Nations and its global agenda. The movement's promotions include "globalization" (redistribution of the world's wealth), "harmonization" (eliminating borders of national sovereignty; regionalization), and population control (See Abortion; Death Culture; New World Order; Planned Parent-hood).

The 1966 Geneva Conference of the World Council of Churches strongly correlated with New Age goals to eliminate capitalism and the free enterprise system (See Global Economics/Banking). Still, plenty of "big business" is involved. Within New Age directories alone, over ten thousand organizations in the U.S. and Canada are listed; many more do not confess ties with the movement.

The New Age movement is soundly linked to the anti-clerical, deistic, republican society of the Illuminati, founded in Bavaria (1776) by a former Jesuit professor. Connected with Freemasonry, the Illuminati seeks to replace Christianity with its own religion of reason (See Naturalism). Some identify today's Council on Foreign Relations as America's version of the Illuminati. Spin-off groups include the occult-driven Club of Rome and the Trilateral Commission, founded by David Rockefeller (1976). Along with these, the Federal Reserve Board has decided New Age ties.

Headquartered in Kansas City, Uniting Spirits is a politically visible New Age group whose intent it is "to heal our planet's universal consciousness." The group's forty-one cities awareness campaign led up to Chicago for the 1996 Democratic convention. Among the group's promotions are radical environmentalism and ecumenicism. Proponents unite to heal self and "Mother Earth," through a quest beginning from within.

New Age Associations: Spiritual

In reality, New Age mysticism is not new at all. It is revisitation of the cosmic gospel of Pantheism, the belief that God is the sum total of all that exists. New Agers interchange the terms mysticism and occultism. A New Ager is a mystic, an occultist, and a pantheist who believes (s)he can attain oneness with the universe and the "Christ-consciousness" by discovering and submitting to self-god with the assistance of initiated adepts, or masters.

To the New Ager, there is no personal God, but rather a god- or life-force which flows through all living things, including plants and animals. Therefore humans are Gods, or part of God. As gods, humans never really die and, consequently, face no personal judgment. Instead, they just keep returning to earth. Reincarnation provides opportunity needed to evolve from embryo-god to ultimate oneness with the god-force. The process involves transformation, or demon possession (See Lucifer; Luciferic Initiation).

Today, Spiritism is practiced by scores of millions worldwide. Having become an organized religion in 1848, it continues to gain acceptance among many of the world's elite, even royalty. Its emphasis is contacting the dead, or actually demons posing as their spirits (known as New Age channeling).

The holistic movement (term coined in 1924) stresses evolution into greater wholes with respect to body, mind, and spirit. Its goal is to balance forces in the universe. This is accomplished by reading auras, engaging in transcendental meditation, and psychic healing practices (i.e., aroma therapy and therapeutic touch massage).

Herbs and vitamins are consumed with similar intent—that is, to "balance forces." In like fashion, most participants in witchcraft believe in manipulating forces of nature, or the New Age god-force. A growing number of medical doctors join Tibetan masters in belief that touch, or *reiki* (RAY key) empowers recipients to mobilize inner resources for healing.

According to attorney and author Constance Cumbey, *Star Wars* is the New Age movement demonstrated on screen. Satan is seen as the "dark side of God," and humankind is encouraged to enter fully into this so-called god of Force.

New Age Association with Nazism

Author of *The Twisted Cross,* Joseph Carr claims that Nazism and the New Age movement are, in fact, synonymous. Carr further documents demonic influences on Adolf Hitler, hailed as Messiah by the Third Reich. Heinrich Himmler was his high priest; the SS Death Head Formation, the clergy. Neo-Nazism is part of the New Age stream. Belief systems intersect on a number of crucial issues: supermaster race (Aryanism), reincarnation, mesmerism, occultism, evolution, deism of man, and, of course, anti-Semitism.

Founded in Europe by Thomas Gretz, the new Kaizen religion pursues unification not unlike that called for by Adolf Hitler, who they say came too soon. At a more opportune time, a new highly spiritual leader from Luxembourg, Alain Porcedda, will emerge. "Group conscious" cult members must be thoroughly identified with the Kaizen Academy, so much so that not even a wink of an eye is permitted in meetings.

New Age: Symbols

As with the ancient mysteries, this new consciousness culture uses code words and symbols. For example, the New Age quantum leap to a higher level of existence (i.e., demon possession via "the naming and the named") is pictured in the rainbow, a symbol of the bridge between the personality (flesh) and oversoul (familiar spirit). Violet is the official New Age color.

As in witchcraft, the number 666 is considered sacred (See Mark of the Beast). Other symbols of the movement include the Ankh ("Key of the Nile"), the unicorn (or Italian) horn, the New Age crystal (obelisk), the crescent moon and star (See Freemasonry; Islamic Fundamentalism), the peace cross, the Sign of the Zodiac, the Rotary Club (Witch's) Wheel, the all-seeing Eye of Horus, Cornuto (hand sign of the "horned one," Satan), Mother Earth, Yin and Yang (Force of Tao), and more. In greeting one another, the slight bow of one's head, with hands pressed together, fingers pointed upward, indicates "the God in me greets the God in you." This gesture is called *Namaste*.

New Age: Literature

Often distributed through health food stores, New Age literature is prolific. One example is *New Age Magazine*, edited by Peggy Taylor. Among the movement's publications are *New Age Journal* and *Mother Earth News*. *Media Spotlight* out of California purposes to destroy Christianity, and widely read occult classics include *The Destiny of the Nations, The Reappearance of the Christ, Discipleship of the New Age,* and *The Secret Doctrine* by Madam Blavatsky. The most popular dictionary is Nevill Drury's *Dictionary of Mysticism and the Occult*.

New Age Movement: Global Agenda

The First Earth Battalion is a computer linked military organization behind the former Iron Curtain. Its *Evolutionary Tactics Manual* instructs toward New Age "transformation" (demon possession); furthermore, it delineates a time frame for world dominion. You see, New Age occultists anticipate mass planetary Luciferic Initiation, pledging loyalty to Lucifer as "God" (actually, demon possession referred to as "transformation"). The Earth will then become a sacred planet under one world government headed by the New Age "Christ," or Antichrist.

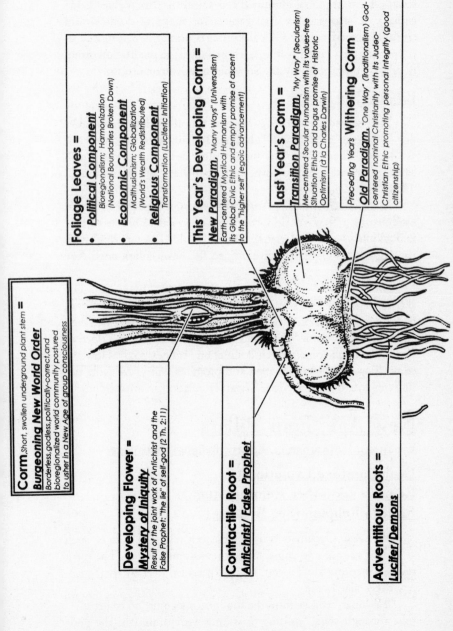

Corm, *short, swollen underground plant stem* =
Burgeoning New World Order
Borderless, godless, politically-correct, and bioregionalized world community postured to usher in a New Age of group consciousness

Foliage Leaves =
- **Political Component**
  Bioregionalism; Harmonization (National Boundaries Broken Down)
- **Economic Component**
  Malthusianism; Globalization (World's Wealth Redistributed)
- **Religious Component**
  Transformation (Luciferic Initiation)

This Year's Developing Corm =
New Paradigm, *"Many Ways"* (Universalism)
Earth-centered Mystical Humanism with its Global Civic Ethic and empty promise of ascent to the "higher self" (egoic advancement)

Last Year's Corm =
Transition Paradigm, *"My Way"* (Secularism)
Me-centered Secular Humanism with its values-free Situation Ethics and bogus promise of Historic Optimism (d la Charles Darwin)

Preceding Year's Withering Corm =
Old Paradigm, *"One Way"* (Traditionalism) *God-centered nominal Christianity with its Judeo-Christian Ethic promoting personal integrity (good citizenship)*

Developing Flower =
Mystery of Iniquity
Result of the joint work of Antichrist and the False Prophet: the "lie" of self-god (2 Th. 2:11)

Contractile Root =
Antichrist/ False Prophet

Adventitious Roots =
Lucifer/Demons

The New Earth (Global Civic) Ethic ignores fundamental values upon which America allegedly is founded, promoting instead a form of global illumined eco-socialism (See Values Education). A strong New Age vehicle for merging political and spiritual objectives, the Global Forum is primarily committed to support of the United Nations, whose New Age meditation group is piloted by Hindu mystic Sri Chinmoy Kumar Ghose.

Biblical Perspective

The "sacred secret" of lawlessness was at work even in Paul's day (2 Thess. 2:7) and will culminate in Antichrist's exalting self as God (2 Thess. 2:4). His supernatural signs and wonders will cause many who fail to love truth to believe his deception (2 Thess. 2:9-12).

As Lucifer incarnate, Antichrist will supposedly triumph in establishing a New World Order, void of so-called Forces of Evil (actually Jews and Christians). Then, the old "Piscean Age" with its obsolete religions will give way to the new, enlightened Age of Aquarius.

Even so, believers need not be alarmed (2 Thess. 2:2). The Bible is clear that God's true plan for peace and harmony will prevail over Satan's counterfeit (See Millennium). When other-minded men and women proclaim "peace and safety" apart from the Prince of Peace, then will come sudden destruction (1 Thess. 5:3). However compelling, the New Age plan and promises will prove sadly defunct in that dismal day (See Great Tribulation, Armageddon).

New Age: Four Pillars
Evolution, Reincarnation, Eastern Religion, Astrology

Evolution (See Evolution.)
Reincarnation (See Reincarnation.)
Eastern Religion (See Buddha.)

New Age Occultists consider Eastern religious leaders, such as Indian swamis and yogis, to be foremost authorities. The most revered mentors are Tibetan monks, presided over by their master, the Dalai Lama.

"Brahman" comes from the root *brih*, meaning "to be great"— this, through yoga, "uniting or yoking with Brahman (the godhead)." In thus yoking with Brahman, the devout Hindu can partake of godhood and, thus, attain the highest state of destiny beyond this physical plane of existence. Toward this pantheistic goal of greatness, there are many paths; but salvation through the shed blood of Jesus is not one of them.

According to Hindu thought, humans presume that they want certain things (discharge of duty, success, pleasure), but what they really want is "being," awareness, joy, and liberation— all attainable, although we are hindered by imperfections and limitations. Life's answer is to transcend the smallness of the finite self by identifying with the impersonal absolute that is at home in the core of each one's being. Individual souls, or *jivas,* evolve toward perfection up the ladder of reincarnation through a sequence of increasingly complex bodies.

While evolving toward presumed greatness, the soul makes choices. To the Buddhist, those who make right choices more closely approach Nirvana, absorption of the finite self into the infinite absolute. To the New Age occultist, more highly evolved personalities have moved from individual to group consciousness. They are "enlightened."

Astrology

"Astrology" comes from two Greek words, *astron* - "star," and *legein* - "speak." It is study of the comparative locale of the planets and stars as they, in turn, influence happenings on Earth. Astrology was a strongly held belief in ancient Babylon and was widely practiced later by Greeks and Romans. Kings and public figures had their own astrologers in medieval Europe. Astrological beliefs are reflected in Jacobean literature, upon whose principles enlightened, or high, Freemasonry stands. The late Lady Diana engaged her own personal astrologer, Debbie Frank, in the last eight years of her life.

At the moment of birth, the astrologer casts a horoscope by charting the position of the sun, moon, and planets relative to the zodiac (band of the celestial sphere divided into twelve equal parts, called signs). Western astrology is based on these twelve signs of the zodiac. To the New Age occultist, astrological charts supply needed information toward making right choices in the evolutionary ladder of progression from embryo-god to supreme oneness with God and the universe. The astrologer assumes the role of counterfeit Holy Spirit in guiding the subject toward his/her mystical goal (See Holy Spirit Imparted).

Biblical Perspective
Evolution

Charles Darwin's deception of "historic optimism" applauds humankind's efforts toward achieving utopia. The historical record proves that, by nature, men apart from divine empowerment wax worse and worse (2 Tim. 3:13); they do not better themselves, as Darwin suggests. Salvation is not of self, lest any presumptuously boast (Eph. 2:9).

The coming thousand-year millennial reign is by no means the utopia New Age occultists anticipate, nor is it the end of the matter for Christians. God's true New World Order will at last consist of a New Heaven and a New Earth with no more tears, death, sorrow, or pain; for the former things shall pass away (Rev. 21: 1, 4, 7). The inheritance promised Christ's Bride will exceed in glory what has even entered the human heart (1 Cor. 2:9).

Reincarnation/Eastern Religion

Claiming never to die or face personal judgment, the New Age occultist believes (s)he will keep returning to earth. Reincarnation will allow additional chances needed to evolve from embryo-god to oneness with the god-force. The Bible, however, warns that it is appointed unto man once to die and after this, the judgment (Heb. 9:27); moreover, earth itself one day will pass away (Matt. 24:35). Finally, and most importantly, God stands alone (Ps. 86:10). Contrary to pantheistic New Age belief, there is no God before Him, beside Him, or after Him (Isa. 43:10-12; 44:6, 8).

Astrology

In the latter times, some will heed seducing spirits and doctrines of demons (1 Tim. 4:1). Whatever the form of superstition, any practice of seeking information apart from God Himself is strictly forbidden (Deut. 18:9-12). A number of terms in the Bible are associated with astrologers—namely, conjurers, necromancers, enchanters, and soothsayers. For their wrongdoing, star gazers and monthly prognosticators shall surely be as stubble (Isa. 47:12-14). Their bogus plan for a coming New Age in the godless New International World Order will surely crumble.

New [International] World Order:
Novus Ordo Seclorum

After the Napoleanic Wars, the Congress of Vienna convened as the first contemporary attempt to create one world government; however, the czar of Russia discovered and subsequently torpedoed the plan. Throughout the first half of the twentieth century, socialists, communists, and capitalist internationalists openly promoted global government. Today they are every bit as zealous and all the more successful.

Code terms for this proposed one world order include: "world law," "collectivist one world state," "interdependence," "convergence," "economic integration," "multilateral institution building," "collective security," "Weltanschauung world view," "new international order," "harmonization/ regionalization" (i.e., eliminating borders of national sovereignty), "globalization" (i.e., redistribution of the world's wealth), "federalized world government," "transnational federal government," "think globally; act locally," "global community/village/vision/nation/neighborhood/civilization/governance/transformation," "unity in diversity," "common future," "New Paradigm," "Third Wave," and "world religion of Open Conspiracy," as described by Fabian Socialist H. G. Wells in *The Open Conspiracy: Blue Prints for a World Revolution* (1928).

Buzz words such as "democracy" and "representation" are used to impart to Americans what Canadian researcher Carl Teichrib identifies as "a skewed sense of reality." To globalists, these words apply exclusively to one world elitist rulers.

New World Order and Conspiracy Theory

All these terms embody *Novus Ordo Seclorum* (Latin for "New World [without God] Order" or "New Order of the Ages"), part of the Great Seal, as inscribed on the one-dollar bill, and an avowed goal of the Illuminati. These so-called "enlightened ones" represented an eighteenth-century Luciferic order founded in Bavaria (Germany) by Adam Weishaupt, a prominent Freemason of the Grand Orient Lodge of France.

This *Novus Ordo Seclorum* will doubtless take form by way of a network of like-minded, high-level officials in pursuit of a common goal; still others believe in a secret cabal of evil men meeting behind closed doors. Alarm over formation of the burgeoning New World Order is not, as some suppose, identified exclusively with turn-of-the-century, right wing hate groups acting in the tradition of the long debunked *Protocols of the Learned Elders of Zion*.

In the *New Freedom* (1913), President Wilson disclosed an organized, interlocked, albeit subtle power that brought fear to some of the biggest Americans in commerce and manufacturing, but none dared call it conspiracy. On 21 November 1933 President F. D. Roosevelt identified "a financial element in the larger centers" which "has owned the Government since the days of Andrew Jackson." More recently, in his masterwork *Tragedy and Hope* (1966), Professor Carroll Quigley (President Clinton's mentor at Georgetown University) documents existence of an international network of Round Table Groups that prefer to remain unknown.

The Eastern Liberal Establishment is an euphemism for a deliberately anonymous membership whose viewpoint is called globalism. At the center of Insider power, influence, and planning, the Council on Foreign Relations, said by some to be America's version of the Illuminati, purposes to abolish national sovereignty for globalism. With the Council on Foreign Relations as their "brain," CFR spin-off groups wield three arms of power: economic (Bilderbergers), spiritual (Club of Rome), and political (Trilateral Commission). The handbook of the occult-driven Club of Rome includes plans for a ten region world government, calling for a New World Economic Order (See Global Economics/Banking). CFR president Leslie Gelb admits "It's one world now."

New World Order and the USA

Although, unlike Gelb, "father of liberal internationalism" Joseph S. Nye, Jr. views the prospect of world government as slim, he nonetheless believes that U.S. choices will no doubt determine its makeup—whether uni-, bi-, or multi- polar; fashioned in economic, and/or military or bio-regional blocs, or exercising multilevel interdependence. Significantly, all agree that the New World Order will not be an era of American dominance, nor will the system be Americanized. Indeed, its very nature necessitates consensus between international capitalism and Marxism.

New World Order and the United Nations/Presidio

The cornerstone of the New World Order is the United Nation's concept of sustainable development, which calls for population control and redistribution of the world's wealth (See Abortion; Death Culture; Planned Parenthood). The New Earth (Global Civic) Ethic promotes its form of global socialism, which excludes national sovereignty and private property rights (See Political Correctness Movement; Values Education).

In his historic address to the United Nations (7 December 1988), Mikhail Gorbachev first spoke openly about a coming New World Order, which he called the "New Paradigm." Former President George Bush has been identified as the first notable Insider to use the term "New World Order" openly and in public, starting with the Gulf War (1990). In a 1991 State of the Union message, Bush extolled "universal aspirations" based on "shared principles" and the "rule of the law." Even now, he added, "the winds of change are with us."

The term "global governance" was used in place of New World Order, considered too charged for the 1995 State of the World Forum sponsored by the Gorbachev Foundation located at the Presidio in San Francisco. Today this "White House on the West Coast" actively works for the New International World Order. The UN's 420-page 1996 report, *Our Global Neighborhood*, outlines a plan and calls for a 1998 Conference on Global Governance to submit needed treaties and agreements for ratification by the year 2000.

The spiritual dimension of the Presidio is evident as conference participants include a Zen Center representative (See Buddha; New Age: Four Pillars), disciples of Pierre Teilhard de Chardin (See New Age Movement), and New Age occultist Maurice Strong, Secretary-general of the Rio Earth Summit Conference (See Radical Environmentalism). Strong advocates making his own Colorado Mecca for mystics, *Baca Grande*, the "Vatican City" of the New World Order.

New World Order and Gods of Olympus

The Olympic Movement claims more nation-states than the United Nations. The official Olympic Symbol of five interlocking rings represents union of the five continents. Tracing back to worship of Zeus, its acclaimed "spirit" is defined by global har-

mony and peace through competition and ceremony soaked in
ancient mystery religion ritual. One such example is passing its
holy torch of enlightenment.

New World Order and Secret Societies/Occultists
(See Ancient Mystery Religions)

Internationally-linked illumined Freemasons are united by a
common code and a clandestine agenda of occult globalism with
a central theme of universality. Another of the most powerful
secret organizations from Yale University, the Skull and Bones,
also aims for an absolute state. David Rockefeller, George Bush
(reportedly a thirty-third degree Mason), and William Buckley
are three of its many famous initiates.

New World Order and New Age Movement

New Age occultists believe global unity to be essential to the
proper flow of the god-force (See Pantheism). The coming Age
of Aquarius will feature cosmic group consciousness under a new
Messiah, actually Antichrist, worshipped as God. Toward harmony and peace, mystics anticipate humankind's taking the quantum leap to its climactic Omega Point, or mass planetary Luciferic
Initiation, which is actually demon possession referred to as "transformation."

New World Order and the Social Services

Social services organizations, such as the Rotary Club, support one world efforts, believed by some to be accomplished by
means of social Darwinism. Charles Darwin's historic optimism
contends that mankind—in his thinking, philosophy, destiny—is
getting progressively better with the passing of time. By extrapolation, Darwin somehow felt assured that man's efforts, apart from
God, will yield a future utopia, a sort of New World Order.

New World Order and Secular Humanism

Humanism exalts man as the measure of all things. Its four
goals include a science-based one world religion, global economics requiring redistribution of the world's wealth, a Declaration of
Interdependence for a coming anti-Christian, anti-American
"world community," and a new species for this New World Order.
Whereas the New Age mystic looks for a new species resulting from a planetary quantum leap to "christhood," the godless

humanist hopes to control his own evolution by means of social and genetic engineering.

Educators Dr. Horace Mann, John Dewey, and Dewey's disciples were instrumental in promulgating humanism's agenda. Among the forty-two professors who signed the *Humanist Manifesto II* was B. F. Skinner, father of Operant Conditioning (basis for many contemporary instructional practices). The 1973 *Humanist Manifesto II* points to the dawn of a New Age toward "transnational federal government."

The international Aspen Institute for Humanistic Studies, a private, non-profit organization, attracts leading officials of the Trilateral Commission, the Rockefeller Foundation, and the White House to attend advanced seminars in global ideology. Most materials developed there find their way into public school textbooks (See Textbook Conspiracy).

New World Order and Education

At the turn of the century, John Dewey's Progressive Education classrooms downgraded the individual while distinguishing the group. Among stated goals of this admittedly godless system were a new economic system and a new world religion (curious in light of Dewey's confessed atheism). Progressivism called for a new race under genetic engineering and carefully structured attitude adjustment and behavior modification (See Values Education). Its motto was "one world; one species."

Published by U.S. educators, the 1948 preliminary draft of a *World Constitution* provided for a "World Council" with a "Chamber of Guardians" to enforce world law. On 5 December 1980 the United Nations General Assembly formulated the Global Education Project, a model for global education and source for teacher training and curriculum development of every nation. At the heart of education restructuring in the United States is this international curriculum based on former UN Assistant Secretary-general Robert Muller's World Core Curriculum.

All members of the Design Teams for this Global Education Project are activists for globalism and New Age philosophy. The esoteric purpose is to bring out children's "personal values" (in conformity, of course, with the group) that they might emerge as planetary "light-bearers" of the coming New Age (See Values Education). The proper worker of tomorrow's New World Order must demonstrate go-with-the-flow collectivism, coupled with politically correct attitudes and behaviors. The Secretary of Labor's Commission on Achieving Necessary Skills (SCANS) pinpoints human capital and resource material for tomorrow's work force. The Outcome-Based Education (OBE) model in today's public school system is designed to bring forth these "proper workers."

Founded in 1951, Seattle's World Affairs Council joins other one world efforts, nationally and internationally, in promoting its Global Classroom concept, thus preparing high school students for an inevitably international future.

New World Order and the Political Correctness Movement

The term political correctness is an umbrella under which a number of other causes unite. Included are civil/gender/sexual orientation rights and radical environmentalism, providing the chief argument for need of a world government. Significantly, the political correctness movement insures the appropriate mindset for the coming New World Order. The movement's program is to tear down Western civilization, specifically European/American culture. Toward this goal, multiculturalism (diversity) redefines America essentially out of existence, thus making room for the "global community."

New World Order and Islamic Fundamentalism; Catholicism (meaning "universality")

According to Iran and her Muslim allies, the Judeo-Christian World Order must be supplanted with a New Islamic World Order by means of *jihad,* thus exerting Iran's military authority in the region and, at the same time, her spiritual authority over the entire Muslim world (See Islamic Fundamentalism).

No doubt Pope John Paul II has his own idea, for he believes himself destined to rule the coming New World Order, which, he claims, is fated to be in place by the end of the present decade.

Biblical Perspective

Whereas the Plan of God moves yielded man from "glory to glory" (2 Cor. 3:18) toward oneness with Christ and the Heavenly Father (John 17), the counterfeit plan moves yielded man from "degradation to degradation" (2 Tim. 3:13) toward pantheistic oneness with the god-force in all forms of life (Rom. 1:25).

Whereas the Plan of God points toward a godly New World Order (Millennial Kingdom; then, New Heaven/Earth, Rev. 20:1-7; 21:1), the counterfeit plan points to an ungodly New International World Order (under one world government, Rev. 13:1, 7). But the wicked shall not inhabit the earth as they suppose (Prov. 10:30). Instead, their expectation will perish (verse 28).

Whereas the Plan of God anticipates the theocratic reign of Christ with His Bride in the Millennium (Rev. 11:15), the counterfeit plan anticipates the dictorial reign of Antichrist, undergirded by his False Prophet (Rev. 13:1, 12).

Whereas the Plan of God allows purchase of wine (blessings of God) and milk (strength of God) without money, or price (Isa. 55:1), the counterfeit plan calls for a cashless society with redistribution of the world's wealth, this under control of Antichrist and his superior race of god-men emissaries (Dan. 11:39).

Whereas the Plan of God is ushered in by believers (1 Cor. 6:2), supported by unfallen angels (Ps. 91:11; Luke 4:10), and in union with the higher stimulus of the Holy Spirit (Acts 1:8), the counterfeit plan is ushered in by sinners (Jude 15), supported by fallen angels (1 Cor. 10:20-21; 1 Tim. 4:1; Rev. 9:20), and in union with Satan (2 Cor. 4:4 with Gen. 3:5). Moreover, the latter is paired with the lower stimuli of enchantments with drugs (*pharmakeia*, or "sorceries," in Rev. 9:21 and 18:23).

Whereas the Plan of God produces holiness unto the Lord, glorifying Jesus Christ (Rev. 21:10-11), the counterfeit plan produces a worldwide pantheistic mystery cult, glorifying Lucifer (Rev. 13:1, 11-12).

Novus Ordo Seclorum

New World [without God] Order; New World Order of Ages

Interdependent collectivist one-world state with enlightened collaborative consciousness

Harmonization (Undermining sovereignty of nation-states)
Bioregionalism (Restructuring around natural ecosystems)
Globalism (Redistributing the world's wealth)
Communization (Concentrating wealth in the hands of few)
Totalitarianism (Concentrating power in the hands of few)
Global Governance (Managing masses by international law)

Philip Isely (WCPA)
Dave Foreman (Wildlands Project)
Gro Harlem Brundtland (Sustainability)
George C. Lodge (Communitarianism)
Mikhail Gorbachev
Thomas Malthus; Paul Ehrlich

CFR
Club of Rome
Trilateral Commission
Bilderberg Group
Presidio
United Nations, WCPA

Central Guiding Principle

New Earth [Global Civic Ethic]

New-world view taught in public education; promotes
enlightened eco-socialism. While giving overriding
preference to the environment and to the world's poor,
it effectively eliminates private property rights.

Historical Components
Secularism (Rousseau)
Naturalism (Pestalozzi)
Permissivism (Horace Mann)
Pragmatism (William James)
Scientific/Social Evolution (Darwin)
Secular Humanism (Dewey)
Pluralism/Reality (Counts, Rugts, Nearing)
Moral Relativism (Rath-Simon Theory)
Added Components, Restructuring
Hegelian Dialectics/Behavior Modification
Certificates of Mastery (National ID)
Polytech Education (School-to Work)
Cradle-to-grave Lifelong Learning
Cosmic Eco-education (Robert Muller)

Philosophical Base

Political Correctness

New-fashioned holistic, integrated, or
"systems thinking" defined by:

Asia- / Afro-centrism
Deconstructionism
Alternative Lifestyle Privilege
Radical Genderism
Radical Environmentalism
Multiculturalism (Diversity)

Religious Base

Neo-Pantheistic Syncretism

Muddles Biblical Christianity with Ecumenicism
Espouses Universalism (e.g., Freemasonry)
IDs "all" as "energy," part of the god-force
Anticipates cosmic illumination with its
quantum leap to group consciousness while
promising New Age egoic advancement
by means of multiple reincarnations toward
Nirvana (Luciferic Initiation)

Central Organizing Principle

U.N. Sustainable Development

Its 3-E's:

Environment
Founded on Lovelock's Gaia Hypothesis
Embraces Bio-centrism, Zero Population Growth
Executes Neo-Pantheistic Eco-Justice
Promotes Eco-activism/ Eco-socialism

Economy
Founded on flawed premise of Malthusianism
Functions by Foundation-omics
Hopes to exact world taxes (Boutros-Ghali)
Seeks to redistribute the world's wealth
Global Eco-nomics favors the "eco" system

Equity
Aims for agrarian "urban clusters" for the masses
Allows for a "ruling elite" of intellectuals and world bankers
(Therefore, some are dubbed more "equal" than others.)
Promotes "tolerance" that is deceptively selective

Nobel Prize

Alfred Nobel was the Swedish chemist who invented dynamite. Under his will, the Nobel Prize is an international honor awarded each year to organizations or individuals. Prizes feature large cash awards. Starting in 1901, Nobel endowment fund interest has been divided annually among persons recognized as having made the greatest contributions in fields of physics, chemistry, medicine, literature, and world peace. Academic committees in Sweden award the first four, and a committee of the Norwegian parliament awards the coveted peace prize. Financed by the Swedish National Bank, a sixth prize for economics was first awarded in 1969.

The Nobel Prize is said to generate free publicity for "one worldism." You see, a high percentage of these prizes is awarded to people recognized for global views, as is the case with the Rhodes Scholarship Fund. Among recent winners are the United Nations peacekeeping forces (1988), the Dalai Lama (Tibet 1989), and President Mikhail Gorbachev (USSR, 1990; See New World Order). One of its most exemplary recipients, the late Mother Teresa, joined the Dalai Lama and Marilyn Ferguson (See New Age Movement; New Age: Four Pillar), Prince Bernhardt (See Bilderbergers) and Robert Muller (See Outcome-Based Education), among other globalists, at the 1985 "Spirit of Peace" Conference sponsored by the United Nations University of Peace. The featured agenda called for a New World Order.

Biblical Perspective

See Rhodes Scholarship Fund.

North Atlantic Treaty Organization (NATO)

The United States is credited with revival of the once devastated Europe by means of the North Atlantic Treaty Organization and the Marshall Plan. Set up in 1949 as an alliance binding Europe to the U.S., NATO offered consolidated defense, principally against the threat of the USSR, to primary Western European and North American states. Since its inception, NATO has grappled with a number of perplexing issues, not least of which is burden sharing.

With the Council of Foreign Ministers as NATO's chief body, its international secretariat is in Brussels, Belgium. Also in Belgium, near Mons, is SHAPE (Supreme Headquarters Allied Powers, Europe), its military headquarters. In 1960 NATO established a permanent multi-national Allied Mobile Force (AMF) with headquarters in Heidelberg, Germany, to move at once to any NATO country under threat of attack.

The Warsaw Pact is NATO's counterpart. Established in 1955, the Warsaw Pact was a military alliance between the USSR and communist states of Eastern Europe. Originally formed in response to West Germany's admission to NATO, the pact was formally dissolved in July 1991.

According to Dr. Jesse Chiang, Professor Emeritus of political science, Seattle Pacific University, NATO expansion is "nothing short of courting disaster." Still, as the major foreign policy legacy of his second term, President Clinton vigorously supports NATO expansion to embrace Poland, Hungary, and the Czech Republic. Even so, limited mainstream media attention was given the 1996 NATO Enlargement Facilitation Act, the July 1997 NATO Summit in Madrid, and the December 1996 foreign ministers meeting which set it.

NATO's stated mission is "peace-keeping." In 1990 the organization declared that nuclear weapons were "weapons of last resort"; furthermore, NATO offered to withdraw all nuclear artillery shells from Europe if the USSR did likewise. In October of 1991 President Bush's unilateral cutback in U.S. nuclear arms correspondingly reduced NATO arms. Keep in mind, however, that the president of the U.S. Committee to Expand NATO, Bruce Jackson, also serves as director of strategic planning for the world's biggest weapon maker, the Lockeed Martin Corporation.

Moreover, prospective new nations of NATO must cut needed social spending to elevate military funding levels. Says Dr. Chiang, to expand NATO is to revive fear and provide excuse for the Russian military to increase spending on arms to match the threat. Expansion makes nuclear disarmament unlikely, even impossible, thus dooming the chances of SALT II and III.

Not surprisingly, NATO is a member nation of the coterie of elite globalists, the Bilderberg group. Furthermore, every U.S.

ambassador to NATO has been a member of the Rockefeller-funded Council on Foreign Relations or its spin-off, the Trilateral Commission. All aim to build a New International World Order.

Biblical Perspective

According to the Great Eschatological Discourse, these latter days will be increasingly encumbered with wars and rumors of war (Matt. 24:6). Despite seemingly noble intent, alliances are by nature brittle and limited. As nations rise against nations and kingdoms against kingdoms (verse 7), the love of many will "cool off" (verse 12). Yet humans continue to seek strength in the inept "arm of flesh," as did ill-advised men and women of old (2 Chron. 32:8).

Undoubtedly, humankind's hostilities will continue to escalate, while God is at work to the contrary to consummate His plan on Earth (Matt. 24:6). Truly, conflicts are destined to intensify, even to the point of Great Tribulation climaxed by Armageddon, surpassing any other time period (verse 21). Ironically, sudden destruction is the promised outcome for those who cry "peace and safety" apart from submission to the Prince of Peace (1 Thess. 5:3).

God's Plan for a New World Order is not the universal community of nations, nor is it "collective security," as envisioned by globalists. Rather, it is Christ's Millennial Reign, featuring unity of the spirit under theocratic headship, not earthly alliance alone, and promising a certain end, once and for all, to godless global aspirations, uprisings, and warfare typical of these last days.

O

Outcome-Based Education (OBE)

OBE Defined

Outcome-Based Education is synonymous with Mastery Learning, Restructuring, the Outcomes-Driven Development Model, Performance or Competency Based Education, and more. It is a major component of Bush's America 2000 and Clinton's Goals 2000 (signed into law March 1994).

Goals 2000 is simply federal control of local schools that makes OBE a national curriculum. OBE changes the way children are trained, evaluated, and graduated. It teaches labor skills, coupled with appropriate attitudes and behaviors to serve well the burgeoning global economic community (See Global Economics/Banking). Eventually, all will be groomed for specific predetermined entry-level occupations. Goals 2000 applies not just to school children, but also to adults who likewise must qualify for the global work force.

Whereas Goals 2000 provides the plan, HR 6 (1994 Reauthorization of the Elementary and Secondary Act) provides the funding. Signed into law by Clinton in May of 1994, the School-to-Work Opportunity Act creates both the Bureau of Apprenticeship and Training, responsible for issuing skills certificates, and a federal data bank of personal information, the Labor Market Information System (LMIS), which threatens citizen privacy rights. The once defeated Careers Act of Congressman, Buck McKeon (1995), has returned, this time diluted into three parts. It repeals the School-to-Work Act, but only in attempt to make Hillary Clinton's Human Resource Development Plan and its federal job placement program the law of the land.

The first National Education Goal affirms that "all children will enter school ready to learn." For this to be the case necessarily presupposes state intervention into every family with infants, toddlers, and preschoolers. Additional goals are 90 percent graduation rate, increased parental involvement, and professional development for educators. Students are to be afforded drug-free, safe schools, and America aims to lead the world in math and science—all by the year 2000. Under Clinton's administration, OBE is progressing at local, state, federal, and global levels. Even if a state has not accepted Goals 2000 funding, OBE is being used in local schools.

OBE: NASDC, NESIC, G-CERF, CSL

Goals 2000 works principally through a non-governmental, nonprofit organization, the New American Schools Development Corporation (NASDC), consisting of corporate sponsors. Under NASDC, eleven "Design Teams" implement education policies in keeping with the six National Education Goals. The Board of Directors for NASDC is replete with members of the Council on Foreign Relations, whose aim is to abolish national sovereignty for globalism (See New World Order).

The National Education Standards and Improvement Council (NESIC) is tantamount to a Washington-controlled national school board; and G-CERF (Governor's Council on Education Reform and Funding) is an unelected committee responsible for drafting a proposal to replace basic education requirements. Another unelected committee, the Commission on Student Learning (CSL), is scheduled to implement them.

OBE: Theoretical Basis

Says Wayne Wolf in the *Iowa Report* (January 1993), the brains behind America 2000 is Dr. Chester Finn, Jr., chief architect of Bush's plan to reform the nation's schools. In theory, OBE borrows heavily from Ivan Pavlov's programmed learning and B.F. Skinner's research in behavior modification. Director of the International Center on Outcome-Based Restructuring William Spady is credited with developing OBE's Skinnerian operant conditioning model.

In OBE, students are grouped not by grade or age, but rather by performance. They are pretested, taught the curriculum, then assessed for mastery. If necessary, the loop of remediation and reassessment is repeated until the desired exit outcome, or goal, is met. In *We Must Take Charge of Our Schools and Our Future* (1991), Dr. Finn advocates specific advantage conferred exclusively on those who meet core national outcomes.

Resting on the assumption that knowledge and skills are hierarchical, and that one needs to learn the basics before going on to more advanced skills, OBE requires every child to master all state-mandated goals in order to graduate to the next level of proficiency. This concept reflects Benjamin Bloom's Taxonomy, which presents moral relativism as the highest possible cognitive goal (See Values Education). Even so, Bloom's Mastery Learning experiment in Chicago proved such a failure that in 1982 it was abandoned in disgrace.

OBE: Political Correctness Movement

In her May 1993 newsletter, Phyllis Schlafly charges that "OBE is converting the three R's to the three D's: Deliberately Dumbed Down." "Understanding and appreciating others in the world community," "self-esteem," "ethical judgment" (albeit situational and self-serving), "change adaptation," and "proper environmental attitudes" up-stage reading, writing, and arithmetic, which now occupy only about one-fourth of the school day. You see, OBE rebuts the conservative 1930s educational theory of Essentialism, which rightly heralded academic standards and discipline.

In the OBE model, individual liberty, majoritarian democracy, and limited government take back seat to tenets of multiculturalism and other politically correct "-ism's." For example, through National Geography Standards, children are effectually molded into rabid environmentalists (See Radical Environmentalism). Indeed, responsible global citizenship becomes the primary purpose for all education.

Until recently, Pennsylvania's Educational Quality Assessment (EQA) was administered to grades 5, 8, and 11. Significantly, only thirty academic questions are posed. Of the 385 attitudinal questions asked, the correct response is rapid emotional adjustment to change—without protest and for the universal good. State-desired responses are rated right or wrong, despite their highly subjective nature.

OBE's mission statement is that "all children can learn." By employing collaborative, or cooperative, learning tactics, and by exchanging bell-curve grading (A-B-C-D-F) for the J-curve (A-B-I), all children appear to succeed. However, affective (emotional, attitudinal), not academic (scholastic), goals produce workers, not thinkers; group members, not individuals.

OBE and Special Education

If a student's ethical judgments are not politically correct, as defined by the state, that student is subjected repeatedly to the learning loop until (s)he "converts" to the worldview. Nonconformists are labeled "at risk" and become subject to special education placement (apparently no longer reserved for students with congenital differences).

OBE and "Coded" Vocabulary

In OBE, the teacher no longer teaches; (s)he "facilitates" as a change agent. Education has little to do with reading, writing, and arithmetic; instead, it stresses adaptability to managed change. Career Education does not necessarily prepare the student for a chosen profession; instead, it fits that student to the workforce needs of the New World Order. Multidisciplinary, thematic curricula produce desired group-conscious attitudes. Students are viewed as "human resources" for a coming "Brave New World," while at the same time, some are encouraged to pursue the "higher self" of New Age mysticism.

OBE, World Curriculum Reform, and Esoteric Philosophy

On 5 December 1980 the United Nations General Assembly created a model for worldwide teacher training and curriculum development—i.e., the Global Education Project, called the University of Peace in Costa Rica.

The United Nations Ambassador from Costa Rica, Carlos José Gutierrez, issued a letter to the General Assembly on 11 October 1989, the content of which affirms that humankind must strive for complete unity with nature (See Pantheism: "All is Energy").

At the heart of restructuring is the Global Education Project, based on the World Core Curriculum of Robert Muller, author of *New Genesis—Shaping a Global Spirituality* (1984), and former UN Assistant Secretary-general. Unbelievably, Muller credited creation of his World Core Curriculum to teachings of Djwahl Kuhl, Tibetan spirit guide for Theosophist Alice Bailey; therefore, the basis for this new education model is taken directly from writings of Lucis (formerly Lucifer) Trust Publishing Company. An avid student of mystic Pierre Teilhard de Chardin, Dr. Muller sustains eleven Schools of Ageless Wisdom nationwide.

Dr. Muller promotes the need for "cosmic education," foreseen by educators such as physician Maria Montessori, a mystic whose system of instructional play fits into an evolutionary social movement, spanning childhood through adulthood (See Charles Darwin). Based on a student's profile, established by means of Alice Bailey's seven-ray multiple intelligences, the student is funneled into a job or career classification to which (s)he is suited to best serve the global community. To qualify, the student must demonstrate cosmic humanism, the belief that all life forms are evolving to a higher state of consciousness (See New Age: Four Pillars, Eastern Religion).

While ushering children into self-realization of the spark of divinity within, the World Core Curriculum promotes such Eastern meditation techniques as guided fantasies into space, or astral projection (See Transcendental Meditation/Altered State of Consciousness). This education system is unmistakably holistic. As such, it interconnects all life forms on the planet. No one life form is superior to another, and the individual's value is only in reference to the whole. Simply put, not to fit into the New World Order renders one alarmingly "expendable."

All members of the design teams for the Global Education Project embrace these notions (See New Age; Radical Environmentalism). They are New Age activists, such as Dorothy J. Maver, who serves on the steering committee of possibly the most significant group behind education reform, the Global Alliance for Transforming Education.

OBE Modeled in Arkansas

Bill Clinton's Governor's School represents the model after which all school districts in Arkansas are to restructure. In addition to promoting politically correct liberal ideologies, the school promotes mystical practices of astral projection (out-of-body experiences), mind-bending manipulation, and New Age relaxation techniques. Although the Bible is outlawed, Zen Buddhist literature is assigned to students, who are encouraged to seek "oneness with the universe" (See Buddha; Pantheism).

OBE and Religious Rightness in the World Community

A stated goal of the UN prize-winning World Core Curriculum is to aid the child in developing and maintaining "a balance between *spiritual* [emphasis added], mental, emotional, physical, and academic development." The esoteric purpose is to bring out "personal" (actually group-shared) values at odds with true Christianity and the Bible (See Authenticity of Scriptures; Political Correctness Movement; Values Education).

OBE and Computer-Assisted Instruction

By federal mandate, the state now develops data banks at the micro-record level for individual students. Data banks log personal family information and biographical data relating to financial status, race, socio-cultural heritage, family structure, physical status and health, drug history, mental astuteness, psychological character, proficiency skills, and non-school performance.

These data are entered while students engage in computer-assisted instruction. With family status and values logged in these data banks, the National Center of Education Federal Data Bank can track student, teacher, and curriculum-linked data through the Drug Free Schools and Community Act (1986). This Exchange of Permanent Records Electronically for Students and Schools (via Internet's electronic superhighway—formatted by SPEEDE/ExPRESS) can be accessed by any educational agency without parental knowledge and, theoretically, by any non-school agency with consent.

OBE and Electronic Computer Resumés

Given OBE, vocational aptitude will be pinpointed and channeled through the education system, and the electronic computer resumé will insure the applicant's placement. Piloted in Indiana, the electronic computer resumé will go to employers from the school district. Job placement or promotions can be denied if the candidate fails to live up to set state standards—again, in the affective domain (truly not measurable, but measured nonetheless). No longer will an applicant be allowed to select his own references.

Domestic and foreign corporations will "think globally" while career-guided workers will "act locally" in response to the projected job market in their own geographical area—all for the good of the New World Order.

OBE and CIM

Legislation has been introduced into states to tie drivers licenses, health care, job permits, and more to "graduation" as evidenced by a Certificate of Initial Mastery (CIM), issued *en lieu* of the high school diploma. Before long, personal information will be transferred to a micro chip, then placed on a card that everyone will need in order to drive, work, marry, or vote (See Mark of the Beast: 666, and Related Technology).

OBE: Today's Student; Tomorrow's Worker

Formed by the U.S. Department of Labor (May 1990), the Secretary of Labor's Commission on Achieving Necessary Skills (SCANS) pinpoints human capital and resource material for tomorrow's workforce, determining what skills will be needed. SCANS became the blueprint for education laws passed in the mid-1990s.

The idea is nationalization of the work force. Tomorrow's proper global citizen and worker must demonstrate go-with-the-flow collectivism, coupled with state-sanctioned, politically correct behaviors and attitudes with regard to morality, spirituality, family, environment, and the like. The national school-to-work system will mandate adult retraining to qualify for required Certificates of Initial/Advanced Mastery. The CIM will indicate that a student has achieved the universally-recognized standard of SCANS work place know-how.

OBE and Volunteerism

President Clinton advocates a national service program for youth. When combined with industrial production and government-mandated service, free public education for all children is part of Karl Marx's *Communist Manifesto* (planks eight and ten).

OBE: The Why-Not's
Outcome Flaws

Whereas most impartial studies of OBE show some achievement gains for the bottom of the class (the system is effective when applied individually in special education), these gains are offset by losses at the top of the class. Robert Slavin of Johns Hopkins University identifies OBE as the "Robin Hood approach to learning," for bright students are kept from advancement as lower achievers are catered to (*Family Voice* [November/December 1993] 29).

When OBE was recently used in Brownsville (Fayette County, PA), ninety-three percent of the teachers and two thousand parents united to discard it from the district. Whereas there are slight improvements in short-term learning by the group as a whole, standardized testing shows no significant long-term comprehension. A John Hopkins University study (1987) found no evidence that OBE resulted in increased academic achievement. The conclusion of their own longitudinal study was that children retained more per hour of instructional time in non-mastery classrooms. In a word, where it has been tried, OBE has failed.

Although the movement promises local control, this means nothing when schools are locked in to national policy and guidelines. Community commissars, not school board members, implement the New American Schools strategy. Finally, through OBE's site-based management, the liberal National Education Association is regretfully empowered.

Use Flaws

If seen only as a method, Mastery Learning makes sense when applied sensibly—that is, in the special education classroom, as traditionally defined, for the sole purpose of strengthening deficient academic skills and discipline. Unlike traditional education, which is time-predetermined (180 days), OBE is achievement-predetermined—that is, all students get A's, or "aim's" (usually requiring only 80 percent accuracy), no matter how long it takes them. This concept is acceptable, and even preferred, for the exceptional student in special education, but certainly not in the mainstream.

As a graduate research assistant at the University of Washington (1979), I participated in a federal grant, CHARTS, and, as such, assessed model special education programs featuring Mastery Learning in several Washington public school districts and in Great Falls, Montana. Given the Direct Instruction (DI) model with continuous assessment of reading, spelling, and math facts, I found OBE learning principles to be effective, not harmful, as some presume. In fact, I employed them successfully in a Christian school's special education classrooms. Be assured, it is not the learning loop itself, but rather the content fed through that loop which is objectionable. Broader aims of Goals 2000 pose the real threat.

Others argue that OBE is not a teaching method at all, but rather a procedure developed by psychologists to modify behavior. Even so, many psychologists oppose the system. They claim that psycho-therapeutic techniques are needed to change attitudes and behaviors relating to self-esteem or adaptability to change. For educators to employ the OBE model is equivalent to practicing psychology without a license.

Given computerized recording of personal data, identification of student learning styles, and tight monitoring of "progress," it is possible for would-be psychologists to use OBE to fine tune political or spiritual sentiment to their own liking. Through Goals 2000, OBE, one stop social clinics, school-to-work, and lifelong learning programs, educrats can and will mold children as they desire.

Because standards for targeted personal qualities are arbitrary, the potential for abuse is enormous. For example, if in evaluating the ability to reach group consensus, a Christian child cannot in good conscience go along with the worldview, (s)he is subject to a sort of persecution. Labeled "at risk," that student may be passed inappropriately into special education.

Biblical Perspective

In many ways, Goals 2000 uses schools to supplant God-ordained family. Toward this end, it seeks to lower the entrance age for kindergarten and to lengthen the school year. Incredibly, America's admittedly godless education system that effectively supplants the Judeo-Christian ethic with its own brand of relativism has presumed to take charge of our children's character development. Moreover, OBE obligates every citizen, regardless of age, to be involved in the educational process; hence, no one escapes its indoctrination. Children and parents alike are required to perform community service, ofttimes conflicting with Christian ministries they would prefer to participate in.

Goals 2000 aims for collaborative, high-quality contribution to the economic and cultural life of the global community. In celebrating diversity, students are required to participate in activities that by nature violate the Christian's call to holiness and separatism (John 15:19; Eph. 5:11). OBE's stewardship toward the global environment requires holistic beliefs that, contrary to the Bible, place all life on equal footing (Matt. 10:31). To be a responsible, involved, cosmic citizen, at one with the universe, as OBE directs, opposes the Biblical admonition to be strangers and pilgrims on earth (Heb. 11:13); in the world, but not of it (John 17:16).

Through Goals 2000 and its proposed national curriculum (OBE), pantheistic premises of New Age theology are being promulgated on cue in America's public education system toward fashioning global citizens (Earth stewards) for a coming New World Order ostensibly built on Antichrist's delusionary lie of 2 Thessalonians 2:11.

ABCs of OBE

O utcome-Based *Egalitarianism* more accurate.

U se of electronic portfolios.

T eam-teaching; peer tutoring; forced community service.

C ompetition de-emphasized.

O ut with diploma; in with Certificates of Mastery.

M ulti-age groupings; mainstreaming (inclusive education).

E xtended school year & class blocks; fewer courses.

B ell Curve *(A-B-C-D-F)* replaced with J-Curve *(A-B-I)*.

A ll succeed; *All children can learn* mission statement.

S ite-based management; team control above local board.

E ducators facilitate; *computers* teach.

D e-emphasis of facts, knowledge (content).

E mphasis on "higher-order" thinking (moral relativism).

D emonstrated outcomes, not Carnegie Units, to graduate.

U nion of *human* resources with the business community.

C ooperative learning; consensus building; collaboration.

A nnual report issued at district, building levels.

T hematic teaching (all classes teach to same theme).

I ndividualism out; collectivism and gender norming in.

O utcomes constant; time to accomplish them varies.

N ew Basics: politically-correct behaviors, attitudes.

P

Pantheism ("All is Energy")

Pantheism originated in the ancient city of Babylon in Mesopotamia (Iraq today). From there it spread rapidly, virtually covering the earth. The Greek word *pan* means "all." *Theos* means "God." Pantheism regards all life forms as divine. The God Pan is worshipped in witchcraft as Lucifer (See Ancient Mystery Religions). Pantheistic tenets are expressed in Egyptian religion, Brahmanism, stoicism, and Neo-Platonism. Its philosophers include Bruno, Spinoza, Fichte, Schelling, and Hegel.

Pantheism and the Earth (See Radical Environmentalism)

Neo-pantheistic Ecotheology starts with the premise that the universe is God. Vice President Gore has written of his own pantheistic awareness of "a constant and holy spiritual presence in all people, all life, and all things." To the pantheist, the fundamental reality of the universe is that the god-force flows through all living entities. In order to maintain nature's fragile balance of energy flow, humankind must be responsible to save "Mother Earth." Toward this end, pantheists tolerate worship of all gods of various cultures, like Gaia, so-called goddess of the Earth. After all, to the pantheist, there is no personal god to whom humankind is accountable (See Multiculturalism).

Pantheism and Animals (See Radical Environmentalism)

Pantheism forms the basis for today's animal rights movement as embraced by Peter Singer of Animal Liberation. The motto of People for the Ethical Treatment of Animals (PeTA) is this: "Animals are not ours to eat, wear, experiment on, or use in entertainment." PeTA co-founder and national director, Ingrid Newkirk, is quoted as having said, "A rat is a pig is a dog is a boy." To the pantheistic animal activist, people have no more rights than animals; all are part of the god-force.

To some, animals are due even more rights than humans, who are historically guilty of "taking dominion" and, consequently, wreaking havoc with energy balance, as defined by pantheists.

The United Nations is taking the lead in correcting presumed ills. Dr. Reed F. Noss, developer of the UN Wildlands Project, describes biosphere core and buffer zones as places where "collective needs of non-human species must take precedence over the needs and desires of humans."

Examples are numberless. Whereas thousands of acres have been set aside in south Alabama for habitat of the Red Hills salamander, humans are being forced to uproot and relocate. In similar fashion, Idaho's Snake River Valley farmers and ranchers are being cut off from their essential water supply in an effort to protect the Bruneau Hot Springs snail, which is no larger than a pencil point.

Pantheism and Energy

To the pantheist, God is the sum total of all that exists. Since energy flows through us, we, too, are Gods, or part of God. Discovering "the higher self" is achieved by means of transformation (i.e., demon possession). Along these lines, New Age author Marilyn Ferguson and José Arguelles preach a PAN philosophy. The PAN (Planet Art Network) is a global association of artists working for New Age transformation and the coming New World Order (See National Endowment for the Arts).

New Age occultists believe that a mass planetary Luciferic Initiation will progress humankind from individual to group consciousness, at which time "enlightened" humanity will suddenly be endowed with psychic powers, promising ability to use the "light" side of the god-force for good ("white magic" in Wicca). No doubt Antichrist will lead the way, being hailed for his psychic powers and telepathic communication, thus proving his "christhood." Nonetheless, in the New Age-to-come, it is alleged that virtually all will exercise such powers. ESP is seen as just another skill people can and will learn (See Age of Aquarius).

The neo-pantheist seeks to steer the energy force. In Zen Buddhism, for example, "divine breathing" is known as *pranayama*, Sanskrit for "controlling the energy force" (See Buddha). Similarly, New Age occultists are encouraged to wear crystals, which they believe to be "life beings" which send out energy used for psychic healing. Also, Therapeutic Touch is lauded as a sort of cerebral biofeedback application. Started by Delores Krieger, this popular New Age treatment is administered by the therapist's hands sweeping along, but not touching, the body of a patient. "Bad" forces are eliminated with the flick of a wrist so as to balance energies therein.

Pantheism and the New World Order

Founder and former leader of the Church of Satan, Anthony LaVey, alluded to Shamballa Forces in reference to the Order of the Knights Templar, precursor to Freemasonry (See Ancient Mystery Religions; Witchcraft/Wicca).

Pantheists believe that Shamballa Forces (Forces of Purification) regenerate humanity, destined to evolve toward liberation (See Evolution; Charles Darwin). Lords of destiny (actually demons) use pain, and even death, as their instruments to purify (See Death Culture). A number of historical figures—the medium of Napoleon, for one—have manifested Shamballa Forces. Others considered to be highly evolved personalities include Bismarck, Mussolini, Hitler, Lenin, Stalin, and Franco, each of whom is a type of Antichrist (See Adept).

These agents of destiny are creators, as it were, of the New World Order. Acting as initiators of cosmic interdependence, they facilitate global unity, recognizing it as essential to the proper flow of the god-force.

Biblical Perspective

God is not an impersonal force, but rather a divine entity to Whom humankind is accountable and with Whom humankind can fellowship (Ps. 145:18). Scripture further clarifies that, although created in the image of God and endowed with infinitely greater worth than any other of God's created life forms, humanity remains distinctively separate from, and subordinate to, this peerless Creator (Gen. 1:26; Isa. 44: 6, 8; Mal. 2:10; Matt. 10:31). God has given humankind dominion (with accountability); even so, He shares His glory with none, be it animal, vegetable, mineral, or even humans, the veritable crown of creation (Gen. 1:26; James 3:7; Isa. 48:11). God alone deserves all praise, honor, and glory (Deut. 4:35).

Moreover, sainthood requires no quantum leap to other-consciousness; however, one must be born from above, thus becoming a new creation in Christ (John 3:3; 2 Cor. 5:17). This is accomplished by confessing and repenting of sin, and believing in and receiving Jesus Christ as personal Savior and Lord (Acts 2:38; Acts 16:31; 1 John 5:1). Spiritual beauty reflected in believers does not mirror the "higher self," nor does it presuppose self-effort (Ps. 45: 13). Indeed, the church is God's handiwork (Isa. 64:8). Her beauty is Christ at work within (Gal. 2:20). Suffering may enhance purification, but the church is not without promise of abundant living (John 10:10). The church's ultimate destiny is to partake of the Divine nature, but only in measure and in strict accordance with the purpose and Plan of God (2 Pet. 1:4).

God is forever God, distinct from His beloved creation and unequaled in His attributes (Deut. 32:39). His ways and thoughts are higher than ours, for who among us can know the mind of the Lord (Rom. 11:34)? In contrast, heaven, earth, and created life forms have origin, limitation, and a certain end (Matt. 24:35). They are not God, or any equal part of God, nor are they to be honored and served as if they were (Rom. 1:25). Humankind can discover and invent, but never create. Remaining unique as a fingerprint, unlike any other, each soul represents frail humanity provisionally redeemed (Matt. 10:30). Although the Creator's mercies are new every morning—indeed, He perpetually makes all things wonderfully new—no new thing spontaneously springs forth under the sun of His creation apart from Him (Lam. 3:23; Rev. 21:5; Eccles. 1:9).

Embracing these truths protects the Christian from pantheistic lies and deception, which are certain to be promulgated increasingly in these last days before the Lord Jesus Christ's *parousia*, or presence (2 Tim. 3:13).

Pike, Albert (1809-1891)

Born in Boston (1809), Albert Pike served as brigadier-general in the confederate army; moreover, he was admitted to the bar. Known for longtime leadership in Freemasonry (1859-1891), Pike ultimately assumed the role of supreme pontiff of Universal Masonry. A great student of the occult, Pike spoke of the *Kabbalah* as a second, more excellent bible; he further claimed, "All the Masonic associations owe to it their secrets and their symbols."

In *Morals and Dogma of the Ancient and Accepted Scottish Rite of Freemasonry* (1871), Pike paired Freemasonry with the ancient mystery religion of Babylon. Pike commended Freemasonry for serving as special guardian of occult secrets, including its hidden agenda to form a Luciferic New World Order. Before Italian nationalist Giuseppe Mazzini died (1872), Mazzini had enticed Pike into the Illuminati and its global revolutionary program. Eventually, Pike headed subversive activities of the Illuminati in the United States (See Council on Foreign Relations).

Pike is credited for having formed a Satanic cult called the New and Reformed Palladian Rite. The idea was to unite all Freemasonry into one international center. Lodges of this supreme rite were called Triangles (See Alice Bailey). Pike set up three Supreme Councils in South Carolina, Rome, and Berlin. Twenty-three subordinate councils worldwide served as headquarters of the international revolutionary movement.

In his 1889 instructions to the councils of the world, Pike directed all initiates of high degrees to maintain the "religion" of Freemasonry in the "purity of the Luciferic doctrine." Pike called "Christians," Hebrews, Moslems, Brahmans (Hindu), and followers of Confucius and Zoroaster to assemble together around Masonry's altars to unite in prayer (See Multiculturalism).

A gifted poet and historian, Pike read and wrote in sixteen ancient languages. His *Morals and Dogma* became the guidebook of the Scottish Rite. As its sovereign grand inspector-general, Pike devoted himself to the Rite until his death (1891). It was he who completely rewrote into their current form the degrees of the Scottish Rite.

Furthermore, between 1859 and 1871, Pike worked out a military blueprint for three world wars and various revolutions throughout the world. These, he believed, would forward the plan of world dominion. Pike felt that a "distant, final war" was necessary for the New World Order to be founded. Apparently, Pike anticipated crisis between Islam and Judaism to spark this conflict of superpowers (See Armageddon).

A preeminent figure in Masonic philosophy, especially American Freemasonry, Albert Pike is appropriately entombed in the "House of the Temple" just thirteen blocks from the White House. Curiously, the actual street layout for Washington, DC takes on the form of key Masonic symbols (Square, Compass, Pentagram, and rule). Apparently, every key federal building has a cornerstone laid in Masonic ritual with specific Masonic paraphernalia placed within each one.

Biblical Perspective

The apostle Paul encouraged Timothy to attend to reading and sound doctrine that, in the end, he might avoid error (1 Tim. 4:13, 16). This last-day admonition warned of "doctrines of demons" spoken in hypocrisy—that is, under intentionally misleading auspices (1 Tim. 4:1). Albert Pike likewise attended to reading and doctrine, but of a different sort. His surreptitious intent was to promote an anti-Christ one world government (Dan. 4:19-27; 7:2-8; Rev. 12:3; 13:1, 5; 17:9-12) with its false religion (See Pantheism; Rev. 13: 11-17; 19:20). The Word of God cautions believers to allow none to deceive them (1 John 3:7), nor are they to be partakers with the disobedient, as neo-gnostic occultist Pike, who was seduced by ancient mysteries (Eph. 5:6-7).

Planned Parenthood

An international family planning organization, Planned Parenthood is a powerful NGO (non-governmental agency), forming an alliance of nearly 170 separately instituted corporations with 900 clinics in forty-nine states. It is known especially for promoting and performing "fully accessible to all" abortions. As a result, Planned Parenthood has come to be known for its "death culture."

The nation's largest chain of abortion facilities is operated by Planned Parenthood, which performs over one hundred thousand abortions per year. This figure does not include the additional six thousand abortions performed elsewhere in the world. Planned Parenthood assisted in forming the National Abortion Federation, a trade association of abortion clinic operators.

Planned Parenthood is authorized to perform abortions on children, give them birth control, and teach children sexual behavior that could, in fact, jeopardize their lives—all this without knowledge or sanction of parents. Our government turns most often to Planned Parenthood for advice on the virtually abstinence-free sex curriculum in public education (See Gay Rights; Values Education; "Safe Sex").

Sustainability, Sanger, and Safe-Sex Sales

The United Nations' concept of sustainable development calls for reduction of the world's population. Founded by Margaret

Sanger, Planned Parenthood serves this principle well. Planned Parenthood fiercely opposes Representative Ron Paul's Amendment to limit use of American tax dollars for international population control—i.e., abortion. In 1998 alone, Congress allocated $385 million to cover costs overseas for family planning.

The radical social agenda of so-called "safe sex" is Planned Parenthood's progeny; moreover, the organization profits some seventy million dollars annually from the sale of birth control pills alone. Planned Parenthood's annual budget well exceeds four hundred million dollars, over a fourth of which comes from government grants. The U.S. government gives tens of millions of tax-payers' dollars to organizations like Planned Parenthood.

New Age Incentives

Some representatives of Planned Parenthood belong to the American Association of the Club of Rome, an elite spin-off group from the Council on Foreign Relations, which calls for dissolution of national sovereignty toward a coming Brave New World. The World Constitution and Parliament Association plans to funnel funds of the new global economics/banking system to countries with zero or less population growth. Such incentive is certain to encourage the agenda of Planned Parenthood in the coming New World Order.

Planned Parenthood has its own New Age trappings. Its former head, Faye Wattleton, encouraged women to feel "the energy" of their womanhood (See Pantheism: "All is Energy"; Genderism). At Gorbachev's World Forum, where she spoke in November of 1997, each participant was given a pendant showing a circle of female witches dancing naked in the moon light (See Witchcraft/Wicca).

Biblical Perspective

(See Abortion; Death Culture.)

Political Correctness (PC) Movement

Touted as "tolerance," the term political correctness is an umbrella under which a number of other "isms" huddle. Its newfashioned revolutionary thinking is often called holistic, integrated, or "systems thinking." United causes include civil/gender/

sexual orientation rights (Gay Rights) and radical environmentalism.

Spawned in the last two decades, the PC program is to deconstruct Western civilization, specifically European/American culture. With some 12,000 members, the Organization of American Historians documents a movement away from traditionally defined history. Indeed, anything "traditional" is the target—Judeo-Christian values, family, work ethic, and the Constitution of the United States.

In public education, political correctness is known by some as higher order ("critical") thinking, or transferable skills needed to succeed in the global work force. Opposers of the movement are tagged racist, sexist, homophobic, and oppressive and are accused of trying to preserve white, heterosexual male supremacy and slave-driving colonialism. Selective revision of history, use of epithets, and labeling opposing arguments as mere "anecdotal evidence" are tactics employed by the movement, whose political agenda supersedes all other considerations.

The conceptual straight jacket of political correctness virtually defines tomorrow's worker in the global community. The 1995 UNESCO Declaration of Tolerance essentially elevates rejection of moral absolutism to the status of legal requirement. So-called higher order thinking is directed towards expediting government control over hiring, firing, and other business practices. Already, the work force development program of Goals 2000 is considering a national job registry whose computer data base contains Myers-Briggs type indicators of the job candidate's political and religious leanings (See Outcome-Based Education).

Honorable-sounding euphemisms preserve the PC agenda despite the term's having become laughable at higher levels of education. You see, intellectual relativism is its base. Simply put, deconstructionism is modern relativism applied to language, thereby disallowing meaningful communication. Truth is unimportant; winning arguments is what matters. Plato called the argument/counter-argument ploy of deconstructionism "antilogic."

The antilogic of today's politically correct crowd is not new. Fifth century Greek philosophers, Sophists, first developed it. These were early humanists known even then for attacking traditional religious beliefs. Protagorus was the leading Sophist who taught that "man is the measure of all things," this being the maxim underlying contemporary secular humanism, multiculturalism, radical feminism/genderism, and Afrocentrism— all part of this liberal movement; all defining the New World Order.

Biblical Perspective

See Deconstructionism/Post-structuralism.

Public Education: Christian to Secular to Mystical

Public Education Christianized (The Old Paradigm)

In a letter to the Ministry of France dated March 1778, Benjamin Franklin called for "a Bible and a newspaper in every house" and "a good school in every district." Article III of the Continental Congress, signed into law by George Washington (1789), defined a good school as one forever encouraging "religion, morality, and knowledge." Thus founded on Biblical principles, traditional public education in America emphasized academic subject-matter curriculum with stress on order, discipline, and individual effort.

Having begun about 1789, and reaching its peak the first decade of this century, America's so-called Sunday School movement set the standard for public education. Speaking for the city of Philadelphia, lawyers argued for obligatory teaching of "what the Bible alone can teach, viz. a pure system of morality" (1844, *Vidal v. Girard's Executors*, 43 US 126, 132); the United States Supreme Court concurred. Though opposition to Bible-based public schooling mounted steadily, another powerful ruling of the Supreme Court (*McCollum v. Board of Education*) likewise established, as late as 1948, that traditional public education in the Western world was in fact church-based, Bible-believing, and piety-instilling, and rightfully so.

Public Education Secularized (The Transition Paradigm)

When in 1850 Horace Mann of Massachusetts sold America on the idea that, in one hundred years, secular education would solve crime and poverty, the Great Awakening (1740-1750) and education reform under Jonathan Edwards and George Whitfield took a dive. How wrong this "Father of Permissive Education" was; nonetheless, with little fight, the church willingly gave up education to the state.

Precipitated by German "Higher Criticism" and Bushnell's *Christian Nurture*, the Liberal Theology movement captivated the mainstream in the nineteenth and early twentieth centuries and, thus, served as the springboard for secularism. Secularism evolved slowly through the influence of many educators—Swiss Johann Heinrich Pestalozzi (1746-1827) and German Friedrich August Wilhelm Froebel (1782-1852) among them. The former advocated Rousseau's principles of natural development, and the latter evolved a new system of education, using instructive play. In Blankenburg (1826), Froebel founded the first kindergarten (German, "garden for children"). By the turn of the century, an even more profound influence was felt under the sway of John Dewey's Progressive Education movement.

Froebel's evolutionary principles; non-Biblical theories such as James' Pragmatic Method, which attacked any attempt to explain life in terms of the supernatural; and Dewey's humanism, in particular, founded modern secular education. Organized in 1919, the Progressive Education Association denounced rote learning, recitation, and conventional textbooks while promoting affective and holistic curricula, cultural relativism, and cooperative consciousness. In the Progressive Education classroom, the individual was downgraded; the group distinguished. Progressivism spread phenomenally during the thirties and forties.

A Fabian Socialist, Dewey wrote, "There is no room for God, and there is no soul. Therefore, there is no room for fixed, natural law or moral absolutes." Among the goals of Dewey's man-centered, godless education system were those of the New Age movement:

• A new economic system, not free enterprise (See Global Economics);

• A New World Order (interdependent globalism, or "communitarianism," as coined by Harvard Business School Professor George C. Lodge in *Managing Globalization in the Age of Interdependence*);

• A new race, its motto being: "one world; one species" (under carefully structured attitude adjustment, behavior modification, and genetic/social engineering); and

• A new world religion (curious in light of Dewey's atheism).

Through the influence of Dewey and his disciples (Harold Ruggs, George Counts, and Scott Nearing), traditional education with its God-fearing, Bible-based instruction toppled. "Pluralism" and "realism" became public education's newest buzz words (See Multiculturalism). Progressive education's slogan became, "Fit the program to the child, not the child to the program"; therefore, *child*-centered supplanted *Christ*-centered education. When Dewey died in 1952, the overpowering Protestant character of the early public schools was extinct.

For the first half of this century and through the early 1960s, the U.S. still boasted the world's premier education system; however, by the mid-sixties, studies showed that student performance had declined. It was then that a recognized expert in analyzing legislation, Maureen Heaton, discovered and exposed an Eisenhower administration document featuring the Delphi Technique of behavior modification. If followed precisely, the document would result in severe limitation of personal freedom with government takeover of every facet of life. Subsequent opposition to Progressivism birthed the back-to-basics movement of the 1970s, which in turn revived Arthur Bestor's Essentialist Theory of the 1930s.

Eighty-five percent of all American children attend public schools, but a walloping twenty percent of all public school educators send their children to private schools. The growing complaint is that "Johnny can't read." Indeed, the Education Department report *A Nation at Risk* (1983) issued the stunning declaration that "If an unfriendly foreign power had attempted to impose on America the mediocre educational performance that exists today, we might well have viewed it as an act of war." Remarkably, the head of America's Communist Party, William Z. Foster, fingered America's Education Department itself as means for developing the new socialist society (*Toward Soviet America*, 1932).

Enter, the New Morality

The U.S. Supreme Court has declared unconstitutional the official use of voluntary, non-sectarian prayer in the public schools; moreover, the Court has outlawed in the classroom school authorized Bible reading and recitation of the Lord's Prayer. According to Senator Jesse Helms, the Supreme Court, in effect, not only has violated the right of free exercise of religion for all Americans; it also has established a national religion in the U.S., the religion of secular humanism.

How true the words of great orator and statesman Daniel Webster: "If Truth be not diffused, error will be." Today, although Johnny still cannot read, Congress allocates tens of millions of dollars in public education for contraceptive-based sex education (See "Safe Sex"). This is true despite overwhelming evidence that these programs contribute to, rather than resolve, society's ills.

Alfred Kinsey's research, published in 1948, forms the basis for today's sex education in America's schools. Having adopted Kinseyan viewpoints, America has suffered huge increase in violent crime, divorce, out-of-wedlock births, child abuse, and teen suicides. That Kinsey documented multiple orgasmic response in study participants as young as five months of age presupposes his victimization of children; moreover, Kinseyan assumptions allow for aberrant sexuality (including bestiality and incest). Still, the Kinsey Institute (Indiana University) and its propaganda arm, SIECUS (Sexuality Information and Education Council of the U.S.), continue to receive funding from the federal government, as well as the Rockefeller and Playboy Foundations.

Enter, Polytechnical Education

In this decade, our government paid for a report extolling virtues of the Marxist-Leninist Polytechnical Education behind the lifelong learning craze of today's education revolution with its cradle-to-grave vision à la Marc Tucker and Hillary Clinton. The socialistic German plan of education, containing elements of the Soviet system, serves as basic model.

Enter, Human Resources for the Global Community

The federal focus has shifted from job training programs for the illiterate and unemployed. Now, it seeks to process all students and, in fact, all workers as human resources for the global job market. The School-to-Work Opportunities Act of 1994 (Public Law 103-239) coupled with Goals 2000: Educate America Act (Public Law 103-227) merge education with the global work force. Eventually, all students will be trained for a specific predetermined entry-level occupation. The work-based learning approach is modeled after the apprenticeship concept of trade schools, not unlike what Dewey and his colleagues called for. "School-site mentors" will direct student career planning no later than the seventh grade.

Public Education Mystified (The New Paradigm)

Years of secularism created the needed vacuum to spark interest in the nineties' cosmic concepts, which promote sustainable society as defined by the Gaia hypothesis (See Radical Environmentalism). With esoteric humanism and world community as its focus, and New Age occultists Drs. Muller and Maver at its hub, today's Outcome-Based Education (OBE) elevates collectivism and responsible global citizenship over academics and concrete intelligence (See Multiculturalism). Introduced in Dr. Muller's book, *New Genesis—Shaping a Global Spirituality* (1984), his own World Core Curriculum presented to the United Nations (1989) reflects the soul of today's educational reform not only in the United States, but worldwide. Political correctness supplants traditional values, the Constitution, and Judeo-Christian faith with a New Earth (Global Civic) Ethic that effectively undermines all that the founding fathers held dear.

Biblical Perspective

Proper perspective toward knowledge places God and His Word at the center of learning, for God is the source of all true knowledge (Prov. 2:3-6; Prov. 1:7); and His Word is truth (John 17:17). In Jesus are hid all the treasures of wisdom and knowledge (Col. 2:3). To teach truth, therefore, each subject must be sound, academically and doctrinally. As such, history is correctly His story; science is His creation; good literature is consistent with His teaching to think on things that are true, honest, just, and pure (Phil. 4:8).

Founders of our country recognized the necessity of weaving Biblical principles into every aspect of life. In seeking religious liberty, they secured by the Constitution the right to speak, teach, and live by these principles. America's move toward secular education undermined this right, and today's budding mystical education is destined to pervert and abuse it (2 Tim. 3:13-14). For some 1.5 million Americans, home schooling has become their choice.

The Bible plainly warns of perilous last days in which heady blasphemers are ever learning, but failing nonetheless to attain knowledge of truth (2 Tim. 3:1-7). To discard America's Christian roots while embracing pantheistic premises of New Age theology is to exchange truth for fables (2 Tim. 4: 3-4). No doubt this is happening on cue worldwide by means of public education bent on shaping politically correct Earth stewards of the New World Order.

R

Radical Environmentalism

The term political correctness is the umbrella under which a number of other "isms" huddle, not least of which is radical environmentalism.

New Ecological Consciousness for the New Ecozoic Age

Once married to Margaret Mead, New Age psychiatrist Gregory Bateson was instrumental in defining the new ecological consciousness, which negates the Cartesian Theory, separating human life from the earth, whose resources God intended to be consumed. The New Ecological Consciousness switches from anthrocentricity (with humankind, the crown of God's creation) to biocentricity (humans subservient to the planet).

Followed by industry and technology, people are viewed as the worst threat to "Mother Earth." Spokesperson for the Rockefeller foundation Merton Lambert is quoted as having said, "The world has cancer, and that cancer is man." Father Thomas Berry further contends that Christianity specifically is mostly to blame for the earth's attrition; moreover, he believes that the new Ecozoic Age will transcend God. Father Berry is a chief spokesperson for Gaia or Ge, goddess of the Earth in Greek mythology. His brand of neo-pantheism is called Ecotheology, which starts with the premise that the universe is god (See Pantheism: "All is Energy").

The Gaia Institute is sponsored by Upper Manhattan's Green Cathedral, that of St. John the Divine, which applies Gaia's interdependence concept to eco clean-up for the federal Environmental Protection Agency. At the Green Cathedral, the National Religious Partnership for the Environment promotes the Green movement in America's churches.

Environmental Crisis: Cornerstone of the New World Order

Radical environmentalists see Gaia-Earth as an interconnected, living ecosystem, whose delicate nature requires the protection of world government. The idea is use of fear and guilt to unite humankind in a common international cause with Nature as its central organizing principle. In collaboration with selected non-government organizations (NGOs), the federal government endorses local "sustainability councils" to reduce consumption, especially energy; restore biodiversity; and retard urban sprawl.

Speaking at the San Francisco State of the World Forum in September of 1995, Mikkail Gorbachev identified the environmental crisis as the international disaster key justifying global restructuring, or *Perestroika.*

Gorbachev's organization, Green Cross International, works closely with the United Nations. Gorbachev insists that by 2002, a type of "Bill of Rights," the Earth Charter, will be imposed through global government to enforce "necessary" environmental regulations worldwide.

The Gaia Hypothesis

In *Goddess Earth,* nationally recognized investigative researcher Samantha Smith exposes the pagan agenda of radical environmentalism. In Greek mythology, Gaia or Ge was the goddess of the Earth. Elaborated in the 1970s by the British scientist James Lovelock and Carl Sagan's ex-wife, Lynn Margulis, Gaia ideology supports the Green Movement claim that modern man is morally responsible for maintaining Nature's fragile balance.

The Gaia Hypothesis of saving "Mother Earth" is the basis for the Endangered Species Act, the United Nation's Biodiversity Treaty, and the President's Commission on Sustainable Development. Because of these, public officials are hindered from taking action without considering the well-being of spotted owls, kangaroo rats, or the Delhi Sands flower-loving fly. Families in United Nations designated biosphere regions of the Wildlands Project can be forced to move so as not to interfere with animal and plant life there, and the term "sustainable" has come to mean global eco-socialism more than conservationism.

The Global Civic [New Earth] Ethic (See Values Education)

Certified products merit the "green label" endorsement more for their company's eco-correctness than for actual eco-impact. You see, the true goal of the radical environmental movement is not clean air and water, as some presume. It is instead formation of what environmentalists call sustainable "urban clusters" in an agrarian society, which in turn will ease totalitarian control of human activities, reproduction, and wealth in the New World Order.

The United Nations plan calls for a 1998 World Conference on Global Governance to submit to the world all necessary agreements to implement by the year 2000. According to the official UN definition of sustainability, the world's poor are given "overriding priority." Because underdeveloped nations are not bound by treaties that developed nations are forced under, the result is redistribution of the world's wealth in favor of those born into unequal circumstances, economically and socially. Conference recommendations rest on the assumption that global citizens are ready to accept this New Earth Ethic, which specifically excludes national sovereignty and private property rights.

Under the New Earth Ethic, the Security Council mission would include environmental security, ensuring compliance by means of an International Court of Criminal Justice. Even now, U.S. soldiers are ordered to guard rain forests and endangered species in Central and South Americas. Undersecretary of state for Global Affairs, Timothy E. Wirth, calls this "a legitimate military issue."

Famed Proponents

Celebrated French oceanographer, the late Jacques Cousteau was a popular champion of radical environmentalism and one world socialism. He openly called for nations of the world to forfeit their sovereignty. The United Nations plans to create an environmental police force of "Green Helmets," placing no limits on government, while extending their powers further into lives of private citizens. The Jacques Cousteau Society has formulated a "Bill of Rights for Future Generations" in an attempt to gather some ten million signatures indicating support of this plan.

The Prince of Wales and Vice President Al Gore are among the movement's influential proponents. In his book, *Earth in Balance*, Gore calls for global restructuring to save the environment. Another vocal spokesperson for the United Nations environmental agenda, also its leader, Maurice Strong, is a New Age occultist associated with Upper Manhattan's Green Cathedral. Perceived by Strong himself as "the Vatican of the New World Order," his Colorado ranch is a hotbed of pagan religious activity. Although himself an oil and steamship billionaire, Strong openly opposes all industrialized society, private property rights, and the Constitutional sovereignty of the United States. He is on the international board of directors of the Better World Society, directed by Ted Turner to convert the world into a global village, free of unsustainable suburban lifestyle. Eating meat, using appliances, and having air conditioning are among those activities deemed unsustainable.

Maurice Strong is an ardent globalist, and a powerful one at that. Former head of the United Nations Environment Programme (UNEP), Strong called for the first UN environmental conference in 1982. He was also secretary-general of the United Nations Conference on Environment and Development (UNCED) held in Rio. Chairman Strong ended the 1992 Rio Summit with these chilling words: "Isn't the only hope for the planet that the industrialized civilizations collapse? Isn't it our responsibility to bring this about?"

Strong's 1996 study with Sir Shridath Ramphal, *Our Global Neighborhood*, appears to carry the globalist agenda to completion on four fronts: environmental, legal, social, and economic. Published by the Trilateral Commission, Strong's *Beyond Interdependence: The Meshing of the World's Economy and the Earth's Ecology* targets the year 2012 for middle class consumption-pattern adjustment.

Global Sustainable Development

Recognized as one of the main references of the UN environmental agenda, *Our Common Future* officially defines sustainability as "development that meets the needs of the present without compromising the ability of future generations to meet their own needs." Global sustainable development is the central organizing principle for politically correct societal conduct by every citizen of the New World Order. It is in actuality a code word for "control." At its heart is the Marxist/Leninist concept, "If you don't produce, you don't consume" (See Death Culture).

Sustainability was first defined in 1987 in a report by the vice president of the World Socialist Party, Norwegian Prime Minister Gro Harlem Brundtland. It has philosophical, economic, social, and environmental implications, demanding that action be taken, even in the face of scientific uncertainty, to reduce consumption, achieve social equity, and preserve biodiversity.

Rio Earth Summit

In June 1992 the United Nations sponsored the largest and most ambitious international conference ever. The Earth Summit in Rio de Janeiro created the Sustainable Development Commission to police the world and, thus, insure global cooperation. The Summit negotiated five major documents:

• Agenda 21 (providing the full agenda for implementing global sustainable development);

• Convention on Climate Control (putting strict regulations on industry and huge taxes on energy consumption);

• Biodiversity Treaty (containing language and provisions of the *Wild Earth* Wildlands Project, threatening national sovereignty and ultimately declaring as wilderness half of all America's land);

• Rio Declaration (redistributing the world's wealth; See Global Economics);

• Convention on Forest Principles (destroying America's timber industry while "managing the world's forests").

These agreements and the New Covenant on Environment and Development work to transform America's Constitutional republic into a social democracy headed by non-elected NGOs.

Agenda 21

Agenda 21 is the far-reaching UN blueprint for global eco-socialism. Endorsed by over one hundred heads of state, this voluminous plan threatens to destroy American property rights, while proposing specific changes in activities of all people. Agenda 21 was elaborated in Turkey at the 1996 UN conference, Habitat II, placing the biosphere at the heart of every human activity.

Habitat II produced the blueprint for environmentally-friendly "urban clusters" and "community sustainability." In the United States, Chattanooga, Tennessee leads the way as model for neighborhood restructuring efforts.

The Biodiversity Treaty: Gore's Global Marshall Plan

Biodiversity describes the variety of genes, species, and ecosystems on Earth. The UN's Biodiversity Treaty is taken directly from the Earth First! blueprint, *The Wilding of America*, as published in its journal, *Wild Earth*. Earth First! works to drive the Green Movement to the radical left. Reliable sources confirm that the alleged "unabomber," Theodore Kaczynski, is a member of Earth First!; moreover, he is suspected of being influenced by the radical environmentalism journal, *A Declaration of War: Killing People to Save Animals and the Environment.* A recent editorial in the *Economist* likewise applauds extinction of the human species for neglecting the world's environment.

The Biodiversity Treaty fingers societies dominated by Islam, and especially Christianity, for nature's having lost its "sacred qualities" (Section 8.3.5). Section 9.2.3.1.2 states, "all living creatures [are] considered equal" (See Pantheism).

Although the treaty did not pass in the Senate, President Clinton has established a Council on Sustainable Development to effect the Earth Summit Programme, pacts, and treaties. The idea is to create a New America with twenty-one bioregions *en lieu* of fifty states. Al Gore's Global Marshall Plan has already been implemented in degrees. If fully implemented, half of all American land would become wilderness. Reserves consist of core and buffer areas, allowing UN jurisdiction to censure human activity within entire ecosystems.

The Biodiversity Treaty establishes legal standing for nongovernmental organizations (NGOs), whose decisions could override elected legislatures. All biodiversity falls under three increasingly powerful NGOs already accredited by the UN: the International Union for Conservation of Nature, created by Julian Huxley in 1948; the World Wide Fund for Nature; and World Resources Institute. These NGOs boast a global network of affiliates. Each designated bioregion is destined to be governed by NGOs, who in turn enforce UN treaties. All biodiversity is to be placed under control of the United Nations Trusteeship Council.

Private Property, Cornerstone of Liberty

The first plank of Karl Marx's *Communist Manifesto* is "abolition of property in land and application of all rents of land to public purpose." In contrast, the Constitution of the thirteen original states called for "life, liberty, and *property* [emphasis added]" as inalienable rights. Ensured by the Supreme Court (23 March 1972), property is the cornerstone of liberty. Foundations of liberty include rule of law, voluntary exchange, limited government, and private property. Nonetheless, under the principle of sustainable development, private property is at risk.

Already, the 1964 Wilderness Act seeks to nationalize private property. "Regulatory Taking" prevents people from using their own property, and most "Condemnations Takings" are in the name of forests or parks. The Endangered Species Act of 1972 provides no just compensation for taking away property rights where endangered species may elect to live. Thankfully, Don Young's American Sovereignty Protection Act (1997) passed the House, marking the first time property rights firmly overcame the Green agenda.

UN World Heritage Convention Protecting World Cultural and Natural Heritage

World Heritage Committee Chairman, Adul Wichiencharoen of Thailand encourages a "holistic approach" to the ecosystem (See New Age Movement). In the eyes of UNESCO, private owners cannot be trusted to guard a world heritage. Therefore, the United Nations is given authority to guide the safekeeping of international sites and monuments recognized for their global value. Hundreds of cultural treasures, wildlife preserves, and historic monuments, such as the Statue of Liberty and Independence Hall, are now regulated by the United Nations, as are tropical rain forests in Australia, the Grand Canyon, Yosemite, Yellowstone National Park, Stonehenge, the Great Pyramids, and Auschwitz concentration camp. Since 1990, the Kremlin, Red Square, and Lenin's tomb have been UN World Heritage Sites.

Without congressional approval or oversight, federal authorities have classified scores of national parks as Biosphere Reserves or sanctuaries. As of 1997, almost 52 million acres of sovereign U.S. park land have been set aside for conservation and scientific study. In all cases, individual rights must give way to collectivism to the point of disallowing "sustainable eco-tourism" in areas of scientific interest.

Environmental Protection Agency

In 1970 the U.S. Environmental Protection Agency was set up to protect "the country from being degraded, and its health threatened, by a multitude of human activities initiated without regard to long-ranging effects upon the life-supporting properties, the economic uses, and the recreational value of air, land, and water."

President Clinton has taken a giant step toward international law by ordering the EPA to enforce massive new regulations, which cost sixty million dollars per year for compliance. Most of the nation's scientists, even Democrats in Congress, oppose Clinton's environmental-pollution model.

Green Parties; Greenpeace

The New Age Green's rallying cry is "Global problems demand global solutions." Radical environmentalism takes a political form in so-called Green parties, which purpose to "preserve the planet and its people." New Age author Fritjof Capra identifies the Green party as among the best vehicles for the ecologically-based one world social agenda.

Through the Green movement, private ownership of land is threatened while the power of government is built. Founded in 1971, Greenpeace is an international environmental pressure group, claiming to be backed by scientific research. Theirs is a policy of non-violent direct action.

French ecologist and author René Dubos coined the popular phrase, "Think globally; act locally." With this in mind, the Green party is best known for its campaign to divide the world into bioregions of common ecological concern. Results include the breakdown of national sovereignty and restructuring of the world's economy. A Washington-based environmental think tank, World Watch, pinpoints the year 2030 as the target date for successful "sustainable society."

Multibillion Dollar Industry

Among the top ten environmental groups are the Nature Conservancy, the World Wildlife Fund, and the National Audubon Society. Such groups hold huge stock portfolios, not to mention real estate. Combined assets of the largest environmental groups total $8.6 billion. An informal coalition of more than 160 private money givers, the Environmental Grant Makers Association, uses eco-regulations for profit. Among others, Ford and Rockefeller Foundations give environmental groups hundreds of millions of dollars yearly.

Environmental Education

Since Americans are not quick to swallow the anti-technology, anti-industry, and anti-private property rights eco-agenda, the Green crowd is foisting it on young Americans, especially by means of public education. Given today's Outcome-Based Education model, defined by the World Core Curriculum, Johnny may not be able to read, but he can (and does) recycle anything and everything.

Perhaps the biggest and most coordinated effort of our century toward ushering in the New World Order under a Green Banner is Earth Day. At a recent Earth Day, Vice President Al Gore encouraged youngsters to plant and hug a tree. The National Education Association has targeted 45 million public education children with Earth Day curriculum featuring home surveys to monitor parent consumption habits. Another Earth Day activity involves guided imagery leading to worship of "sacred Mother Earth" (See New Age Movement).

The Environmental Education Act (signed into law by Bush, 1990) created the EPA's Office of Environmental Education. Sixty-five million dollars was appropriated for five years of Green education programs designed to produce politically eco-correct kids, veritable change-agents-in-the-making for the New World Order. Youngsters now see themselves as the Earth's champions and protectors; computer networking allows global communication. With teachers, World Heritage Youth produced education kits, distributed in 1997 to schools worldwide. Of many environmental groups for youth, Kids for Saving the Earth has the greatest membership.

Buried in the National Geography Standards of Goals 2000 are items designed to transform youth into rabid environmentalists. Students are encouraged to choose environmental projects as their community service in fulfilling "mandatory volunteerism" requirements. Even young school children are alarmed and outspoken about deforestation of the planet, acid rains, ozone depletion, global warming, and the greenhouse effect.

- *Deforestation:* Deforestation is destruction of forests without planting new trees to replace those lost. A quarter of the net carbon releases in the atmosphere is attributed to forest clearance, said to worsen the greenhouse effect. One of the world's leading experts on deforestation in the Amazon, Dr. Evaristo Eduardo de Miranda, disagrees with those who lament South America's alleged loss of some fifty thousand acres of rain forest a day. Satellite photos prove to the contrary that, over the past two hundred years, only about ten percent of the rain forest in Brazil has been cut back. Despite alarmist claims, the Amazon rain forest is not in danger of being destroyed.

• *Acid Rains:* In some places, acid rain is known as "poor man's fertilizer." Environmentalists claim that destructive chemical changes in the ground water can be felt thousands of miles from the source of automotive exhaust fumes and industrial activities (such as burning coal). To the contrary, a half-billion dollar study conducted by our government from 1980-1990 found that acid rains, caused by sulfur dioxide and oxides of nitrogen, are not destroying lakes and streams, crops and vegetation. The study concluded that "there is no evidence of widespread forest damage from current levels of acidic rains in the United States." Acknowledged expert Dr. Ed Krug agrees.

• *Ozone Depletion:* The ozone layer is said to be in the upper atmosphere shielding all life on this planet with but an eighth of an inch of pale-blue gas. More accurately, ozone is all around us. Some scientists claim that more than three percent of the ozone layer has been destroyed, threatening to disrupt the world's food supply and to increase the risk of skin cancer.

Industrialization is thought to be responsible for large, irreparable holes in it over the north and south poles. However, so-called "holes" in the ozone layer existed long before the Industrial Age which is blamed for them.

Occurring as a result of volcanic activity, major storms, *El Niño,* and sun spots, ozone layer ebb-and-flow is quite normal. While it may be being destroyed in the stratosphere, it is at the same time being replaced. Some thirty years ago, before widespread use of now banned chlorofluorocarbon gases (CFCs), these facts were well established by meteorologist Gordon Dobson (1956) and two Frenchmen (1968).

Astrophysicist at the Harvard-Smithsonan Astrophysical Observatory, Sallie Baliunas has exposed ozone-depletion fraud by those distorting technology to fit a political agenda. To protect the ozone, a treaty has already banned production of freon, the basis for all refrigeration and air conditioning. Ironically, CFCs are what make these appliances energy efficient. Some fear that, in time, proposed environmental regulations could unnecessarily result in serious restrictions on automobile use and removal of air conditioners and refrigerators from homes.

• *Global Warming and the Greenhouse Effect:* Caused by production of carbon dioxide in the air, preventing escape of solar radiation absorbed by the atmosphere and the earth, the greenhouse effect results in a rise of the earth's temperature. Biocentric thought blames humankind for industrial use of oil, gasoline, coal, natural gas, and the like, although no evidence proves that human activities have had any effect whatsoever on the weather. In fact, temperatures on earth are largely governed by fluctuations in solar activity.

If so-called global warming were to cause polar ice caps to melt, cities like New York would be under water. Computers may indicate that global warming is an actual threat; but then, according to Dr. Patrick Michaels of the University of Virginia, computer analysis is based on the earth's being flat. Furthermore, today's computers can include only two of fourteen components that make up weather.

Finally, global warming occurred before the automobiles blamed for it. Besides, car exhaust greenhouse gasses have little effect on nature when compared to the huge output from major volcanoes and ocean evaporation. Remember, too, that global cooling was the pressing issue of the 1970s. If global warming were a valid concern, the earth would have warmed two to four degrees Celsius over the past one hundred years. This plainly is not so.

To the contrary, evidence shows that snow cover in the Northern Hemisphere including the arctic caps has, since 1966, grown eighteen percent. In fact, U.S. government satellite and balloon measurements show a very slight cooling of .037 degrees Celsius, and a new study at Washington D.C.'s George C. Marshall Institute concludes that significant global warming at the hands of humankind is unfounded.

Eighty-one percent of the scientific community (including Drs. Fred Singer, Patrick Michaels, and the late Dixie Lee Ray) agree that global warming cannot be proven absolutely. In excess of 4,000 scientists have signed the Heidleberg Appeal asking governments to refrain from policy-making until global warming can be further researched. The Liepzig Declaration, which openly disputes global warming claims, has been signed by hundreds of climatologists worldwide. Over 15,000 credible scientists associated with the "Petition Project" out of Oregon concur further that increases in atmospheric carbon dioxide actually benefit natural plant and animal environments.

El Niño

El Niño is a condition caused by warming waters in the western Pacific. Scientists attribute changing weather patterns of the 1990s to *El Niño*. According to Dr. Walter Brown, former National Science Foundation Fellow with the Massachusetts Institute of Technology, years of scientific research contradicts Theories of Interglacial Periods. Whether the earth is heading into an age of global warming or ice, radical environmentalists will no doubt find ample evidence for their political causes even in the face of scientific uncertainty.

Biblical Perspective

That environmental issues are trifling is not the point. In reference to end-times, Jesus predicted famines, pestilence, and earthquakes of devastating proportion (Matt. 24:3-14). In his book *Countdown to Rapture,* investigative reporter and news analyst, Salem Kirban, examines undeniable changes in the world's resources and its environment. It is true, for example, that more famines have taken place in the last two hundred years than in all of the previous seventeen centuries since Christ's first coming. The environmental research group, World Watch, estimates that the violent weather of one year (1998) cost more than losses from weather-related disasters throughout the entire eighties.

According to God's Word, woe is proclaimed upon earth's inhabitants, not because of technology, industry, or an out-of-balance ecosystem, but rather because of the Devil himself and his flood of deception, lies, and persecution (Rev. 12:12, 15). While those who fear God's Name are promised reward, the true destroyers of earth are themselves promised destruction (Rev. 11:18).

Biblically, the earth as we know it is destined to pass away. God never intended for it to last forever, for a New Earth will take its place (Rev. 21:1).

While on earth, Christians are called to be scrupulous stewards of God's creation. They are to tend, keep, and subdue the earth for life's necessities (Gen. 1:28; 2:15).

Whereas God has purposed that humanity take dominion over "every living thing that moves upon the earth," Green ideology elevates nature over humankind. Radical environmentalists exonerate brown bears for their fishing, and wolves for eating meat, but not humans. In God's economy, humans are of infinitely greater value than other life forms (Matt. 10:31); however, biocentric thought assigns greater intrinsic value to the eco-system when compared with even a billion human bodies—this, according to Green biologist David Graber.

Radical environmentalism's passion to save what remains of our natural world perverts genuine Biblical stewardship with worship of the creation rather than its Creator (See Pantheism). Paul admonished Pastor Timothy to avoid such "godless chatter" and "oppositions of science falsely so called" (1 Tim. 6:20). In his letter to the Romans, Paul maintains man is without excuse (1:20) when attempting to change the glory of God into a corruptible image (1:23), worshipping and serving the creation more than the Creator (1:25). The Bible clearly forbids worship of Nature (Isa. 42:8). Still, Vice President Gore writes in his book that man can gain "new insights" by understanding a "religious heritage" based on the "worship of a single Earth goddess who was assumed to be the fount of all life."

No doubt radical environmentalists are more interested in promoting the visibly leftist agenda of a spiritually-driven New World Order with its Global Civic (New Earth) Ethic than in taking responsibility for the environment under the guise of saving whales and rain forests. At the forefront of global integration, radical environmentalists cultivate guilt and fear toward uniting humankind into "one [biocentric] mind," serving to empower and enable the work of the coming one world dictator, known in scriptures as the coming Antichrist (Rev. 17:13).

Rapture v. Second Coming (Contrasted)

Biblical Perspective

Rapture: Real or Reverie?

The word "rapture" is not Biblical. For this reason, some question its Scriptural validity, thinking it to be an invention of the nineteenth century. "Rapture" is derived from the Latin *rapere,* meaning "to seize" or "to carry off" (by force) and from the Greek *harpazo,* meaning "caught up" or "snatched away." Significantly, *harpazo* is found in the Greek New Testament.

Other Scriptural terms relating to the Rapture include the "earlier out-resurrection from among the dead" (Phil. 3:11, 14), the "first resurrection" (Rev. 20:5-6), "the glorious appearing of Christ" (Titus 2:13), "the presence of Christ" (1 Thess. 4:15), "the high, upward calling" (Phil. 3:14), keeping "from out of the hour of the trial" (Rev. 3:10), "arising" and "coming away" (Song 2:8-14), and "the taking away" (Greek Middle Voice, indicating "for self-interest," Matt. 24:39).

Rapture Defined

Simply put, the Rapture is hair-trigger taking of the last-day Philadelphia Church from out of encroaching Tribulation. Its time frame is Antichrist's first appearance on earth, typified by great deception with concurrent falling away of even true believers (See Manchild; Rev. 3:10; 2 Thess. 2:3). At the Rapture, the Lord Himself will come down from Heaven with a shout, the voice of an arch-angel, and the trump of God, used historically to signify an event of importance (1 Thess. 4:16). First, the dead in Christ shall rise from their graves. Prepared believers who are still alive will join them in being snatched away quickly, as if the object of a pickpocket. Having met their Lord "in the air [spiritual realm]," and themselves having put on immortality, these forever will remain with Jesus (1 Cor. 15:42, 49, 51, 52, 54; 1 Thess. 4:15-17).

Rapture—Pre-, Mid-, or Post-Trib? (See Tribulation)

Neither Old nor New Testament passages mention Christ's Bride as participating in Israel's time of trouble, which includes Great Tribulation. Whereas Christ's prepared Bride will escape Tribulation, Israel will complete unfinished business with God during it (See Seventy Weeks of Daniel).

Indeed, the Rapture evidences onset of Tribulation. Scriptures clearly indicate that it will be pre-tribulational (Rev. 3:10, 17:12; Luke 21:28; 2 Thess. 2:7-8; Matt. 24:37-39; 2 Pet. 3:4; 1 Thess. 5:9). Grammatical, historical, and contextual methods of Biblical interpretation likewise support a pre-trib Rapture.

The Rapture is the hope of the church, a singular source of continuous comfort to believers, especially these last days (1 Thess. 4:17-18), for the Bride of Christ will be kept from out of "the hour of the trial" which shall come upon all the world, to try them that dwell upon the earth (Rev. 3:10). Throughout this season of unparalleled trouble, the Lord will hide His own in a secret tabernacle, or pavilion (likened to the honeymoon tent). No doubt with prophetic view of the Rapture, Psalm 27:5 reads, "within a rock will He set me on high."

Rapture: For All or Some?

This earlier out-resurrection happens to those who, having previously answered Christ's call to Bridehood, are prepared and looking for His appearance (Phil. 3:11, 14; Rev. 22:17; Titus 2:13). That believers exist in the Great Tribulation is best explained by a partial rapture (Rev. 13:7). Christ's Philadelphia Bride (not Laodicea, Rev. 3:10; 14-22) will be hidden from the wrath to come upon all the Earth (Luke 21:36; Isa. 26:20, 21; Ps. 27:5). She will instead partake of the marriage feast of the Lamb (Isa. 26:20; Rev. 19:7) and will assume a number of prodigious roles—heavenly (judging fallen angels, 1 Cor. 6:3) and earthly (ruling and reigning with Christ during the Millennium, Rev. 20:5-6, 22:15, 19:15). In contrast, believers found wanting at the time of the Rapture may yet make Heaven their home, but first must endure martyrdom in the Great Tribulation (Rev. 6:9-11).

Rapture: Its Day and Hour

Matthew 24:44 lets us know that the Rapture will take place at a time not specifically anticipated. Only the Father knows when the Rapture will occur (Matt. 24:36). Of the day and hour knows no man (nor angel of Heaven, nor even the Son, according to the best manuscripts).

Rapture: Imminent or Soon?

Imminence presupposes no necessary happenings prior to the Rapture. To the contrary, specific requirements defining maturation and functioning within the Body of Christ, as delineated in Ephesians 4:3; 11-16 (also, Isa. 52:6-8; Rev. 12:5) clearly suggest pre-Rapture prerequisites not yet attained. Other Scriptures require a first revealing of Antichrist and establishment of world government before the Rapture (2 Thess. 2:3; Rev. 12:1-5).

Parousia: *Rapture or Second Coming?*

The King James Version has incorrectly translated the Greek word *parousia* as "coming" (thus intimating the Second Coming). However, *parousia* is best translated "presence" or "to be beside" so as not to confuse the Rapture with Christ's Second Advent. For example, Matthew 24:3 asks the vital question, "What shall be the sign of your presence?" 1 Thessalonians 4:15 tells us that those alive at His presence will not go before those already dead, for at the Rapture the dead in Christ will ascend first.

Similarly, in 2 Thessalonians 2:1, the appropriate translation, "presence," relates to the Greek word, *episunagogay*, meaning "to collect together with stress upon the place (the spirit-realm)." All three passages refer to Christ's presence at the Rapture, not His Second Coming.

How does the Rapture differ from the Second Coming?

To differentiate between the Rapture and the Second Coming, one must examine keys to time, persons, terms, impact, places, motion, and visibility.

Time Keys. The timing of the Rapture is developed from proper interpretation and harmonization of many Scriptures. In Luke 21:28-36, we see that the Rapture comes when "these things" (signs of His presence) begin to come to pass. The summer (referring to Tribulation) is now at hand. Believers are to pray that they might flee Tribulation and stand before the Son of Man. In contrast, the Second Coming parallels Armageddon— this being after the three and one-half years of Tribulation, followed by an additional three and one-half years of plagues (Zech. 14:4, 9, 11). Premillennialism rightly teaches that the Second

Coming occurs before Christ's thousand-year reign from Jerusalem on earth (See Millennium).

Person Keys. Although adequately prepared and looking for Christ's appearing, the bowed-over, pre-Rapture Bride-in-the-making is depicted in Scripture as in need of escape, covering, and protection (Luke 21:28, 36; Matt. 25:10; Luke 21:36; Mark 13:35). With but a little strength, she takes full advantage of the wide-open door of ministry set before her. Moreover, she effectively restrains the work of Antichrist, but is unable to thwart it completely. Later, at Christ's Second Coming, she is transformed into a victorious warring army treading the wine press of the fierceness and wrath of Almighty God, thus sealing the doom of Satan (Lucifer), Antichrist, and his False Prophet (Rev. 19:1-15; Jude 14; 1 Thess. 3:13).

Term Keys. Terms of endearment and comfort announce the Rapture with its well-disposed concealing of the Bride in the secrecy of Christ's bridal chamber for but "a little moment" until the Tribulation's passing (Ps. 27:5, 31:19-20; Song 2:10-14; Is. 26:20-21). On the contrary, terms of woe, destruction, killing, wailing, gloom, doom, and vengeance typify the Second Coming of Christ with His Bride, previously snatched away to escape such things (Joel, Isaiah, Revelation).

Impact Keys. The Rapture features escape, for the Manchild of Revelation 12 is snatched up to God while the Mother-Church herself is forced to flee to the wilderness of Tribulation. (See Manchild Ministry).

Believers are to watch and pray always that they, too, may be strengthened to flee *ek* ("from out of") Tribulation (Rev. 3:10) and stand before the son of Man (Luke 21:36). With regard to the Second Coming, however, there is no escape. According to Revelation 9:18-20, one-third of humankind is killed, and the rest are without repentance.

Place/Motion Keys. The Rapture takes place going "up" into the air (spirit realm) (1 Thess. 4:17; Rev. 12:5), but the Second Coming takes place coming "down" onto the earth (natural realm) (Rev. 19:11-15).

Visibility Keys. Because the Rapture is instantaneous, it is too quick to be seen and is, therefore, invisible to nonparticipants. Whereas the Rapture mysteriously takes one, leaving the other behind (Matt. 24:40), the Second Coming is visible to all. It is announced with lightening coming out of the East and shining even unto the West (Matt. 24:27). All men see the Son of Man coming in a cloud (of witnesses) (Heb. 12:1) with power and great glory (Luke 21:27).

Summary

The Rapture and the Second Coming clearly happen at different times and in differing ways. While the Rapture precedes Tribulation, the Second Coming precedes the Millennial Reign of Christ. Whereas hope, comfort, and escape attend those raptured, judgment and destruction with no escape for unregenerate humankind will haunt the Second Coming. The motion of the Rapture is "up" (into the spirit realm), but the motion of the Second Coming is "down" (into the earthly realm). Only prepared believers looking for Jesus see Him at the Rapture, but the whole world sees Jesus and His previously out-translated Bride at Christ's Second Coming.

The Rapture, Second Coming, and Globalism

The Rapture is significant to the study of globalism in that its participants finally escape the putrid harvest of end-time ungodliness and, in so doing, render a death blow to the headship of Antichrist, whose recovery at best is temporary (1 Cor. 15:51-57; Rev. 13:3). By the same token, the Second Coming effectively overturns Satan's counterfeit global network (the New World Order under Antichrist) while, at the same time, it ushers in God's more excellent plan for theocratic global government under Jesus Christ and His Bride (See Millennium).

Reincarnation

Referred to as transmigration or metempsychosis, reincarnation exists in many philosophies and religions, even beyond those of the ancient Egyptians and Greeks. One of the four pillars of the New Age movement, reincarnation helps define Theosophy, Buddhism, Hinduism, Jainism, and certain "Christian" heresies, such as the Cathars. Following physical death, the human soul (or the spirit of a plant or animal) is said to live again in another life form. The status of each subsequent reincarnation supposedly reflects one's quality of life preceding it.

To New Age occultists, adepts are considered highly evolved enlightened ones. Once embryo-gods, adepts have ascended the reincarnation ladder multiple times and are equipped, therefore, to watch over and guide the progress of humanity toward its Omega Point, or mystical goal (See Age of Aquarius). To some, adepts are spirit beings (actually demons) with whom New Age occultists, or mystics, interact once they have entered an altered state of consciousness.

Having achieved Luciferic Initiation, the adept is master of esoteric philosophy, which embraces secret occult doctrines and practices. Having triumphed over matter, presumably by mastering self, the adept finds his/her consciousness shifted from self to group. As such, (s)he has repeatedly reincarnated until, finally, (s)he has reached Lucifer's dream of being one with God and one with the universe (See Pantheism; Radical Environmentalism).

Biblical Perspective

Scriptures are clear on the issue of reincarnation: "It is appointed unto human kind once to die" (Heb. 9:27). Humans do not live and die; live and die; but they do reproduce "after his kind" (Gen. 1:11, 12, 21, 24, 25; 6:20; 7:14; Lev. 11:14-16, 19, 22, 29; Deut. 14:13-15, 18). For this reason, a human could not have been a primate in some "past life," nor will anyone, not even a so-called adept, become a God in some future life of "higher existence." The Scriptural concept of "partaking of the Divine nature" is counterfeited in this fallacy (2 Pet. 1:4). Each one has but a single life to live, either for or against the Most High God; and judgment follows (Matt. 12: 30; Gen. 14:18 [*El Elyon*]; Heb. 9:27).

Reincarnation is but one branch of the tree of strong delusion, nurtured globally by Antichrist and substantiated by "wonders of falsehood." Its belief advances New Age mysticism of the New World Order. In New Age theology, the adept is "Custodian of the Plan," the counterfeit of the Plan of God. For these reasons, it is germane to the study of globalism (2 Thess. 2:9-11).

Revived Roman Empire;

Kings without Kingdoms

Biblical Perspective

About six hundred years before Christ, Daniel anticipated the major world governments to follow Babylon—namely, Medo-Persia, Greece, and Rome. In the seventh chapter of Daniel, the prophet saw a vision of four great beasts, diverse from one another, and coming out of the sea "of peoples, nations, multitudes, and tongues" (Dan. 7:3; Rev. 13:1; 17:15). The first was like a lion, representing Babylon (verse 4); the second, like a bear, portrayed Medo-Persia (verse 5). Next, the leopard indicated Greece (verse 6); and the ten-horned beast, picturing Rome, was source to the "little horn," a prophetic description of Antichrist (verse 8), whose appearance will exceed his fellows, and whose mouth will speak very great things (Dan. 7:20; 2 Thess. 2:4).

Daniel had seen another image, as recorded in Chapter Two (verses 31-33). This great image's head of gold likewise represented Babylon; its breast and arms of silver illustrated Medo-Persia; his belly and thighs of brass depicted Greece; and his legs of iron denoted Rome. Charlemagne, Mussolini, and Hitler tried to revive ancient Rome, but none could accomplish what only Antichrist can at his given time. In Daniel's vision, the feet (part iron, part clay) anticipated a future world rule under Antichrist, which will resemble that of ancient Rome in its religion, scope of influence, nature of sway, and destined collapse.

Religion

The ancient Roman Empire, which lasted for about 800 years, was a political, economic, and military entity held together religiously by the Roman Catholic (meaning "universal") Church. The mix of clay with iron in Daniel's vision could depict the glue (clay) of the end-time eco-religious system coupled with the dictatorial reign of Antichrist (iron) (See New Age Movement).

In yet another illustration, the iron of fading totalitarianism, mingled with the miry clay of democracy, bears striking resemblance to today's United States of Europe, soon to become the United States of the World. What is now happening with the European Community almost guarantees the economic dominance of Western Europe in the New World Order. Although the United Nations, Council on Foreign Relations, and Trilateral Commission all are headquartered in New York, the Hierarchy of Europe appears ultimately to be in charge.

Under Constantine, first emperor to adopt nominal Christianity, ancient Rome was temporarily reunited, but the Gospel was compromised with a muddle of pagan practices and beliefs. Scholars claim that three-quarters of Roman Catholic ritual originated in paganism. Three examples include votive offerings, holy water, and images.

Under Antichrist and his False Prophet, the world will be united once again by a syncretistic religious system with pantheism at its core (See Radical Environmentalism: Gaia). Rome Revived will follow the lead of each previous global kingdom represented by Daniel's image in that it will resurrect mysteries of ancient Babel, mother of all religious abominations, whose sensuality, opulence, and worldly power continue even to this day and beyond (Rev. 17:5).

Indeed, the Council of Europe's official poster depicts the European Community as the Tower of Babel under construction with twelve upside-down pentagrams above it. Representing the twelve nations of the new United Europe, the "stars" are Pentacles of Witchcraft, symbolizing the Goat of Mendes, Satan himself (See Ancient Mystery Religions, Light and Goat Motifs). The caption reads, "Europe: Many tongues; one voice."

Scope of Influence

Traditionally founded in 753 B.C., Ancient Rome became a kingdom, later a self-ruling republic, occupying the Italian peninsula, then most of Europe, the Near East, and North Africa. At its peak, the Roman Empire stretched from Britain to Mesopotamia (Iraq today) and the Caspian Sea. As Ancient Rome spanned the earth, so will Revived Rome under Antichrist's dictatorial reign, beginning with the European Community (Rev. 13:7, 8). In *Bolshevism and World Peace* (1918), Russian Communist Leon Trotsky wrote, "The task of the proletariat is to create a U.S. of Europe as foundation for the U.S. of the world."

Nature of Sway

In art, architecture, literature, law, and engineering, Ancient Rome influenced Western Europe throughout the Middle Ages, the Renaissance, and thereafter. Similarly, Revived Rome will stamp its trademark on the world. In the seventeenth chapter of

John's Revelation, we read about "ten horns" of worldly power. In this context, Antichrist is depicted as the king who will rule "a short space" (verses 11-12). Many theologians pair these ten power sources with Daniel's ten toes. Having "one mind," these "kings without kingdoms" will rule for "one hour" with Antichrist, to whom they willingly forfeit their power and strength (verses 12-13).

Globalist Zbigniew Brzezinski identifies progressive regionalism as a precondition for eventual and genuine globalization. Perhaps the ten toes of Daniel's image represent ten global megaregions: Europe, Far/Middle East, North/South Americas, South/Central Asia, New Zealand, South/Central Africa into which the world will be divided under Antichrist. The Constitution for the Federation of Earth proposes an administrative structure of twenty world electoral and administrative regions with ten mega-regions.

Many would agree, however, that a more likely interpretation identifies these "kings without kingdoms" as industrial monopolists and international bankers, who act as kings with no visible kingdom as they manipulate the world's economy to suit their own ends.

Cartel capitalism is dominated by mega-magnet international financiers, whose global interests, influence, and connections spell astonishing power. Take, for example, the House of Rockefeller comprised of globalists whose billions of dollars in assets maintain considerable leverage over hundreds of billions more. The Eastern Liberal Establishment stands for the powerful political, economic, academic, and mainstream media partnership essentially controlled by it.

Through the Council on Foreign Relations, the Rockefeller family has extended its influence in government, the Federal Reserve, communications, and education. John D. Rockefeller made his first move on education when, in 1902, he formed the tax-exempt General Education Board. Since then, incredible Rockefeller funds have promoted globalism and socialism in America's public education system. The Brothers Rockefeller continue to use their massive wealth to create and promote what they openly call the New World Order.

Philanthropy is essential to growth of wealth and, therefore, power—this by means of "scientific giving" to foundations. The

Rockefellers are not alone in such practices, or in their one world mission. Many capitalist families have become so intermarried with the Rockefellers that by 1937 one could trace a virtually unbroken line of biological relationships from the Rockefellers through half of the sixty wealthiest families in our nation.

The Rockefellers have both competed and cooperated with the dominant banking family of Europe, the Rothschilds. Since the late 1700s, the Rothschilds have allied with Freemasonry and its one world agenda to expand their banking operations. During the late 1800s, they began financing American industrialists. Through the Rothschild-Rockefeller-Carnegie chain, much of America's corporate wealth can be traced to Europe's "old money" and one world interests of Freemasonry.

Destined Collapse

Clearly, Rockefeller-Carnegie-Ford Foundations all function as "kings without kingdoms." Because money is their God, they have no practical use for the religion of masses. In due course, the final act of these "kings without kingdoms" will be to make desolate Antichrist's cohort, the False Prophet-whore of the New Age religious system. As God previously destroyed Babylon (60 B.C.) for her spiritual whoredoms, He likewise will use these "kings" to judge and destroy end-time Babylon, this time permanently (Isa. 13:19-20; Rev. 17:16).

Emperors of ancient Rome ruled by military, not civil power; similarly, Rome Revived will be distinctive for its "devouring and breaking in pieces." Believers no doubt will feel its fury (Dan. 7:19; Rev. 13:7). Although not indefinitely, the coming New World Order will, for a season, usurp the rightful place of Jerusalem, physically (as the City of God) and spiritually (as the people of God).

Revived Rome's demise will be even more astounding than the collapse of Ancient Rome, when Constantinople fell to the Ottoman Turks in 1453. Then, Antichrist's brutal international order will be shattered by Jesus Christ, "a stone cut out without hands" (or born of a virgin, Dan. 2:34-35). Thereafter, in the Millennium, Christ will restore Jerusalem, national and spiritual (See Israel; Rapture/Second Coming). It is Christ, the Lamb, Who shall utterly overcome, for He alone is Lord of lords and King of kings—with or without kingdoms of their own (Rev. 17:14).

Rhodes Scholarship Fund

A South African born in the U.K. (1853), Cecil John Rhodes was a politician who served as prime minister of Cape Colony and an industrialist who made his fortune using Black slaves in diamond mines of South Africa. Aiming at the formation of a block of British territory from the Cape to Cairo, and of a South African federation, Rhodes was responsible in 1885 for the annexation of Bechuanaland (Botswana). Moreover, in 1889 he formed the British South Africa Company, which occupied Mashonaland and Matabeleland, thus forming Rhodesia (Zambia and Zimbabwe).

In 1891 Rhodes established the secret Society of the Elect to advance the cause of a New World Order by absorbing and then applying the world's wealth to its development. To forward his dream that the United States be reannexed to the British Empire, Rhodes established a foundation to provide education in England for bright young Americans. Under his will, the Rhodes Scholarship Fund was founded at Oxford University for scholars from the Commonwealth, Germany, and the U.S. While himself studying at Oxford, Rhodes was a fervent disciple of Professor John Ruskin, who called himself "the reddest also of the red."

A thick associate of the Rothschilds, Rhodes hobnobbed with European Freemasonry. The Illuminati on faculties of colleges and universities wanted to cultivate students of exceptional ability, especially those from well-bred families. Those recommended for special training in internationalism were awarded the Rhodes Scholarship, among others. They were persuaded that their exceptional talents and aptitude guarantee their right to rule over less gifted counterparts, who are unaware of what is good for them. With the mind to create a new culture favoring ruling elites in the world community, these scholars eventually became strategically placed experts who advised top executives to undermine governments and religions they were elected or appointed to serve.

Biblical Perspective

Glory, honor, and peace are due those who "work good"

(Rom. 2:10). To acknowledge accomplishment is acceptable, and even pleasing to God. The Lord Himself commends the dutiful for being "good and faithful," and He even promotes them to positions of leadership (Matt. 25:21). It must be noted, however, that true honor comes from God alone (John 12:26; Ps. 49:12). He is no respecter of persons, not even the ruling elite of the New World Order (Acts 10:34). Concordant evil powers at odds with the plan and purpose of God will fail, as will the glory of their misplaced approbation (Rev. 14:8-10; Hosea 4:7).

Rosicrucians

A highly secret cult of the early 1300s, the Rosicrucians came to be known as the Order of the Rose Croix. Little is known of its true beginnings. We do know, however, that initiates merged with, and eventually took over, stone mason guilds of Europe. The Rosicrucians retained many symbols from the building trade. Dogma of the corrupt military and occult order, Knights Templar, is intermingled with the Rose-Croix (Albert Pike. *Morals and Dogma* [Richmond: L.H. Jenkins, Inc., 1920]. 820).

The document *Fama Fraternitatis* is an allegory of the Order's alleged history. Its mythical character, Christian Rosenkreuz, was said to have studied the occult in his travels to Syria and Egypt. Thereafter, he returned to Europe to spread this illumination. However, he was not well received. As a result, he went home to Germany, hoping to establish a society of believers (Albert G. Mackey. *An Encyclopedia of Freemasonry* [New York: The Masonic History Co., 1921]. 639).

Rosenkreuz's fictionalized life was apparently symbolic of the Knights Templar. The Rosicrusian's intent in sharing it was not to increase its ranks, but rather to monitor Europe's openness to the occult—this, without revealing the Order's true identity. Only decades later did the Order expand by publicly enlisting candidates for initiation. It seems that the tale was readily recognized as true. In response, a number of societies emerged, each claiming to possess occult secrets of Rosenkreuz. Having circulated this fable merely to run a credibility check, the Order did not themselves embrace gullible enthusiasts; therefore, these burgeoning societies were not considered to be true Rosicrucians.

Some modern Masons deny connection with the Knights

Templars and the Rosicrucians; however, this disclaimer is unlikely in that the York Rite's last three degrees are Knights of the Red Cross, Knights of Malta, and Knights Templar. Moreover, the Scottish Rite eighteenth degree, Sovereign Prince of the Rose-Croix, together with its seventeenth degree, is called the Chapter of Rose Croix. Freemasonry purposes to unite the world in its esoteric doctrine and global agenda.

Biblical Perspective

Christians are not to attend to stories and endless genealogies, which prompt needless questions and fail to convey the truth. This type of error is to be expected increasingly in these last days. Therefore, watchful believers are to avoid old wives' stories, lest they be turned away from sound doctrine (1 Tim. 1:4; 2 Tim. 3:13; 1 Tim. 4:7; 2 Tim. 4:3; Titus 1:9).

S

"Safe Sex"

In the 1940s Dr. Alfred Kinsey revolutionized American culture, while systematically undermining Judeo-Christian morality with his aberrant ideas about human sexuality. Trained as a zoologist, Kinsey based his research on interviews with child molesters, prostitutes, and homosexuals. He considered the sexual conduct of animals to be his standard for human sexuality, further believing that society should not stifle any sexuality. Such assumptions allow even for bestiality and incest.

Having investigated the work of the Kinsey team and Institute, Judith A. Reisman exposed illegal experimentation on virtually hundreds of children, even infants of only five months of age, as documented by Kinseyan Table 34. Co-author of *Kinsey, Sex and Fraud: The Indoctrination of a People,* Dr. Reisman concluded that Kinsey's research was fraudulent; nonetheless, his agenda is foisted daily on our children under pretense of safe-sex instruction through nationwide public education programs. For example, in Seattle (August 1995) the late Superintendent John Stanford approved formation of a district "Sexual Minority Advocacy Council." With the Seattle-King County Public Health Department, SMAC promotes same sex intercourse through "safe-sex" classes and presentations.

With an initial grant from the Playboy Foundation, the sex education arm of the Kinsey Institute, SIECUS (Sexuality Information and Education Council of the United States), was founded in New York (1964). Although promotion of Kinseyan views by SIECUS is said to have ignited the hurtful sexual revolution of the 1960s, SIECUS continues to receive funding from the federal government and the Rockefeller Foundation (See Revived Roman Empire; Kings without Kingdoms). Zero Population Growth and the Planned Parenthood Federation of America are among many organizations that endorse SIECUS.

The government and today's mainstream media would have us believe that "everyone's doing it," but teen panelists for *USA Today* report to the contrary. According to a Time-Cable News

Network survey, about seventy percent of teens thirteen to seventeen years old had not had sex. As if to promote early sexual activity, "safe sex" is the incessant theme of music lyrics, television commercials, movie plots, magazine articles, and public education efforts. Public schools have become Medicaid providers, and Medicaid/Medicare reimbursements include dispensing condoms with empty promises of "safe" sex. It may be true that using a latex condom each and every time does provide some protection, but its faithful use cannot guarantee immunity against AIDS. The taxpayer-funded "America Responds to AIDS" safe-sex campaign promotes a number of concepts that simply do not ring true (See Gay Rights).

For example, a federal program started in 1970 (Title X of the Public Health Service Act) continues to provide even controversial forms of birth control to America's poor. In so doing, Title X leaves parents completely out of the picture, even if their child is brought by a pedophile to receive contraceptives from a clinic.

The politically correct crowd believe that too many people on earth outstrip her resources (See Radical Environmentalism; Death Culture). Especially when coupled with Kinseyan nonproductive sexual gratification at any age, this Thomas Malthus idea fits hand-in-glove with the United Nations concept of sustainable development, as defined in *Our Common Future.* Sustainable communities and moral relativism earmark the New World Order.

Biblical Perspective

No illicit sex is "safe." This is why God's Plan calls for a man and woman to give one another the gift of chastity at the onset of their legal, monogamous, heterosexual—and, yes, even fruitful—marriage, its bed undefiled (Heb. 13:4). These last days are defined instead by pleasure-loving and moral incontinence (2 Tim. 3:1-7). Duped by mockery of God's immutable Word with calculated intent to topple Judeo-Christian morality, global citizens are herded mindlessly into a New World Order as they willingly buy into the Kinseyan brand of moral relativism, which undermines God's Plan by degrading the very crown of His creation (2 Pet. 2:1; See Authenticity of Scriptures; Political Correctness Movement; Values Education).

Seventy Weeks of Daniel

Biblical Perspective

The Seventy Weeks of Daniel (or "70 sevens") is simply a name applied to a specific period of time (490 years) referred to in Daniel 9:24-27. These verses contain a complete history of Israel from Daniel's time to that of the Messiah.

Although they have been interpreted in countless ways, and remain somewhat of a mystery, these Seventy Weeks are crucial to understanding all Biblical prophecy. Daniel himself was not given perfect understanding. He asked, "My Lord, what shall be the end of these things?" (12:8). To this, God answered, ". . . the words are closed up and sealed till the time of the end" (12:9). Still, some erroneously insist that Daniel wrote only about events that had already happened. Others believe that the 490-year period culminated with Jesus' death. It is more likely, however, that this prophecy is yet to be fulfilled, for God's reply to Daniel indicates that the Seventy Weeks prophecy plainly looks into the distant future.

Daniel's Intercession

Daniel's study of Jeremiah (Chapter 25) regarding the seventy years of captivity compelled him to pray for God's intervention on behalf of His people. Daniel begged God to shorten the time of their grief (Dan. 9:1-19). God's answer to Daniel came in a vision. The angel Gabriel revealed to Daniel that the nation of Israel would be restored to her homeland after her period of captivity. This would be followed, many years later (before final judgment), by the Coming of the Messiah. God further disclosed that His people would be restored to glory as a nation within a period of seventy weeks of seven years each (a total of 490 years).

God's Answer

These 490 years are divided into three groups: 7 weeks (49 years), 62 weeks (434 years), and 1 week (7 years). During the first seven weeks (49 years), the returned exiles, although interrupted, were to complete construction of the city of Jerusalem, its Temple most specifically. The next 62 weeks of seven years (434 years) would mark the time for Messiah's three and one-half year ministry.

Some scholars believe the 490 years began with the decree of Cyrus in 536 B.C. (Isa. 44:28). They also believe the first 69 weeks (483 years) of this prophecy end roughly with the beginning of Christ's ministry in A.D. 26. Others argue that the beginning point is the order of King Artaxerxes to Nehemiah (Neh. 2:5-8), which places the return of some of the exiles at 445 B.C. In this view, the first 483 years end at Jesus' triumphal entry into Jerusalem. Whatever the case, we can know for certain that the end of the 483 years brings us generally to the time of Christ's ministry.

Happenings within the Prophesied 490 Years

The seventy weeks of years are determined (Dan. 9:24):

- To finish the transgression (Heb. 9:15; Isa. 53:5);
- To make an end of sins (John 1:29);
- To make reconciliation for iniquity (Heb. 2:17);
- To bring in everlasting righteousness (Isa. 51:6, 8; Joel 3:17);
- To seal up the vision and prophecy (Isa. 61:1-3; Luke 4:17-21); and
- To anoint the Most Holy (Mark 1:9-11).

All six aspects take place within the Seventy Weeks. To summarize, the first forty-nine years started with the command to rebuild the Temple following the return from captivity, and the work continued (apparently with stop-gaps) until the Temple was finally rebuilt. The conclusion of the next sixty-two weeks landed in about A.D. 26, which serves as kick-off point for Christ's ministry.

Jesus was cut off at Calvary in the middle of the final seventieth week, the first half of which was represented by Christ's three and one-half year ministry (Dan. 9:26). The last half of the seventieth week will take place during the final three and one-half years of the Great Tribulation (period of plagues), during which time the Lord will confirm the covenant with many (144,000 representatives from each of the twelve tribes of Israel). Plagues start with the homecoming of Two Witnesses (Messianic Jewish and Gentile) and end with the Second Coming of Christ.

Therefore, the time from the going forth of the command-ment to restore and to build Jerusalem unto Messiah, the Prince, shall be 490 years in total (Isa. 44:28; 45:1, 13; 2 Chron. 36:22-23; Ezra 1:1-4).

Conclusion

The Seventy Weeks of Daniel are significant for a number of reasons. First, the prophecy underscores biblical authenticity, for most of the prophecy has transpired just as God told Daniel it would, despite astronomical odds to the contrary. Next, the proph-ecy gives us a glimpse into the future, for God promised to reveal Daniel's vision more fully in these last days. Finally, the Seventy Weeks confirm the fact that God has not discarded national Israel, as some say; He has a continuing plan for her.

Solipsism (Self-God)

In philosophy, solipsism is a view that maintains that self is the only thing that can be known to exist; others merely reflect one's own consciousness. New Age "visioneers" discover this self through renewed relationship with the planet, known also as the Earth goddess Gaia (See Radical Environmentalism).

Prominent educator, globalist, and occultist Dr. Robert Muller defines the self as "the Earth become conscious of herself." Muller promotes such fanciful ideals in his New-Age, UN-backed Glo-bal Education Curriculum. The World Core Curriculum for which Muller received the UNESCO Peace Prize is at the heart of today's education reform in America and throughout the world (See Outcome-Based Education).

Solipsism embraces the notion that I must feel good about myself. In psychology, narcissism is an exaggeration of normal self-respect and involvement; hence, the "Me Generation," with its "Imperial Self." In preparing youngsters to become good world citizens, today's Outcome-Based Education Model puts more emphasis on misplaced self-esteem than it does on basic skills.

Self-esteem has become the unremitting mantra of mystics and secularists alike. Both camps believe individuals should real-ize their own desires (See "Safe Sex": Kinsey). Whereas secular humanists express their religious emotions in "a heightened sense of personal life," New Age occultists journey inward in search of the "higher self."

Good global citizens of the New World Order are committed to "collective thought." Some anticipate a coming Age of Aquarius by means of mass planetary Luciferic Initiation, ultimate mystical experience of "the self." Wrongly presumed to reflect one's own creative mind energy, collective thought is more accurately achieved through Hegelian Dialectic, or group consensus under peer pressure (See Pantheism: "All is Energy").

Biblical Perspective

God's Word makes it clear that no one rightly "hates his own flesh" (Eph. 5:29). In fact, believers are admonished to love themselves; but, in so doing, they are commanded to make no provision for harmful carnal desires or self-will (Matt. 22:39; Rom. 13:14). To expedite the birth of the New World Order requires death of the old one with its outmoded Golden Rule (See Values Education). These last days are defined by a counterfeit form of self-love, even to the point of pantheistic self-deification by means of earned egoic advancement. In time, Antichrist will exalt himself as "God," and many will fall prey to his lie (2 Tim. 3:1-2; 2 Thess. 2:3-4; 11).

Spirit Guide/Guide

See Adept/Initiated Adept.

T

Teachers' College, Columbia University

From 1904 until the end of his life, atheist John Dewey taught aspiring educators at the Teacher's College at Columbia University, where he served as head of its education department. It was he who brought notoriety to this previously obscure institution.

Perhaps more than any other man, Dewey molded educational thought in the early part of the twentieth century, and he controlled education in Western civilization for about fifty years. The first president of the American Humanist Society, Dewey authored and signed the first *Humanist Manifesto* (See Humanism/Secular Humanism). A Fabian Socialist, Dewey held to the Marxist concept, and he embraced Darwinism. That Dewey's agenda was intended to supplant the nation's public school system with a form of socialism was the finding of an investigation conducted by the Reece Committee in the early 1950s.

Rockefeller and Carnegie funded, the Teachers College at Columbia University exalted and expounded Deweyism while raising some of the most radical advocates of Dewey's so-called Progressive Education system. Dewey's disciple, Professor George Counts of Columbia University, opposed forces of social conservatism and promoted a "New Social Order."

Because Dewey's alma mater served as the model for teacher training programs in colleges and universities across the United States, many believe that much of what is wrong with America's public education system today is traced to the Teachers' College at Columbia University. It is estimated that as many as one-fourth of all present high school superintendents, and nearly half of all teacher-college heads, have received advanced degrees there. Today, Columbia University boasts a reputation for promoting Marxism. Her president is George Rupp, and her budget includes tens of millions to promote leftist causes.

Although the group called Progressive Education Association disbanded during the fifties, its philosophies remain the basis of all modern public education. Dr. Max Rafferty called Progressive Education, as disseminated from the Teachers' College, Columbia University, "the old pagan philosophy of hedonism refurbished in modern technology." When Dewey died in 1952, the overpowering Protestant character of the early public schools had completely disappeared.

Biblical Perspective

(See Public Education: Christian to Secular to Mystical: Biblical Perspective.)

Textbook Conspiracy

The international Aspen Institute for Humanistic Studies is a private, non-profit organization where leading officials of the Trilateral Commission, the Rockefeller Foundation, and the White House go for advanced seminars in global ideology (See New World Order). A former president of the institute admitted that most of the materials they develop sooner or later find their way into textbooks, which are used by over forty million American youngsters.

Textbooks and Global Indoctrination

Throughout the last several decades, globalists have effectively employed the billion-dollar textbook industry to promulgate their agenda. Many textbook publishers are represented on the Council on Foreign Relations, founded by the Rockefellers and their allies. The Rockefellers themselves have spent millions of dollars creating and rewriting textbooks to suit their own global interests (See Revived Roman Empire: Kings without Kingdoms). Publishing house founder, D. C. Heath, put it well when he said, "Let me publish the textbooks of a nation, and I care not who writes its songs or makes its laws."

While nearly half of all high school graduates remain functionally illiterate, today's students focus their studies on liberal socialism, big government, and the "global village." While undermining patriotism and free enterprise, textbooks promote global politics and economics (See Global Economics/Banking). For example, *Building America* was so chock full of Marxist propaganda that, despite Rockefeller subsidy and NEA support, the California legislature prohibited appropriation of funds for its use in the classroom.

Textbooks and Political Correctness

The term political correctness is an umbrella under which a number of other "isms" huddle. The movement's program is to deconstruct Western civilization, specifically European/American culture. Anything "traditional" is the target (e.g., the Constitution of the United States). Causes thus united include civil/gender/sexual orientation rights and radical environmentalism— all central themes of textbooks employed in classrooms throughout America today. Texts such as Walter McDougall's *United States History: In the Course of Human Events* (West Publishing Company) emphasize politically correct multiracial history and victimization of African Americans and women (See Afrocentrism; Genderism).

In the name of multiculturalism (diversity), America cooperated with the USSR in the 1977 Textbook Study Project. Together, they came up with a Marxist-Leninist concept known as Polytechnical Education, which melds academics with vocational training. The U.S./USSR Education Exchange Agreement was signed in 1985, then again in 1988 (See Outcome-Based Education).

Textbooks and Revisionist History Standards

Developed by the National Center for History in the Schools (1994), the Goals 2000 history standards were announced and then condemned by the U.S. Senate. To neutralize opposition, the Council for Basic Education reviewed and subsequently tinkered with them. As a result of Gary Nash's efforts, more than thirty states have adopted these standards, effectively robbing students of their national heritage. You see, revisionist history completely ignores Western culture, failing even to address the Reformation and making little mention of the Renaissance and the Enlightenment. While George Washington is dismissed as more of a symbol than a hero, Soviet dictator Gorbachev is credited for single-handedly ending the Cold War.

Textbooks and Evolution

Although strong evidence supports creationism (not outlawed in the Scopes Trial of 1925, as some assume), it is completely absent from America's high school biology textbooks. Instead, evolution is taught exclusively. The theory is presented as fact although discredited by such world famous scientists as Albert Einstein.

Biblical Perspective

In the Christian classic *The Battle for the Mind,* Dr. Timothy LaHaye shows that American education was never intended to be godless; nonetheless, textbooks today freely omit "under God" in quoting Lincoln's Gettysburg Address (e.g., Laidlaw's *Our Nation's History*). Believers are to "learn not the way of the heathen," nor are they to "enquire after their gods" (Jer. 10:2; Deut. 12:30), yet the National Science Foundation's federally-funded *Man: A Course of Study* included a story for fifth graders about a man who consults with spirits that tell him to save his own life by eating his wife. The course's primary developer, Peter B. Dow, challenged "the notion that there are 'eternal truths' (e.g., Ten Commandments) that must be passed down from one generation to the next."

In these last days, men and women are more in love with pleasure than with God (2 Tim. 3:4). Not surprisingly, a Michigan Department of Public Health booklet reads, "Sex education should work to impart competence, not necessarily constraint." Since it does not take thirteen years (kindergarten through grade twelve) to teach "the facts of life," it becomes apparent that the true goal of sex education is "morals modification" (See Planned Parenthood; "Safe Sex").

Today's new morality wars against the Judeo-Christian ethic. For example, the Bible lets us know that God "has no pleasure in the death of him that dieth" (Ezek. 18:32). Still, a number of textbook publishers feature death and dying themes (See Death Culture; Values Education). For example, in 1969 Simon and Schuster released an *Inner City Mother Goose:* "Jack be nimble/ Jack be quick/snap the blade/and give it a flick/grab the purse/it's easily done/then just for kicks/just for fun/plunge the knife/and cut/and run."

Several years ago, a member of the American Board of Professional Psychology testified before the U.S. House Subcommittee on Education, exposing contempt for parents as being "shockingly apparent in many of the courses funded under Title III" and promoted by the National Institute of Mental Health. The Bible warns that "there is a generation that curseth their father and doth not bless their mother" (Prov. 30:11). As we fast approach the twenty-first century, God-given parental roles and rights are increasingly supplanted by the "global village," embracing instead their "Gaia-Mother Earth" (See Radical Environmentalism).

The basis for today's Outcome-Based Education movement is the award-winning World Core Curriculum, based on occult teachings of the transchanneler Alice Bailey, who founded Lucifer (Lucis) Publishing Company. In *Education in the New Age* (page 87), Bailey pinpoints textbooks as vehicles for the coming New Age of cooperative consciousness, inspired predominantly by pseudo-love of the planet.

Theosophy/Theosophical Society

Theosophy derives its name from the Greek word meaning "divine wisdom." The term itself traces to the Orient, especially India. Its underlying belief is pantheistic, proclaiming all life forms to be fundamentally one through a supreme existence (See Pantheism: "All is Energy").

Theosophical doctrines were influenced by Buddhism's wheel concept of spiritual progression, culminating in universal salvation and reconciliation. Neatly plugged into the highest levels of Freemasonry, Theosophy is likewise a form of ancient Gnosticism, plaiting religious, philosophic, and scientific thought into the tangled braid of today's New Age movement (See also Ancient Mystery Religions).

Theosophy promotes a divine plan for the world and, with this in mind, encourages study of comparative religion. As in Spiritism and Rosicrucianism, Theosophy anticipates a one world religious system featuring universal brotherhood; consequently, the society plays an important role in conditioning humanity to accept the forthcoming New World Order.

Lucis (formerly Lucifer) Trust is an off-shoot of the society, whose world membership of over 30,000 is active today in more than sixty countries. The modern American history of Theosophy began in New York (1875) under the leadership of Helena Petrovna Blavatsky and, later, Annie Besant.

A Russian-born daughter of nobility, Madam Blavatsky is known best for her literary contributions to the society. Her occult classic, *The Secret Doctrine,* is still regarded by Theosophists as divinely inspired. According to the Society's literature, there exists a brotherhood of ascended masters in remote Tibet. These masters allegedly have undergone multiple reincarnations and are, therefore, highly evolved. These are said to have possessed Blavatsky, using her to disseminate their now-restored spiritual truths. *The American Theosophist* is the official magazine for members of the Theosophical Society in the USA, which is headquartered in Wheaton, Illinois.

As with Christian Science, Unity, and other pantheistic systems, Theosophy knows no personal God to whom humans are accountable. As embryo-gods, Theosophists fancy themselves part of the god-force, progressing toward a culminating Omega Point of enlightenment. Following her death, Blavatsky's disciple, Annie Wood Besant (1847-1933), carried the torch. According to Besant, all men become "Christs;" the voice of the God within is "your voice."

Biblical Perspective

Theosophy refutes every fundamental doctrine of Biblical Christianity. Instead, the Theosophist glories in a higher form of revelation to mark the soon-coming Age of Aquarius, that of group consciousness. Chiefs of the society regard Christians as being "particularly pernicious" for lacking acquiescence with this illusory notion.

While rejecting the atonement of Christ's cross, Theosophists trust instead in self-god (and karma), discarding the authority of Holy Scriptures for vain, empty deceit (Col. 2:8). As such, Theosophists join others in these last days who have a form of godliness, but deny its true power, centered in the cross of Calvary (2 Tim. 3:1, 5).

In assessing the worth of any belief system, one principle prevails—that is, let God be true, and every opposing man (or demon spirit) a liar (Rom. 3:4). As Christians, we are to touch no unclean thing; instead, we must withdraw from those who contravene the one living God and His holy, inerrant Word (Isa. 52:11; Matt. 24:35; See Authenticity of Scripture).

Transcendental Meditation (TM)

Altered State of Consciousness

An eighteenth century philosophy of Immanuel Kant, pantheistic Transcendentalism has reappeared in the United States as both a mystical and social doctrine. In fact, it has served to shape American ideals of self-reliance, reformation, and Utopian idealism.

TM is based in part on Hindu meditation. The idea is to transcend one's body and ordinary perceptions of time and space. In this highly aroused state, one moves in and out of consciousness. "When all the senses are stilled, when the mind is at rest, when the intellect wavers not—that, say the wise, is the highest state" (*Katha Upanishad,* II, iii, 10).

This so-called "highest state" is practiced by aboriginal healers, Afro-Brazilian spirit mediums, witch doctors, and New Age occultists. Popularized in the late 1960s by the Beatles, Transcendentalism was introduced to the West by Maharishi Mahesh Yogi, who claims that its worldwide practice is bringing universal peace. The TM movement falsely claims credit for dramatic transformations sweeping Eastern Europe at the close of the Cold War.

A mind-training, centering technique, meditation is decidedly Eastern. The Hindu posture considered conducive to meditation is the world-famous lotus position in which the legs are crossed so that each foot reposes, sole up, on its opposite thigh. The spinal column is completely upright; and hands are arranged in the lap one on top of the other, palms up with thumbs touching.

Meditators are given a special word or phrase (mantra) that they repeat over and over to themselves. This practice is intended to bring about a state of well-being and relaxation. Coupled with New Age meditative music, repetition of the mantra induces a trance state. The quickest way to contact "spirit guides," and most powerful occult technique known, meditative visualization encourages participants to create their own reality. Psychologists and medical doctors are among the foremost promoters of "visual imagery" for healing everything from poor self-image to the most deadly diseases.

TM, forms of yoga, visualization, and other centering techniques are taught today in top management seminars, not to mention America's public school classrooms. Ideal communities of perfect peace are being established around the world. For example, Triangles of Theosophist Alice Bailey experiences organized meditation, allegedly linking energies of light and goodwill worldwide.

Biblical Perspective

Transcendental Meditation is not to be confused with reverent meditation on God's Word, which requires continuous cognition (Ps. 1:2; 119:148; 1 Pet. 1:13). Although the genuine peace of God passes all understanding, Christian meditators appropriate it, not by slipping in and out of consciousness, but rather by keeping their minds honed (Phil. 4:7; 2 Tim. 1:7).

End-time believers are to hold fast to established principles of Christian tradition, which do not include assuming the lotus position, engaging in Eastern centering activities, or repeating mantras (2 Thess. 2:15; Matt. 6:7-8). God commands them, for their own safety, not to learn from the heathen. Rather, they are to withdraw from them (2 Cor. 6:17). When New Age occultists suggest interchange with mediums and spiritists who "whisper and mutter," believers should instead consult the one true God (Isa. 8:19, NAS).

Trilateral Commission

The membership of the Trilateral Commission is composed of some three hundred twenty-five leaders of the world's three economic superpowers, North America, Western Europe, and Japan; hence, the term "trilateral." The Commission meets twice yearly to encourage their economic interdependence. Many private organizations link with the Trilateral Commission to form what is known euphemistically as the Eastern Liberal Establishment (Insiders).

Whereas the Council on Foreign Relations is the "brain" behind globalism, CFR spin-off groups wield three arms of power:

economic (Bilderbergers), spiritual (Club of Rome), and political (Trilateral Commission). At the center of Insider power, influence, and planning, the Council on Foreign Relations holds the Eastern Liberal Establishment together; furthermore, its avowed aim is to abolish nationalism for globalism. Along these lines, CFR member and Trilateralist Richard Gardner has called for "piece by piece" erosion of national sovereignty in bringing forth the "house of world order" (See New World Order; United Nations).

Not surprisingly, most of the Commission's important French participants belong to the Grand Orient Lodge of Freemasonry, and its largest contributor is the Ford Foundation (See Illuminati). General Electric, General Motors, and Xerox are among its supporters (See Revived Roman Empire; Kings without Kingdoms).

In 1973 David Rockefeller founded the Trilateral Commission and solicited the support of leading bankers, businessmen, labor leaders, and politicians throughout the world. The commission's founding director, Zbigniew Brzezinski, drafted its charter. Brzezinski's philosophy continues to dominate the Trilateral Commission, as well as the executive branch of the U.S. government, yet he praised Marxism and favored occult writings of French Jesuit priest Teilhard de Chardin. In the Penguin paperback *Between Two Ages,* Brzezinski gave form to the coming "Technetronic Era" reflective of the school-to-work system entrenched in today's education reform (See Outcome-Based Education).

Four thrusts of the Commission's "Triangle Papers" follow:
1. Renovated world monetary system;
2. Redistribution of the world's wealth;
3. Stepped-up trade with communists; and
4. Greater international controls.

In uniting Japan, Canada, the U.S., and the European Community, the Commission underwrites one world government whose eco-socialism promises to supplant sovereignty of nation-states with that of multinational corporations (See Global Economics/Banking; Radical Environmentalism).

Authorities agree that, together with the Council on Foreign Relations, the Trilateral Commission virtually runs our government. Says Salem Kirban (*Satan's Angels Exposed*), secrecy, power, and force are three strivings shared by the CFR, the Bilderbergers, and the Trilateral Commission. Former professor of economics at California State University, and later a research fellow at Stanford University, Dr. Antony Sutton warned of the commission's threat to our nation's sovereignty and financial security (*Trilaterals over America*).

Biblical Perspective

(See Biblical Perspective for Insiders/Eastern Liberal Establishment; Council on Foreign Relations.)

U

United Nations

Formed during the classical period at mystic Delphi in Greece, the Amphictionic Council served as predecessor of today's United Nations (UN). Ostensibly embracing international peace, security, and cooperation, the UN succeeds the League of Nations, formed after the First World War in attempt to arbitrate international dispute. Two weeks after Pearl Harbor, the Council on Foreign Relations (CFR) acted through the State Department to establish the United Nations. Each founder belonged to the CFR, the brain behind globalism.

UN Charter (See Political Correctness Movement)

The Post War Foreign Policy Committee served as planning commission for the UN and its charter, which was drawn up in 1945. Fashioned with regional governance in mind, the UN Charter boasts four objectives, the first of which is tolerance. Next, united strength promises to maintain worldwide peace and security, this with use of armed forces in the common interest. Finally, the UN purposes to promote the social and economic advancement of all people by redistributing the world's wealth. A powerful non-government organization, the International Union for the Conservation of Nature (IUCN) serves as official advisor to the UN.

UN and Globalism (See New World Order)

The UN's original resolution was to maintain peace by its Security Council's preservation of wartime alliances among the U.S., USSR, and Britain (with France and China also permanent members). The intent was to warm up Americans to the idea of global government, but with outbreak of the Cold War, this failed to happen. The UN has since played what is perceived by many as a positive role in disaster relief, development assistance, and cultural cooperation. The UN is seen by some as a kind of International Red Cross, with UN Day celebrated each 24 October.

• Globalism and the World Constitution and Parliament Association

Convening at the highest levels, the United Nations now stands poised at the center of the New World Order. Notwithstanding, some authorities believe that the World Constitution and Parliament Association is destined to replace the UN, whose chief objective is no secret. It aspires to become a one world government with one world laws, courts, schools, military complex, and churches (minus Biblical Christianity). Toward this end, the WCPA has implemented the lion's share of a number of sessions planned to usher in the New World Order.

• Globalism and the Eastern Liberal Establishment

With its headquarters in New York City, the United Nations is an association of nation-states joining more than 126 organizations and agencies worldwide. Its Security Council is the UN system's supreme organ.

John D. Rockefeller, Jr., donated the land for the UN building on the Hudson. The Rockefeller family predominantly controls the Eastern Liberal Establishment, whose expressed mission is globalism at the price of national sovereignty (See Revived Roman Empire; Kings without Kingdoms).

• Globalism and the Global Commons (See Radical Environmentalism)

The UN's trusteeship of Global Commons includes outer space, the atmosphere, nonterritorial seas, and environmental systems that support human life. Ecologist Garrett Hardin concluded in his seminal 1968 essay that "Freedom in a commons brings ruin to all." He called for totalitarian measures. Nearly three hundred environmental treaties already administered by the UN give it extensive authority over the global commons, and NAFTA is at work on an agreement to surrender national sovereignty to a global Environmental Protection Agency controlled by the UN.

UN Scandal

UN associates are not without scandal. Secretary-general of the UN's founding conference, Alger Hiss, was imprisoned in 1950 for allegedly having spied for the USSR. Similarly, former UN Secretary-general Kurt Waldheim was discovered to be a

Nazi foot soldier in Yugoslavia during World War II; he served as an intelligence officer in an army unit responsible for transporting Jews to death camps.

Americans do not elect the president of the UN, any member of the UN General Assembly, or any UN representative for that matter; but 68 percent of America's national parks, wildlife preserves, and historic monuments are now regulated by the UN. Although there are 185 nations in the UN, UN employees live tax-free in the United States, and U.S. citizens pay for fully one-fourth of the UN's operating budget.

UN's Levying Global Taxes (See Global Economics/Banking)

In the fall of 1997 media mogul Ted Turner, long involved in environmental causes, announced his billion-dollar donation over the next ten years to fund United Nations humanitarian programs around the world (See Mainstream Media). However, UN rules forbid this donation to be substituted for the estimated $1.5 billion debt supposedly owed the UN by the U.S.

To address the UN's total debt of about $2.3 billion, and with encouragement of world leaders as Mikhail Gorbachev, Boutros Boutros-Ghali introduced the concept of global taxation by adding a surcharge to airline tickets, or by charging a small fee for exchange of foreign currency.

Founder of the 250,000-member Christian Action Network Martin Mawyer warns that if Mr. Boutros-Ghali's successor, Kofi Annan, is empowered to levy global taxes, he will, in fact, lead a sovereign one world government. The U.S. Constitution allows only Congress to "lay and collect taxes," but Hillary Clinton flew to Stockholm in 1997 to lobby for a UN tax which will support world dictators and UN bureaucrats while allowing the UN to grow even bigger than the American government. In Copenhagen the UN revealed its plan for global taxation to help finance the international restructuring paradigm, as called for in the agenda of radical environmentalists.

UN Sustainable Development
(See Radical Environmentalism)

In 1987 the UN began its final drive to restructure nation-states into what has come to be known as the Global Village. That year, it issued a report on alleged environmental disasters

prompting need for global political transformation to support
sustainable development. Sustainability is a specific ruling principle, whose intent is to define supposedly voluntary, politically
correct conduct for all world citizens. According to Dr. Beverly
LaHaye of Concerned Women of America, sustainable development is a specious term the UN uses to say that wealth and
resources must be redistributed, and populations must be controlled (See Global Economics/Banking; Death Culture). The
idea is to establish down-sized "urban clusters," or global commons, subject to appointed federal agents and unelected members of private, non-government organizations (NGOs).

The UN Constitution parallels the 1997 USSR Constitution
(Chapter #2, Article 18), which completely describes "sustainable
development." In 1996 the UN's plan, described in a report entitled *Our Global Neighborhood,* favored "global governance," a
form of global socialism to be implemented by the year 2000.
The UN-funded Commission on Global Governance made up
of some of the world's most influential people completed a three-
year study whose recommendations, founded on the Global (New
Earth) Ethic, exclude national sovereignty and private property
rights (See Values Education).

Totalitarian Military Complex (See Armageddon)

The CFR-controlled U.S. State Department has purposed
to implement a program of total general disarmament. In *The
Most Secret Science,* retired Air Force Colonel Archibald Roberts
claims that, under this plan, the U.S. will finance and man what
he calls "a totalitarian UN military complex." Indeed, the UN's
ultimate authority, its Security Council, purposes to field a standing army with authority over all military forces worldwide.

The three-year UN Commission on Global Governance,
released in late 1995, recommends a rapid deployment force to
respond immediately while more conventional peace keeping forces
are assembled. According to Cliff Kincaid, author of *Global Bondage,* the UN is presently drafting plans for a one world government to accompany its world army.

The UN is gaining more power and control each year, often
at the expense of national sovereignty, and certainly in overt
defiance of our U.S. Constitution. A number of provisions within
sundry existing executive orders render feasible importation of

UN troops to uphold the law in cases of "increased international tension or financial crisis."

While serving as UN Secretary-general, Boutros Boutros-Ghali was considered by some to be the most influential individual on earth. With ambitious globalist designs and limitless resources, financially and militarily, he was accountable to no one. Mr. Boutros-Ghali encouraged increased commitments of money and troops by the West, particularly from the U.S., placing lives of American military personnel in the hands of foreign commanders.

UN's All-encompassing Infrastructure

The United Nations already represents a limited form of world government. In addition to its peace keeping forces, the UN's comprehensive infrastructure includes the International Criminal Court (not American-style justice), and specialized organizations, such as the World Health Organization, International Monetary Fund (global welfare), and World Bank (See Global Economics/Banking). Along with the Institute of Pacific Relations and the Council on Foreign Relations, the United Nations Association is a political think tank used by the International Banking Cartel to advance its global agenda (See Revived Roman Empire; Kings without Kingdoms).

The UN oversees UNESCO, the United Nations Educational, Scientific, and Cultural Organization, created in 1946 by its first Secretary-general, Sir Julian Huxley. Innovations of UNESCO include Biosphere Reserves; the "right" kind of tolerance; and lifelong learning, following the school-to-work pattern developed in the former USSR and implemented in the Outcome-Based Education model (See Political Correctness; Radical Environmentalism). Although the U.S. is not a member of UNESCO, and Congress has no role in biosphere nominations or approvals, U.S. taxpayers have contributed as much as $5 million in one year alone (1995).

UNESCO has purposed to introduce an international or global perspective in primary schools "to be incorporated into existing curricula, whenever possible." Serving as an UNESCO model of proper global citizenship, the April 1997 Vancouver Congress opened doors for its repeat across North America with intent to birth a new era in cosmic education (See Public Edu-

cation: Christian to Secular to Mystical). Already, controversy in
America has begun over a proposal to replace the traditional
pledge with a Pledge of Allegiance to the United Nations. "Education for Global Citizenship" features renewed relationship with
the planet. Tactics employed include "mind mapping" to force
group consensus and "visioneering" energy toward transformation, a term used by New Age occultists in reference to demon
possession (See Luciferic Initiation).

UN and New Age Occultism (See Ecumenical Movement;
Antichrist; False Prophet) Well connected to Freemasonry, and
founded in 1922 by notable New Age occultists, Lucis (formerly
Lucifer) Trust is a non-profit, tax-exempt educational corporation which endorses, supports, and seeks to strengthen the UN.
Accordingly, the UN has a meditation room sporting symbols of
Babylonian occultism (See Ancient Mystery Religions). Here
Hindu mystic Sri Chinmoy Kumar Ghose leads the UN Meditation Group, encouraging adherents of all world religions to
awaken to the "god within" (See New Age Movement; Pantheism). At a Spiritual Summit Conference, whose keynote speaker
was Dr. Margaret Mead, the UN's resident guru led ambassadors, Hopi medicine men, Shinto priests, and a Unitarian minister in meditation.

Popes John XXIII and Paul VI joined the Dalai Lama,
Muslim Anwar el-Sadat, and Buddhist UN Secretary-general U
Thant to form the Temple of Understanding, known as the United
Nations of World Religions. Housed at the Cathedral of St.
John the Divine in upper Manhattan, it seeks to facilitate one
world religion. Its director of international programs is a Catholic priest, and endorsers include the United Lodge of Theosophists (See Alice Bailey; Dr. Annie Wood Besant; Madam Helena Petrovna Blavatsky).

The new Secretary-general of the United Nations, Kofi
Annan, from Ghana, Africa, chose occultist Maurice Strong to
reform the world body. Director of the Temple of Understanding
in New York, Strong systematically points to presumed environmental fears in the name of Gaia, goddess of "Mother Earth."
Through UNESCO, Strong is grooming the world's youth,
tomorrow's global citizens and world servers to embrace Gaia.
Toward this goal, the UN has sponsored an Environmental Sab-
bath for the Goddess Earth, Gaia.

UN and Education Reform (See Public Education; Outcome-Based Education) In *My Testament to the UN*, prize-winning creator of the World Core Curriculum and occultist Robert Muller quotes the UN's resident guru as having called the UN "the vision-light of the Absolute Supreme." As former UN Assistant Secretary-general, Dr. Muller views the UN's spiritual dimension as inevitable. In fact, he dubs himself "Father of United Religions."

Muller is a fellow responsible in part for building Thanks-Giving Square in Dallas, a UN-sponsored meditation garden depicting humankind's divine oneness (See Pantheism). In "A Letter to All Educators in the World," Dr. Muller extolled the UN along with former UN Secretary-general U Thant, a devout Buddhist who openly praised Lenin, as means for human evolution. In calling for a new education aiming for global citizenship, Muller affirms his planetary civic commitment to world government with the right and duty to represent him in all matters pertaining to the universal good.

Muller's cosmic-minded, spiritually oriented World Core Curriculum has already been translated into Dutch, German, Italian, Russian, and Spanish and is being used by groups and individuals in Africa, Argentina, Australia, Brazil, Canada, Costa Rica, Ecuador, Guatemala, Holland, India, Mexico, New Zealand, the Philippines, Russia, the United Kingdom, and the United States. The number of schools using Muller's New Age curriculum exceeds thirty; each is an official UN school. Clinton's Goals 2000 campaign is expected to pave the way for Muller's World Core Curriculum to take hold in American public education.

UN and the Family (See Abortion; Death Culture; Planned Parenthood; Political Correctness; Safe Sex) The United Nations 1995 Fourth World Conference of Women in Beijing was the largest international gathering of women ever. Not surprisingly, the UN has blacklisted pro-family Christian organizations, such as Concerned Women of America, for its agenda featured politically correct, albeit Biblically incorrect, genderism defined in its documents as male, female, homo-, bi-, and trans-sexual. Conference participants proposed "Equal Rights Amendments" in the national constitutions of all governments, further requiring gender awareness for all educators and textbooks free of traditional sex-stereotypes (See Textbook Conspiracy).

The conference's stated objective was "to change and transform the world by the year 2001." Its platform mandated America's domestic policies and laws not unlike the yet-to-be-ratified 1989 UN Convention on the Rights of the Child that limits and restricts parental authority, and, in so doing, threatens freedom of religious expression to "train up a child" aright, according to Biblical admonition.

Among the conference's advancements were gay rights and family planning. Already President Clinton has lifted the ban on funding UN population control programs, and Planned Parenthood is working hard to funnel U.S. moneys into the UN Fund for Population Activities, which backs China's policy of forced abortions.

The agenda of the UN 1996 World Food Summit in Rome was as much about population control as it was food. Once again, the idea was to reduce population through abortion and acceptance of childless radical feminism and homosexuality on the pretext of finding ways to make sure every person has enough to eat (See Political Correctness; Gay Rights).

UN and the Global Village

Beginning in 1987, the UN began its final drive to restructure the world's nations into one Global Village. Worldwide political transformation that supports sustainability is the UN's answer for presumed environmental disasters, poverty, and overpopulation. Recent conferences held around the world (Vienna, Cairo, and Copenhagen) addressed rights of children over their parents, forced abortion and sterilization, and global taxation.

The idea is for everyone to shift in attitude and behavior "within the dictates of natural ecology," even in the face of scientific uncertainty (UN Habitat II Conference, Istanbul). Indeed, the scientific community has reached no consensus to warrant need for the nearly 300 environmental treaties already administered by the UN.

To many, the UN is a paper tiger unable to stop, for example, the Bosnian-Serbs massacre; however, for the first time in history, the UN responded with severe steps almost unanimously to oppose Iraq when she aggressively entered Kuwait, thus raising hopes of a coming New World Order.

Biblical Perspective

Builders of the infamous Tower of Babel were said to be "one" and, therefore, of limitless capability. For this reason, God confounded their languages (Gen. 11:6-7). Many scoff at the contemporary notion of nations united as one. In so doing, they fail to notice that the impossible was proved to be possible the week of events surrounding Lady Diana's untimely death in Paris. In Greece and Turkey at the time, I marveled at the singular global response to this needless tragedy.

Countless mourners around the world viewed Princess Diana's funeral on television, the eve of which Mother Teresa breathed her last. Possibility of global unity never before realized became reality, as the world in one accord grieved the loss of two of her most beloved humanitarians.

The uniting of peoples and nations is not what God opposes. It is rather their union apart from, and in direct opposition to, their would-be Savior and Lord, Jesus Christ. This objection is not rooted in human pettiness, for God's ways are far above the ways of man (Isa. 55:9).

It is based instead on God's rightful concern for His Name and for the well-being of those who presently bear it, or will bear it in the near future and throughout eternity (Phil .2:9-11).

Unity among peoples of the world is clearly a Biblical principle (John 17:21-23). In Christ, there is neither male nor female, bond or free (1 Cor. 12:13). God respects no person, or group of persons, above others (Acts 10:34). His boundless love is extended to all (John 3:16), even while they are yet in sin (Rom. 5:8), and His glorious plan for theocratic globalism will soon be realized in Christ's forthcoming Millennial Reign; however, it will not sanction belief in Hindu gods, Shiva and Ram, as the late Mother Teresa erroneously proclaimed at the Pashupati Temple in 1984 (Acts 4:12).

The "one mind" apart from God, as described in Scripture, ultimately involves relinquishment of power and strength to Antichrist, whose primary task is to promote Satan's deception while undermining the work and Plan of God (Rev. 17:13). Inspired and empowered by Satan, this lawless one will bring "strong delusion" while leading the final rebellion against God Himself (2 Thess. 2:9; Matt. 24:24-25). Those who fall prey to

Antichrist's brand of global unity will not only miss out on the blessing, but also will experience certain wrath of God for participating in blasphemy and for motivating others to do so (Rev. 14:9-11).

Because of Satan's deceptive and seductive ways, Christians are admonished to "believe not every spirit," but rather to "try the spirits" to ascertain whether or not they are of God (1 John 4:1-14). Out of love alone, the Father has sent the Son, not to condemn, but to save the world (1 John 4:9-10). Our rightful response is to set aside fear (1 John 4:18). We are to love our brother, yes, but with "love unfeigned," avoiding the "spirit of error" (1 John 4:20-21; 2 Cor. 6:6; 1 John 4:6). This requires a single eye for the blessed hope and glorious appearing of our great God and Savior, Jesus Christ (Titus 2:13).

V

Values (Affective) Education

America's Founding Values Proclaimed

Known for his oft-repeated battle cry, "Give me liberty, or give me death," Revolutionary leader Patrick Henry acknowledged that our great nation was founded "not by religionists, but by Christians; not on religions, but on the Gospel of Jesus Christ." This fact was evidenced in the first colonial grant made to Sir Walter Raleigh (1584); in the first charter of Virginia, granted by King James I (1606); in subsequent Virginia charters (1609 and 1611) and various ones granted to the other colonies.

In the 1830s French statesman Alexis de Tocqueville studied America's remarkable prosperity. This historian and social philosopher published the classic two-volume work *Democracy in America,* crediting America's goodness for her greatness. Without it, he warned, she will cease to be great, for faith in morality is America's "surest pledge of freedom."

America's Founding Values Undermined

Before the time of German philosopher George Hegel (1770-1831), moral absolutes remained unquestioned; Hegelian theory declared no fixed rights or wrongs. As a result, moral, cultural, sociological, or ethical relativism now permeates Congress and the courts, the mainstream media, the professions, the entertainment industry, and public education (Dr. James Dobson. *Focus on the Family Newsletter* [Colorado Springs: Focus on the Family] 2).

In lamenting the loss of America's founding values, Jewish medical educator David C. Stolinsky rightly reasons that hesitancy to go out after dark is not in fear of evangelicals forcing us to read the New Testament, but rather in fear of gangs taught that nothing is superior to their own needs or feelings. Indeed, the work of the Barna Research Group involves extensive surveys of "Generation X'ers," over three-fourths of whom reject altogether the notion of absolute moral truth [George Barna, *Generation Next* (Venture: Regal Books, 1995), p. 31]. According to Joseph Fletcher's "situation ethics," me-centered circumstances determine whether an action is right or wrong.

The Hegelian mindset is keenly evident in sex education promulgated through public schools. Kinseyan sexologists produce and approve curricula, through which students undergo hours of sexual "attitude reassessment" until their value systems are effectively restructured to hallow "the self" (See Safe Sex; Solipsism).

America's Founding Values "Clarified"

Values, or affective, education is not new. It has been prevalent for decades in America's public education system. Based on the Raths-Simon Theory of Relativism, its three underlying assumptions follow:

1. Religion, family, and society have all failed to convey necessary values to children; therefore, teachers ("change agents") must facilitate their conveyance;
2. Values necessary for children are humanist survival values; and
3. A person can find an effective set of values unaided by culture or history.

The definitive text for values education is Sid Simon's *Values Clarification* handbook from the Center of Humanistic Education. On page eighty-three, Simon writes, "The child should be protected from moralistic crap." Along these lines, children are to be considered "ill" when they first come to school because they embrace their parents' assumed-to-be outdated values. Students are taught instead to evaluate and "clarify" their own beliefs by reaching conclusions based on the following seven criteria for choosing, prizing, and acting upon values:

• Choosing

1. Values must be freely chosen, not taught.
2. Values must be chosen from alternatives, none of which are fixed or are of more importance than others.
3. Values must be chosen after careful consideration of the consequences of each alternative.

• Prizing

> 4. Values must be prized, or cherished.
>
> 5. Values must be publicly affirmed.

• Acting

> 6. Values must be acted upon.
>
> 7. To establish a value as the chosen behavior, it must be acted upon regularly.

Commonly employed instructional tactics include "educational diagnostics" to determine the extent to which children have been oriented, "Magic Circles," diaries, role playing, open-ended questions, problem-solving exercises, and even use of the computer. First developed in the late 1950s, consensus is a Soviet term for "collective opinion." Collaborative approaches of the hot new consensus process are also called conflict resolution, Hegelian dialectics, and the Delphi Technique.

Because teachers are prohibited from favoring any moral stand, peer pressure heavily influences student decisions. One of Simon's exercises asks students to plant themselves on a values continuum regarding premarital sex. On one end is Virginal Virginia, who wears white gloves on every date. On the other is Mattress Millie, who wears a mattress strapped to her back. The preferred somewhere-in-between position requires acting upon this under peer pressure.

Supposedly free to make their own choices of right or wrong, children are wheedled into the popular position that the woman in Simon's famous Alligator River scenario "did the right thing" in necessarily having sex with the boatman in order to cross the Alligator River to meet her lover on the other side. Because values must be publicly affirmed, and then acted upon, it is difficult for students to back down should they reevaluate their original stance.

Values are presumed to be chosen from limitless alternatives; however, in reality students are given only limited choices. For example, in Simon's system, a student may be asked, "Which would you rather do on a Sunday morning—sleep late, watch TV, or play with a friend?" Going to Sunday school is not presented as an admissible option.

America's Founding Values Supplanted (See Outcome-Based Education)

Radical values adjustment is required for development of human resources in the school-to-work plan of Goals 2000. Through the process of "values clarification," students are instilled with transferable skills needed to succeed in the global work force. Today's United Nations-funded Commission on Global Governance, *Our Global Neighborhood,* embraces a New Earth (Global Civic) Ethic. Based on core values said to unite all people despite backgrounds, this new ethic is a form of global eco-socialism with intent to bring justice and equity to people born into unequal economic and social circumstances by taking wealth from the rich and then distributing it to the poor. Ignoring fundamental values upon which America is founded, it specifically excludes national sovereignty and private property rights.

Ongoing restructuring efforts in America today call for removal of prayers surrounding sessions of Congress as well as the phrase "In God We Trust" from currency. Some urge the elimination of Christmas as a national holiday, not to mention the rank of military chaplain from the armed forces. Sadly, an unanimous 1997 U.S. Supreme Court decision struck down the Communications Decency Act, hoping to rid the internet of obscenity, perhaps America's only unregulated business today.

Biblical Perspective

The Bible warns of teachers who go astray by forsaking the straight path of moral absolutism. Among them are change agents of values education who fail to acknowledge God's Word as the plumb line for truth (2 Pet. 2:1, 2,15). Given no real guidance or correction, their students are induced to call evil good—and good evil (Isa. 5: 20). Take, for example, Sid Simon's provocative lifeboat scenario. The question is posed, "Whom [of a specified group] do we eliminate for the good of the whole?" No allowance is made for solutions to save; rather, the student's "free" choice has imposed upon it firm parameters with an unmistakable message that some have less value, thus less right to live, than others.

In the 1820s, gifted orator Daniel Webster issued the somber warning that "if truth be not diffused, error will be." He added, "If the power of the Gospel is not felt throughout the length and breadth of the land, anarchy and misrule, degradation and misery, corruption and darkness will reign without mitigation or end."

Webster's chilling words reflect end-time Biblical prophecy that ungodly seducers of our nation's youth will wax worse and worse, deceiving and being deceived (2 Tim. 3:13). Simply put, world citizens-in-the-making are being groomed, wrongly so, to eliminate the one true God in exchange for the universal god-force, and to elevate the supposed good of the New World Order over God's unalterable moral code (See Pantheism).

W

Witchcraft/Wicca

(See Ancient Mystery Religions: Freemasonry/Witchcraft/New Age.) Wicca is an Old English term from which we get the word "witch." One who engages in witchcraft is said to possess and exercise magical powers. If the intent is evil, that one practices "black magic." On the other hand, if the intent is "benign," (s)he practices what is termed "white magic." A warlock means "one who breaks faith," but is more often used by non-witches to refer to a male witch.

Practice of sorcery, magic, witchcraft, or Shamanism is based in pantheism and, thus, dates back to the ancient mysteries. A shaman is a ritual leader who acts as intermediary between society and the supernatural world. Also known as a medicine man, seer, or sorcerer, the shaman is expected to use so-called white magic to cure illness and control spirits, good or evil. Forming the basis for much of today's mythology associated with witchcraft, the Book of Enoch is extra-biblical, apparently written as early as the second century B.C.

The Herbal Connection

Deuteronomy 18:10 of the New American Standard version of the Bible uses "sorcerer" for "witch," and "sorcerer" comes from a Hebrew word meaning "to cut up (as herb)." Even today's so-called traditional practitioners are recognized for having considerable skill in herbal medicine. Witchcraft practices include use of poisons and philters (blood leeching); nevertheless, in 1976 the World Health Organization recommended integration of traditional healers into the health teams of African states (See United Nations).

The "Christian" Connection (See Ecumenical Movement)

Obi or obeah is the witchcraft of Black Africa imported to, and practiced in, the West Indies. Both Obi and Voodoo combine Roman Catholicism with West African religious tradition.

Followed in some parts of Africa, South America, and the West Indies, Voodoo also arose on seventeenth-century slave plantations.

The Freemasonry Connection

It is fair to say that many high-ranking Freemasons are known to be practitioners of witchcraft. For example, the sex-magic cult OTO (*Ordo Templi Orientis*) claims illumination to all Masonic secrets and, in fact, was founded by a Freemason from Australia.

Thirty-third degree Mason Aleister Crowley headed and gave shape to Wicca. Crowley called himself "the Beast 666" and was known worldwide as "the wickedest man on earth" (See Mark of the Beast: 666). Crowley died a heroin addict in England in 1947. Self-styled "king of the witches" in London, Freemason Alex Sanders is regarded as one of the most influential leaders of Wicca after Freemason Gerald B. Gardner.

Whereas Gardner founded traditional Gardnerian Witchcraft, Alex and Maxine Sanders founded Alexandrian Witchcraft.

Anton Szandor LaVey was an ex-carnival worker who studied the works of Freemason Aleister Crowley. In 1966 he founded and became high priest of the Church of Satan in San Francisco; ex-members later founded the Church of the Satanic Brotherhood. Referred to as the "Black Pope," LaVey agreed to act as official adviser for the film *Rosemary's Baby,* said to be the "best paid commercial for Satanism since the Inquisition." By February of 1989, his Satanic Bible had sold well over a half-million copies.

In his book *The Satanic Rituals—Companion to the Satanic Bible,* LaVey admitted that "virtually every occult order has many Masonic roots." For example, Wicca is the national organization the Masonic Golden Dawn. LaVey recognized the Golden Dawn as source for invocations found in his Satanic Bible (See Great Invocation). Moreover, world-renowned, twentieth-century witches Janet and Stewart Farrar credit the Golden Dawn for giving rise to today's cult explosion.

The Entertainment Connection

At the 1997 Atlanta Conference on prophecy, David Benoit exposed rampant sorcery and witchcraft in children's television programs. He quoted a prominent witch as having labeled Disney's film, *Pocahontas*, "the most pagan-positive film in history."

More frequently than not, witches today are associated with the apple-bobbing, taffy-pulling children's holiday of Halloween. They are seen as silly-looking, essentially harmless old ladies, or even sweet and pretty young ones, as portrayed in a popular television series of bygone years. For this reason, many are surprised to learn that witches include Halloween as one of their eight major festivals. In fact, they celebrate it as their new year. Halloween, or the Vigil of Samhain, is a November Eve witch's holiday considered to be the day of the year most suitable for magic or demonic activity.

Originally, Halloween was a Druidic festival. The Druids were a pagan priesthood of ancient France and Britain who drenched their altars with blood of human burnt sacrifices. It was believed that on this eve of the Druidic new year, the Lord of Death permitted wicked souls under his dominion to return to their earthly homes. The living offered sacrifices to appease these wicked dead and, thus, avert any pranks they were inclined to play.

Recent data affirm that even dabblers in witchcraft are very susceptible to inflicting physical and emotional harm to self and others. According to noted Christian psychologist Dr. James Dobson, potential gateways for teen involvement include heavy or "black" metal rock music, "slasher movies," games such as *Dungeons & Dragons*, video arcades, the personal computer, and unsupervised parties.

The Immorality Connection

Satanists are highly organized, secretive law breakers involved in drug abuse, prostitution, human sacrifice, and other acts of "satanic ritual abuse" (SRA). Some participants are termed "generational" in that one generation indoctrinates the next into Satanic cult rituals. Additional unsavory practices include summoning demons (Conjuration); casting evil spells (Cantrips); and eating human flesh (Anthropophagy). Cult "breeders" bear children for ritual sacrifice; moreover, they blaspheme God at black masses, while observing a perverted Catholic mass to ridicule Christianity. Throughout the eighteenth and nineteenth centuries, small groups in Europe known as Hellfire Clubs reintroduced black masses and other Satanic practices, including sexual immorality (See Safe Sex; Values Education).

Biblical Perspective

(See Ancient Mystery Religions; New World Order)

In the Bible, a witch is usually a woman in league with evil spirits and whose ancient craft is condemned as abomination in both Testaments (Deut. 18:9-14; 1 Sam. 28:3, 9; 2 Kings 23:24; Isa. 8:19). Old Testament law required that practicing witches be put to death (Exod. 22:18). Paul saw to it at Ephesus that, for the sake of believers, even the witches' books were burned (Acts 19:18, 19). Many secular sources condemn the Christian church for having persecuted witches in Europe between the fifteenth and seventeenth centuries, and also in North America at the Salem witch trials.

Witchcraft's tie-in with globalism becomes evident when her structure, symbols, associations, and practices are compared with those of the worldwide New Age Movement and Freemasonry. Belief systems of witches, New Age mystics, and illumined Freemasons consist of Luciferic doctrine. All three promote one world government, featuring a "superior race of god-men," who inspired by Antichrist despotism, seek to rule the world (See Adept/ Initiated Adept). Pagan Earth religion witches number an astonishing quarter-of-a-million in "Christian" America alone. Many are politically active in seeking to save "Mother Earth," central organizing principle motivating formation of the New World Order (See Radical Environmentalism).

World Constitution and Parliament Association (WCPA)

In 1959 the World Constitution and Parliament Association (WCPA) was founded near Denver, Colorado. Its key figure and Secretary-general since 1966 is Philip Isely. Under Isely's direction, the association has assembled a Provisional World Parliament. A total of five sessions were originally planned to usher in a New World Order. At its third session (1987), a Provisional World Presidium and World Cabinet were appointed to serve as executive branch of its anticipated one world order. The Fourth

Provisional World Parliament was scheduled to convene in late September 1997.

Design and Action for a New World is the primary document circulated by the WCPA to promote its global agenda; furthermore, the WCPA has drafted a World Constitution. The *Constitution for the Federation of Earth* was first adopted in 1977 during a meeting of the World Constituent Assembly, at which time the document was signed by some one hundred thirty-five participants from twenty-five countries. Calling for a democratic federal world government "for the good of all," this Constitution is intended to be a sort of "mother board" for the coming New World Order, the need for which is triggered by a purported environmental crisis (See Radical Environmentalism). Work to prepare this document began in Milan (1965), and its final ratification campaign was officially launched in Portugal (1991).

The *Constitution for the Federation of Earth* reads like an occult manual. It comes as no surprise, then, that the WCPA enjoys such a large network of support from the New Age movement. Yogi Shanti Swaroop of India serves as its official "Spiritual Liaison," and eco-educator Dr. Robert Muller is among its distinguished endorsers. Influenced heavily by Theosophist Alice Bailey and mystic Teilhard de Chardin, Muller was presented the Peace Education Prize by UNESCO in 1989 for his work in developing the World Core Curriculum (See Outcome-Based Education; Public Education; United Nations).

The WCPA's *Diagram of World Government* under the *Constitution for the Federation of Earth* calls for a ten region world government, paired with a "New World Economic Order," borrowed directly from the Club of Rome's handbook (See Global Economics/Banking). The spiritually-driven Club of Rome pledges worldwide peace and prosperity at the expense of national sovereignty; it further envisions a cashless society not unlike the Biblical account of the Mark of the Beast.

Toward this end, the WCPA is calling, albeit indirectly, for elimination of our armed forces to the extent that America would be unable to withstand attack by a United Nations "Peace" Force. Correspondingly, for over three decades, top leaders have systematically yielded U.S. military strength to the UN under the "Arms Control and Disarmament Act" passed in 1961.

Global efforts of the WCPA are protected under the U.S. Constitution, the very document it seeks to supplant. Already, the WCPA has begun its public campaign with slick, full-page advertisements and radio interviews. Activist Dick Sutphen admonishes fellow mystics to join "family, friends, and associates" in infusing its New Age concepts and awareness "into every area of their personal world—from the office to the bridge club; from the [public] schoolroom to the Little League" (*New Age Activist*, Vol. 1, No. 1, Summer 1986 newsletter).

Of itself the WCPA is not especially powerful, but make no mistake—although it aspires to appear "grass roots," its imposing infrastructure consists of the money center banks, major foundations, the Council on Foreign Relations, and the World Federalist Association. It has even been suggested that the UN is destined to be replaced by the WCPA, whose membership includes prestigious statespersons, educators, financiers, and more, nearly one-fifth of whom are associated with the United Nations. In cooperation with its Global Ratification and Elections Network, the WCPA has coaxed almost six hundred organizations from some ninety-five countries to join its collaboration efforts called "networking for change."

Biblical Perspective

See United Nations.

World Future Society (WFS)

The World Future Society is where the political, spiritual, and economic aspects of one world government can all merge, for it functions as a kind of clearing house for all global organizations and societies. The *Futurist* magazine is its bi-monthly publication. The WFS in effect has become the "world forum" called for in the Club of Rome's 1972 book, *The Limits to Growth*. The handbook of the occult-driven Club of Rome includes plans for a ten region world government, calling for a "New World Economic Order" (See Global Economics/Banking).

The greatest number of connections with the World Constitution and Parliament Association comes through the World Future Society. Key figure of the WCPA, Philip Isely belongs to the World Future Society. Also a member, Lucile Green is fourth signer of the WCPA *Constitution for the Federation of Earth* and founder/co-chair of the World Government Organization Coalition.

Canadian socialist Maurice Strong is the powerful director of the World Future Society. A member of the Club of Rome, Strong serves also as trustee of the Rockefeller Foundation; and his name is associated with the Aspen Institute for Humanistic Studies. As former head of the UN Environment Programme (UNEP) and Secretary-general of the UN Conference on Environment and Development (UNCED) held in Rio De Janeiro (1992), Strong is known appropriately as the great-grandfather of radical environmentalism. His study with Sir Shridath Ramphal, *Our Global Neighborhood,* appears to carry the global agenda to its expected zenith.

The World Future Society sponsors a yearly symposium, which, since 1980, has focused on "thinking globally, while acting locally." Movers and shakers of the New Age community attend. Among the most important symposiums to date was Worldview '84, which proved to be nothing short of a world government planning session. Additionally, the WFS has hosted World Game events to promote need for a cooperative New World Order on campuses and communes in Boston. In 1991 the Rockefeller Brothers Fund hosted a successful series of World Game workshops on Capitol Hill for consulates, ambassadors, and staff members of the United Nations.

Biblical Perspective

See United Nations.

"Even so, come, Lord Jesus."
(Revelation 22:20)

Select Bibliography

Economics/Politics

Allen, Gary. *The Rockefeller File.* Clackamas, OR: Emissary Publications, 1976.

Greider, William. *One Word, Ready or Not: The Manic Logic of Global Capitalism.* New York, NY: Simon & Schuster, 1997.

Hansen, Carol Rae, editor. *The New World Order: Rethinking America's Global Role.* Flagstaff, AZ: Arizona Honors Academy Press, 1992.

Kah, Gary. *Seattle Conference Video.* Noblesville, IN: Hope for the World, 1995.

Kidd, Devvy. *Why a Bankrupt America?* Arvada, CO: Project Library, 1994.

Lalonde, Paul and Peter. *Racing Toward the Mark of the Beast.* Eugene, OR: Harvest House Publishers, 1994.

Lindbergh, Charles A., Sr. *Lindbergh on the Federal Reserve.* Costa Mesa, CA: The Noontide Press, 1989.

Tamedly, Elisabeth L. *Socialism and International Economic Order.* Cardwell, ID: The Caxton Printers, Ltd., 1969.

"Unknown $9.1 Trillion Company." *North Bridge News.* The Liberty Tree (Nov. 1995): Vol. 1, Issue 14.

"Why is America Bankrupt? The Truth, The Solution." *Why Are You Volunteering?* Boulder, CO (1993).

Education

Baxter, Ern. et. al. *Secular Humanism: Man Striving to be God.* Milford, MI: A New Wine book co-published by Integrity Publications and Mott Media, 1980.

Bernhoft, Robin, Ph.D. *Outcome-Based Education: Lobotomy by Robin Hood.* Seattle, WA: PERC, 1992.

Blumenfeld, Samuel L. *NEA: Trojan Horse in American Education.* Phoenix, AZ: Research Publications.

Counts, G. S. *The Social Foundations of Education.* New York, NY: Charles Scribner's Sons, 1934.

Dager, Albert James. "America 2000: Education Reform for the New World Order." *Media Spotlight* (1993).

DeWeese, Tom. *The DeWeese [Insiders] Report, Volume 2, Issue 5.* Chantilly, VA: Newsletter of the American Policy Center, September/October 1995.

DeWeese, Tom. Interview with Brannon Howse, 15 December 1996. *Goals 2000, School-to-Work and The Careers Act* (1997).

DeWeese, Tom. "Special Report: The Truth About Outcome-Based Education (OBE), Assault on Student Learning." Supplement to the *DeWeese Report* (1997).

Fields, Melanie K.; Leslie, Sarah H.; Hoge, Anita B. "When Johnny Takes the Test." Des Moines, IA: *The Christian Conscience*, 1995.

Gabler, Mel and Norma. *What Are They Teaching Our Children?* Wheaton, ILL: Victor Books, A Division of SP Publications, Inc., 1987.

Gabler, Mel. *Values Clarification: Does It Build or Destroy Basic Values?* Pensacola, FL: A Beka Book Publication, Pensacola Christian College.

Hefley, James C. *Are Textbooks Harming Your Children?* Milford, MI: Mott Media, 1979.

Horowitz, David. *150 Years of Evil: Marx's Manifesto.* Washington, DC: Accuracy in Academia, 1998.

Huck, Susan L. M. "Your Children and America's Established Religion, Secular Humanism." *American Opinion* (January 1980).

Hyles, Jack, Ph.D. *Satan's Bid for Your Child.* Hammond: Hyles-Anderson Publishers, 1973.

Kennedy, D. James, Ph.D. *A Godly Education,* Ft. Lauderdale, FL: Coral Ridge Ministries.

Kennedy, D. James, Ph.D. *Education: Public Problems and Private Solutions.* Ft. Lauderdale, FL: Coral Ridge Ministries, 1993.

Kjos, Berit. *Brave New Schools.* Eugene, OR: Harvest House Publishers, 1995.

LaHaye, Tim. *The Battle for the Mind.* Old Tappan, NJ: Fleming H. Revell Company Power Books, 1980.

L.A. Rouche, Lyndon H., Jr. "Will You Allow Your Child to be Spiritually Molested?" *The New Federalist* (Aug. 1993).

Luksik, Peg. "Outcome-Based Education Not Good for State's Pupils." *The Tribune Democrat* (1993).

Luksik, Peg, and Pamela Hobbs Hoffecker, *Outcome-Based Education: The State's Assault on Our Children's Values.* Lafayette, LA: Huntington House Publishers, 1995.

McGraw, Onalee. "Secular Humanism and the Schools: The Issue Whose Time Has Come." Washington, DC: The Heritage Foundation *Family Choice in Education: The New Imperative (Critical Issues Series),* 1976.

Morris, Barbara. *The Religion of Humanism in Public Schools.* Boston, MA: Houghton Mifflin Company, 1961.

Public Education Research Council. Seattle, WA: PERC, 1992.

Tabor, Ron. *Outcome-Based Education.* Olympia, WA: Parents and Taxpayers Across Washington State to Elect Ron Taber State Superintendent of Public Instruction, 1996.

U.S. Department of Education. *Grant Award Notification.* Washington, D.C.: Office of Elementary and Secondary Education, 1996.

Wolf, Wayne. "The Myth of Local Control." Des Moines, IA: *Des Moines Iowa Report,* 1993.

Freemasonry

Ankerberg, John and Weldon, John. *The Secret Teachings of the Masonic Lodge.* Chicago, IL: Moody Press, 1990.

Bluemel, Craig. *Announcing the Birth of the New World [Without God] Order.* Seattle, WA: The Bible Answer Stand Ministry, 1996.

Brown, Vilas Jay. *The Ancient York Rite of Freemasonry as Worked in America and the Ancient Arabic Order Nobles of the Mystic*

Shrine, Including Ladies Organizations. Portland, OR: Freemasons, 1961.

Campbell-Everden, William Preston. *Freemasonry and Its Etiquette.* New York, NY: Weathervane Books, 1978.

Clausen, Henry C. *Inspector Inquisitor Thirty-First Degree; Master of the Royal Secret Thirty-Second Degree.*

Curtis, Bill. *Secret Societies.* A & E Network: The Unexplained, 16 July 1998 and 18 February 1999.

Decker, Ed. *Freemasonry: Satan's Door to America?* Issaquah, WA: Free the Masons Ministries.

Decker, Ed. *The Dark Side of Freemasonry.* Lafayette, LA: Huntington House Publishers, 1994.

Holly, Dr. James L. *The Southern Baptist Convention and Freemasonry Volume II, Including the Complete Text of Volume I.* Taylors, SC: Faith Printing Company.

Mackey, Albert G. *An Encyclopedia of Freemasonry.* New York, NY: The Masonic History Co., 1921.

Marrs, Texe. *Dark Majesty, The Secret Brotherhood and the Magic of A Thousand Points of Light.* Austin, TX: Living Truth Publishers, 1992.

Pike, Albert. *Morals and Dogma of the Ancient and Accepted Scottish Rite of Freemasonry Prepared for the Supreme Council of the Thirty-third Degree, for the Southern Jurisdiction of the United States and Published by Its Authority.* Richmond, VA: L. H. Jenkins, Inc., May, 1920.

Rice, John R. Lodges, *Examined by the Bible.* Murfreesboro, TN: Sword of the Lord Publishers, 1971.

Shaw, Jim. *The Deadly Deception.* Lafayette, LA: Huntington House Publishers, Inc., 1988.

Spence, Lewis. *An Encyclopedia of Occultism.* Secaucus, NJ: The Citadel Press, 1960.

Still, William T. *New World Order: The Ancient Plan of Secret Societies.* Lafayette, LA: Huntington House Publishers.

Webster, Nesta H. *Secret Societies and Subversive Movements.* London: Boswell Printing & Publishing Co., Ltd., 1924.

General References

American Heritage Dictionary of the English Language, Third Edition. New York: Houghton Mifflin Company, 1992.

Amplified Bible. Grand Rapids, MI: Zondervan Bible Publishers, 1987.

Bowen, William. *Globalism: America's Demise.* Lafayette, LA: Huntington House, Inc., 1984.

Breese, David. *7 Men Who Rule from the Grave.* Oklahoma City, OK: SW Radio Church, 1980.

Bryant, T. Alton. *The New Compact Bible Dictionary, Special Crusade Edition.* Minneapolis, MN: The Billy Graham Evangelistic Association, 1967.

Celebration of Sovereignty. Seattle, WA: Hope for the World, October 1996.

Concise Columbia Encyclopedia. Columbia University Press, 1991.

Davis, June N. *Scripture Keys for Kingdom Living.* Denver, CO: Scripture Keys Ministries, 1992.

Elliott, Stephen P., et. al.. *Webster's New World Encyclopedia,* revised edition of the Ninth Edition, 1990 of *The Hutchison Encyclopedia.* New York: Prentice Hall, 1992.

Fagan, Myron. *The Illuminati Take-Over* tape series, transcribed and edited by Debra Rae, 1996.

Levy, David M. *The Tabernacle: Shadows of the Messiah—Its Sacrifices, Services, and Priesthood.* Bellmawr, NJ: The Friends of Israel Gospel Ministry, Inc., 1993.

Levy, David M. *Malachi: Messenger of Rebuke and Renewal.* Bellmawr, NJ: The Friends of Israel Gospel Ministry, Inc., 1992.

Nelson, Thomas. *Nelson's Illustrated Bible Dictionary.* Nashville, TN: Thomas Nelson Publishers, 1986.

PC Study Bible for Windows, Reference Library Edition. Seattle, Washington: Biblesoft, 1994.

Prophecy Conference of the Decade with Hal Lindsey, Chuck Missler, et. al. Seattle, WA: SEA-TAC Red Lion, July 1995.

Rotherham, Joseph Bryant. *The Emphasized Bible.* Grand Rapids, MI: Kregel Publications, 1981.

Ryrie, Charles C., Th. D. *The Starter Study Bible: New American Standard.* Iowa Falls, IA: Word Bible Publishers, 1977.

Seiss, J. A. *The Apocalypse: Lectures on the Book of Revelation.* Grand Rapids, MI: Zondervan Publishing House, 1973.

Smith, Jerome H. *The New Treasury of Scripture Knowledge, Revised and Expanded.* Nashville, TN: Thomas Nelson Publishers, 1992.

Thompson, Frank C., D.D., Ph.D. *The New Chain-Reference Bible, Fourth Improved Edition.* Indianapolis: B.B. Kirkbride Bible Co., Inc., 1964.

Van Impe, Dr. Jack & Rexella. *Daniel—Final Endtime Mysteries Unsealed, Parts 1-4.* Troy, MI: Jack Van Impe Ministries International, 1993.

White, E.G. *Will America Survive?* (formerly, *The Great Conspiracy*), excerpts in "What's Behind the New World Order; How It Will Affect You," 1996.

Worrell, A.S. *The Worrell New Testament: A.S. Worrell's Translation with Study Notes.* Springfield, MO: Gospel Publishing House, 1980.

Wuest, Kenneth S. *The New Testament, An Expanded Translation.* Iowa Falls, IA: Riverside Book and Bible House, 1961.

Young, Robert. *Young's Analytical Concordance.* Grand Rapids, MI: Associated Publishers and Authors, Inc.

Geo-Politics/Ecology/Environment

Allen, Gary. *None Dare Call It Conspiracy* (and *The Rockefeller File*). Rossmoor, CA: Concord Press, 1971.

Chiang, Jesse, Ph.D., Professor Emeritus of Political Science, Seattle Pacific University, Seattle, Washington. "An Inquiry Into NATO Expansion for Security and Stability in Europe" (1 July 1997).

Cohen, Tim. *The Anti-Christ and a Cup of Tea.* Nobilesville, IN: Hope for the World, 1998.

DeBell, Garrett. *The Environmental Handbook, Prepared for the First National Environmental Teach-in.* New York, NY: A Ballantine/Friends of the Earth Book, 1970.

DeWeese, Tom, President of the American Policy Center. "The DeWeese Report." *Insiders Report* (May 1995): Volume 2, Issue 1.

DeWeese, Tom. "Scaring Children 'Green,'" interview with Phyllis Schlafly, 30 July 1994. *Environmentalists in the Classroom (1997).*

DeWeese, Tom. "OBE & the Green Agenda," an address, 24 October 1996. *How to Rip Apart & Restructure a Nation* (1997).

DeWeese, Tom. "The Most Dangerous Man in the World," an address, 30 September 1996. *Assault on the Classroom (1997).*

Froese, Arno. *How Democracy Will Elect the Antichrist.* W. Columbia, SC: The Olive Press, 1997.

Kah, Gary H. *En Route to Global Occupation.* Lafayette, LA: Huntington House Publishers, 1992.

Kincaid, Cliff. *Global Bondage: The U.N. Plan to Rule the World.* Lafayette, LA: Huntington House Publishers.

Lindsey, Hal. *Planet Earth - 2000 AD, Will Mankind Survive?* Palos Verdes, CA: Western Front, Ltd., 1994.

McManus, John F., "Conspiracy for Global Control." *The New American* (16 September 1996): Vol. 12, No. 19.

Smith, Samantha. *Goddess Earth: Exposing the Pagan Agenda of the Environmental Movement.* Lafayette, LA: Huntington House Publishers, 1993.

Medical

"Advice about AIDS." *A Seattle-King County Department of Public Health Publication* (September 1985): 1-8.

"AIDS." *Plymouth Rock Foundation Fac-Sheet* #42.

Bennett, William J. *AIDS and the Education of Our Children.* Pueblo, CO: United States Department of Education Consumer Information Center, 1987.

Cameron, Dr. Paul. *Exposing the AIDS Scandal.* Lafayette, LA: Huntington House Publishers.

Concerned Women for America. *The Shocking Truth behind the Government's Safe-Sex Lie.* Families First! Resource Center (1994).

Coral Ridge Ministries. Media Inc. *Why It Matters: Questions and Answers about Free Speech, the Homosexual Agenda, and "Truth in Love"* (1998).

Drake, Donald C. "Testing AIDS Drugs." *The Seattle Times* (Monday, 2 November 1987): Section F.

Falwell, Dr. Jerry. *Almost Born: The Shocking Truth about Partial-Birth Aborion.* Forest, VA: Liberty Alliance, 1998.

"Horizons." *US News and World Report* (12 January 1987): 60-70.

King County Medical Society. *Tel-Med Tapes (19—): #5065* (general description of AIDS); *#5069* (risk reduction practices); *#5070* (AIDS virus antibody test).

McIlhenny, Chuck and Donna. *When the Wicked Seize a City.* Lafayette, LA: Huntington House Publishers, 1993.

National Right to Life Committee, Inc., 419 Seventh Street, NW, Suite 500, Washington, D.C., 20004-2293.

Pekkanen, John and Ursula Naccache. "A Special Report, AIDS: The Plague that Knows No Boundaries." *Readers Digest Association, Inc.* (1987): 49-60.

"Q and A about AIDS." *A Seattle-King County Department of Public Health Publication* (September 1985): 1-13.

Randall, Jan. *Morality Curriculum: The Whole Man, Scope and Sequence,* Seattle, WA: CCBTC Publications, 1985.

Reuters. "Abortion Rate Down." Seattle, WN: *The Seattle Times,* 3 January 1997.

Stutzman, D. R. *AIDS: Questions and Answers.* Seattle, WA: CCBTC Publications, January 1988.

Surgeon General of the U.S. Public Health Service. *Report on Acquired Immune Deficiency Syndrome.* Olympia, WA: Washington State Department of Social and Health Services, 1986.

Yarber, William L. *AIDS: What Young Adults Should Know (Student and Instructor's guides)*. Reston, VA: American Alliance for Health, Physical Education, Recreation, and Dance, 1987.

Yarber, William L. *STD: A Guide for Today's Young Adults (Student and Instructor's guides)*. Atlanta, GA: Division of Sexually Transmitted Diseases, Center for Prevention Services, Centers for Disease Control, 1985.

Military Technology

Lindsey, Hal. *The Final Battle*. Palos Verdes, CA: Western Front, Ltd., 1995.

McAlvany, Don. *The Fourth Reich, Toward an American Police State*. Oklahoma City, OK: Southwest Radio Church, 1993.

Missler, Chuch, et. al., *Preparing for the Coming Computer Crisis*. Seattle, WA: Doubletree Hotel, SEA-TAC, 13 August 1998.

New Age

Baer, Randall. *Inside the New Age Nightmare*. Lafayette, LA: Huntington House Publishers.

Bennett, Hal Zina, Ph.D. "The Inner Guides." *Magical Blend* (Issue 16): 40.

Bluemel, Craig. *New Age Symbols and the Meanings—A Warning*. Seattle, WA: The Bible Answer Stand Ministry, 1996.

Carr, Joseph. *The Twisted Cross*. Lafayette, LA: Huntington House Publishers, 1985.

Cumbey, Constance. *Hidden Dangers of the Rainbow*. Lafayette, LA: Huntington House Publishers.

Cumbey, Constance. *A Planned Deception: The Staging of a New Age "Messiah."* East Detroit, MI: Pointe Publishers, Inc., 1985.

Froese, Arno. *The Coming World Religion, Cassette #F-69*. W. Columbia, SC: Arno Froese.

Into the Sun. Ramona, CA: Lemurian Fellowship, 1998.

Moriarty, Michael A. *The New Charismatics, A Concerned Voice Responds to Dangerous New Trends*. Grand Rapids, MI: Zondervan Publishing House, 1992.

World Goodwill Newsletter. "A Matter of Energy," No. 1-2, ISSN 0818-4984. Quarterly bulletin, 1992.

Yarker, John. *The Arcane Schools.* Belfast, Ireland, 1909.

Newsletters/Magazines

Access to Energy. Cave Junction, OR: Oregon Institute of Science and Medicine, March 1997 (vol. 24, no. 7).

Accuracy in Academia. *Campus Report.* Washington, DC: 1999.

Campaign Watch, A Publication of Campaign for Working Families, Washington, DC: Campaign for Working Families, 1998.

Capitol Watch. Washington, DC: An Emergency Campaign, 1998.

Christian Broadcasting Network (CBN). *News Facts and News Report.* VA: 700 Club, 1996-1998.

Christian Coalition. Chesapeake, VA 23327-1990: POB 1990, 1996-1999.

Concerned Women for America. Washington, DC: *Family Voice,* 1995-1999.

Countdown . . . The Christian Intelligence Journal. Palos Verdes, CA: Hal Lindsey Ministries, 1995-1997.

Dobson, James, Ph. D. *Citizen.* Colorado Springs, CO: Focus on the Family, 1994-1999.

End Times News Digest. Medford, OR: Omega Ministries, 1994.

Facts for Freedom. Seattle, WA: Action Gram, June 1996-1999.

Franz, Wanda, Ph.D. Washington, DC: *National Right to Life Committee,* Inc., 1995.

Froese, Arno. *Midnight Call.* West Columbia, SC: Midnight Call Ministries, 1995-1999.

God's News Behind the News. St. Petersburg, FL: Cathedral Caravan, Inc., 1995-1999.

Hooper, Kathy. *Let's Talk Prophecy.* Roswell, GA: Kathy Hooper Ministries, 1996-1999,

Grant, Dr. Robert G., Ph.D. Washington, DC: *Christian Voice,* 1996-1997.

Impact, Published for Friends Reclaiming America One Heart at a Time. Ft. Lauderdale, FL: Coral Ridge Ministries, 1995-1999.

Insiders Report. Chantilly, Virginia: American Policy Center, 1995-1999.

International Intelligence Briefing. Palos Verdes, CA: Hal Lindsey Ministries, 1995.

Irvine, Reed, *AIM Report.* Washington, DC: Accuracy in Media, Inc., 1995.

Kah, Gary. *Newsletter.* Noblesville: Gary Kah, 1995-1999.

McAlvany, Donald S. *The McAlvany Intelligence Advisor,* 1995-1997.

Missler, Chuck and Nancy. Personal Update, *The Newsletter of Koinonia House.* Coeur d'Alene, ID: Koinonia House, 1995-1997.

New American. Appleton, WI: The Review of The News, Incorporated, 1993-1997.

This Nation. Forest, VA: Christian Action Network (POB 606), 1996.

United We Stand America, The National Newsletter, May, 1996.

World, Volume 9, Numbers 18, 21, 24, 1994.

Religious/Spiritual/Moral

Bernstein, Henrietta. *Cabalah Primer.* Marina Del Rey, CA: DeVorss & Company, 1987.

Bluemel, Craig. *The Jewish Cabala, Spiritual Inspiration for the New World Order.* Seattle, WA: The Bible Answer Stand Ministry, 1996.

Boettner, Loraine. *Roman Catholicism.* Philadelphia, PA: The Presbyterian and Reformed Publishing Company, 1961.

Brown, Dr. Walter. *In the Beginning.* Phoenix, AZ: Center for Scientific Creation.

Christian Defense Fund Staff. *One Nation Under God, America's Christian Heritage.* Springfield, VA: Christian Defense Fund, 1997.

Coles, Robert. *The Spiritual Life of Children.* Boston, Mass: A Peter Davison Book, Houghton Mifflin Company, 1990.

Crews, Joe. *The Beast, the Dragon, and the Woman, Twelfth Edition.* Frederick, MD: Amazing Facts, Inc., 1991.

Duncan, Homer. *Evolution: The Incredible Hoax.* Lubbock, TX: Missionary Crusader.

Duncan, Homer, *Humanism in the Light of Holy Scriptures,* Lubbock, TX: Missionary Crusader, 1981.

Duncan, Homer. *Secular Humanism: The Most Dangerous Religion in America.* Lubbock, TX: Missionary Crusader, 1980.

Graham, Billy. *Storm Warning.* Dallas, TX: Word Publishing, 1992.

Hall, Manly. *The Adepts in the Eastern Esoteric Tradition.* LA, CA: The Philosophical Research Society, Inc., 1998.

Harris, M.H. *Hebraic Literature.* New York, NY: Tudor Publishing Co., 1943.

Hunt, Dave. *Global Peace and the Rise of Antichrist.* Eugene, OR: Harvest House Publishers, 1990.

Kah, Gary H. *The Demonic Roots of Globalism: En Route to Spiritual Deception.* Lafayette, LA: Huntington House Publishers, 1995.

Kinman, Dwight L. *The World's Last Dictator.* Woodburn, OR: Solid Rock Books, Inc., 1993.

Kirban, Salem. *Countdown to Rapture.* Irvine, CA: Harvest House Publishers, 1977.

Kurtz, Paul. *Humanist Manifestos I and II.* Buffalo, NY: Prometheus Books, 1979.

Lalonde, Peter and Paul. "Startling Proofs—Does God Really Exist?" Niagara Falls, ON: This Week in Bible Prophecy, 1997.

Lindsey, Hal. *Apocalypse. Code.* Palos Verdes, CA: Western Front Ltd., 1997.

Lindsey, Hal. *Planet Earth: The Final Chapter.* Beverly Hills, CA: Western Front Ltd., 1998.

Martin, Walter. *The Kingdom of the Cults.* Minneapolis, MN: Bethany Fellowship, Inc., Publishers, 1977.

McGregor, J. P., Th. B., Th. M., et. al. *Speaking in Other Tongues: A Scholarly Defense.* Seattle, WA: CCBTC Publications, 1986.

Nelson, Thomas. *Nelson's Illustrated Bible Dictionary.* Nashville, TN: Thomas Nelson Publishers, 1986.

Payels, Elaine. *The Gnostic Gospels.* New York, NY: Vintage Books (A Division of Random House), 1981.

Reisman, Dr. Judith A., and Edward W. Kinsey Eichel, *Sex and Fraud, the Indoctrination of a People.* Lafayette, LA: Huntington House Publishers.

Richter, Allan D. *Eve of the End.* New York, NY: A Hearthstone Book, Carlton Press, Inc., 1994.

Repa, Barbara Kate. "Assisted Suicide: A Tough Pill to Swallow." *The Nolo News* (Summer 1996): 8-9.

Scholem, Gershom. *Kabbalah.* New York, NY: A Meridian Book published by the Penguin Group, Penguin Books, 1978.

Showers, Renald. *Maranatha: Our Lord, Come!, A Definitive Study of the Rapture of the Church.* Bellmawr, NJ: The Friends of Israel Gospel Ministry, Inc., 1995.

Smith, Huston. *The Religions of Man.* New York, NY: Perennial Library, Harper & Row, Publishers, 1965.

Smith, Samantha and Brenda Scott. *Trojan Horse. How the New Age Movement Infiltrates the Church.* Lafayette, LA: Huntington House Publishers, 1993.

Wyman, Hastings, Jr. "The Gay Agenda." *The Washington Blade* (4 March 1994): 35.

Social/Cultural

Cockcroft, James D. *Marian Wright Edelman.* Grolier Electronic Publishing, Inc., 1993.

Coral Ridge Ministries Media, Inc., Post Office Box 407132, Fort Lauderdale, Florida 33340-7132.

Hart, Benjamin. *Faith & Freedom, The Christian Roots of American Liberty.* Alexandria, VA: Christian Defense Fund, 1997.

Howard, Philip K. *The Death of Common Sense: How Law is Suffocating America.* New York, NY: Warner Books, A Time Warner Company, 1996.

LaHaye, Beverly. *Who But a Woman?* New York, NY: Thomas Nelson Publishers, 1984.

Luce, Clare Boothe Policy Institude. Quarterly Newsletter. Hendon, VA: Clare Boothe Luce National Office, 1998.

Thibodaux, David, Ph.D. *Beyond Political Correctness: Are There Limits to This Lunacy?* Lafayette, LA: Huntington House Publishers, 1994.

Wardner, James W. *The Planned Destruction of America.* Longwood, FL: Longwood Communications, 1993.

Witchcraft/Satanism

Cavendish, Richard. *Man, Myth, and Magic.*

Chaplin, P. James. *Dictionary of the Occult and Paranormal.*

Dobson, Dr. James. "Satanism." *Information from Focus on the Family* (1992): 1-12.

Kirban, Salem. *Satan's Angels Exposed.* Huntington Valley, PA: Salem Kirban, Inc., 1980.

Lady Queensborough, *Occult Theocracy.*

Park, Irene A. *Seven High Pagan Masses and Halloween.*

Pollard, Jeff. "Halloween: Whose Celebration Is It?" *The Evangelist* (October 1984).

Warnke, Michael A., *Schemes of Satan.* Tulsa, OK: Victory House, Inc.

Wright, Robin G. "Halloween: Satan's Celebration." *Christian Life* (October 1985).

Index

A

D ——————

F

G

M

S

Y

Z